Adventure Time
and Philosophy

Popular Culture and Philosophy® Series Editor: George A. Reisch

For full details of all Popular Culture and Philosophy® books, visit www.opencourtbooks.com.

Popular Culture and Philosophy®

Adventure Time and Philosophy

The Handbook for Heroes

Edited by
NICOLAS MICHAUD

OPEN COURT
Chicago

Volume 87 in the series, Popular Culture and Philosophy®, edited by George A. Reisch

To order books from Open Court, call toll-free 1-800-815-2280, or visit our website at www.opencourtbooks.com.

Open Court Publishing Company is a division of Carus Publishing Company, dba Cricket Media.

Printed and bound in the United States of America.

ISBN: 978-0-8126-9858-9

Library of Congress Control Number: 2014952049

Contents

A Few Short Graybles

♫ C'mon and grab your friends. We'll go to very distant lands. ♫

There may be no two sentences that better describe philosophy than the introduction to *Adventure Time*.

Philosophy is tough. It can be baffling, daunting, and even scary.

Philosophy is the quest to solve the most difficult questions we can ask. On that quest, the monstrous problems loom . . . who we really are, the meaning of life and death, how we can know the truth, whether we have any free will, the nature of time, the existence of God, . . . everything (and even what "everything" means).

Philosophers, those adventurers who dedicate their lives to trying to overcome these problems, often find themselves in very distant, not to mention weird and often lonely lands—the lands of unpopular ideas, dissident theories, crazy questions, and even crazier answers.

Philosophers may think of themselves as heroes but they are often seen as villains or even monsters—objects of hatred for supposing that the Earth might not be the center of the universe, that the gods might not exist (or if they do exist, might not care what we do), that free will could be an illusion, that science may be missing something important . . . Philosophers may suddenly find themselves unpopular. That's why it's best to go on this adventure with a friend.

Exploring *Adventure Time* is especially fascinating. We will try to figure out whether Finn was fated to lose his arm, if the Ice King is actually such a bad guy, and what it really means to be evil—just to name a few deep questions the show asks us. *Adventure Time* is chockablock with philosophical questions.

Most fans of *Adventure Time* are grown-ups but children like it too. Children are willing to ask honest questions, and seriously consider answers that seem absurd at first. Like philosophy, *Adventure Time* deals with ideas and questions that look and sound crazy. Those are the questions like "How small can something be?" "What does 'evil' really mean?" and "If I jump really high, can I end up in space?"

You start looking at the crazy answers when you realize that the obvious, non-crazy answers are usually wrong. Matter isn't solid, the Earth's moving, and even time can be bent and distorted. These are the kinds of thoughts that *Adventure Time* isn't afraid of . . . in fact, those thoughts are treated, just as they should be, like they're fun!

Adventure Time takes no crazy thought for granted. Everything humans have taken for granted during their short time on the planet has turned out to be mistaken. Common sense often leads us away from the truth. And the more we study, the less we know.

Adventure Time isn't a *kids' show*. But it does speak to children and to those grown-ups who are still able to think like children—knowing that the world's full of things they don't know about, willing to consider and reconsider everything. Thanks to *Adventure Time*, even old, bearded, and wizened philosophers might occasionally remember why they got into this business in the first place . . . because the world is a wonder, a mystery, and an adventure. We can't conquer it, we can't win it, and we can't beat it, but we can *play* in it.

So. Let me invite you on an adventure, the kind of adventure that never ends . . . a fun adventure into the weird, wild, and dangerous.

Welcome to *Adventure Time and Philosophy*!

I

Nasty, Brutish, and Sweet

1
The Finn-losophy of *Adventure Time*

JOHN V. KARAVITIS

Once again, the boys are facing an unimaginable magical foe. The creature has six arms, two hundred legs, and a bad attitude. One of its poison-spitting tentacles reaches toward an unnamed princess . . . And the boys have seen all they need to! Leaping from Jake's back, Finn shouts, "Hero Time!" as his grass blade slices through the writhing tentacle. The hideous beast gathers into itself, whimpering as Finn lands with his arms cocked at his hips. Jake, who shaped himself into a shield around the princess, unfolds and fist-bumps Finn, "Yeah, man!" Finn turns to the princess, ready to bask in her gratitude, and then steps back, buffeted by her scowling face. "Dog-cabbage-it! You rutabaga heads! My boyfriend was trying to help me tie my shoe. I'm a princess. I shouldn't have to tie my own knots! What were you thinking?"

The Land of Ooo is a world of both science and magic; of beautiful, young princesses, and evil, old wizard kings; of deepest friendships, and darkest dangers. In many ways, it's not at all like our world. In many ways, it's just like it. And one fact is true in both worlds: thinking takes more time and more effort, but it's often wise to look before you charge and start hacking off limbs. . . .

A strange world, this Land of Ooo, where science and magic exist side-by-side. Science and magic represent two conflicting views of how the world works, one that requires time, effort, and deep thought, and the other that is much easier and often more appealing. We will explore Finn's view of how the world works—his "Finn-losophy"—and how that view explains the way Finn lives his life.

"Come along with me," gentle reader, on an adventure of our own in the Land of Ooo. Like Finn, let's explore what it means to believe in magic and what it means to believe in science. And, by the end of our adventure, we'll see how our view of the world, as either magical or scientific, affects how we behave in the world—and our future.

Episode A: Science Hasn't Left, but Magic Seems So Right!

The Land of Ooo is a post-apocalyptic world where both science and magic exist. At the very beginning of the title sequence, remnants of science and technology are clearly visible. These imply that science is still a part of the world. But we also see evidence of magic being perhaps an even greater part of this world. We see the Ice King flying; the citizens of the Candy Kingdom (who are made of . . . candy, of course!); Marceline Abadeer, the Vampire Queen, transforming; and Jake, with legs stretched long, Finn riding on his back.

On the one hand, magic is everywhere in the Land of Ooo. Everyone Finn deals with is either non-human or possesses magical powers. Jake the Dog has the power to shrink, stretch, and change his form into various shapes. The Ice King can fly and freeze objects. Marceline can fly, move things with her mind, shape-shift, and she lives by depriving red objects of their color. The Magic Man from Mars has magical powers in general. Flambo the Flambit can cloak Finn and Jake in a flame shield to protect them while they are in the Fire Kingdom. Finn and Jake encounter magic, and make use of it, constantly.

On the other hand, there are numerous examples of science in the Land of Ooo, and of Finn's and Jake's acceptance of and reliance on science. We see cell phones, a telephone line, VHS tapes, PCs, videogames, holographic phones, holographic books, a holographic newspaper, computer worms, robots, a rocket ship, a Martian spaceship, a re-animation serum, cloning, mutations, and the results of Princess Bubblegum's various experiments and scientific investigations. There is even an annual technology fair![1]

---

[1] "Death in Bloom."

The presence of Finn's and Jake's friend and roommate, Beemo, reinforces their acceptance of science in a world filled with magic. An autonomous, intelligent, and consciously-aware PC, who looks like a cross between a personal computer from the mid-1980s and a video game controller, Beemo is not just their friend and roommate. He acts as Finn's calendar–alarm clock, and he's also their video game console and VHS tape player. (Just don't ask where the tapes are inserted!) When Beemo accidentally deletes an important core system driver file from his memory, the three of them make a trip to the factory where he was created to get a replacement copy. The factory still exists, and it is staffed with many other similar automatons.[2]

Don't Be RIDICULOUS! There's ALWAYS a Good Explanation!

Science and magic each represent a unique way of viewing how the world works. An important theme in *Adventure Time* is that how you view the world affects how you behave in it. The branch of philosophy that deals with the nature of the world and how it works is called "metaphysics," and, of course, the branch that explores how we should behave is called "ethics."

Of all of Finn's and Jake's acquaints, Princess Bonnibel Bubblegum is the staunchest proponent and defender of science. The Candy Kingdom's creator and ruler, she's always conducting experiments or applying science to understand events. The series begins with Princess Bubblegum trying to create a serum that would bring back the dead—a "decorpsinator" serum.[3] When the Ice King kidnaps Finn and Jake, she and Lady Rainicorn work to rescue them. She has anticipated every contingency. *"But I've spent hours calculating every possible danger, and am well-prepared."* Armed to the teeth with advanced weapons, she seeks to assure Lady Rainicorn that they will prevail in their quest to free them. *"Lady, it will be fine. We've got SCIENCE!"* she confidently proclaims.[4]

---

2 "Be More."
3 "Slumber Party Panic."
4 "Lady and Peebles."

When the Magic Man steals Jake's perfect sandwich creation, and then traps himself and it in a slo-mo bubble, Princess Bubblegum uses science to explain what he's done. *"He's using a molasses-based super-covalent sub-atomic bond, slowing an-y-thing that enters its field. But only if the molasses is at room temperature."*[5]

Throughout the series, Princess Bubblegum persistently denies that magic exists. When Starchy falls ill, and is tended to by the Princess, he refuses medical treatment from her. He demands to be cured by magic instead. The Princess denies that magic exists. She tells Starchy *"All magic is scientific principles presented like mystical hoodoo. Which is fun, but it's sort of irresponsible."* She then playfully pretends to apply magic to cure him, but Starchy is offended that the Princess would so callously disrespect his beliefs.

Forced to seek a "cold spell" in Wizard City, she, Finn, and Jake are all captured and brought before the Grand Master Wizard. Rather than admit that *"All wizards rule"* in exchange for their freedom, she defends science and denies that magic is real. She shouts at the Grand Master Wizard *"All magic is science! You just don't know what you're doing, so you call it magic. Well, it's ridiculous."* At the end of this episode, not having obtained a cure for Starchy's illness, she yet again falls back on science—on the placebo effect—which "cures" him.[6]

On a few occasions, Princess Bubblegum does appear to explicitly acknowledge the existence of magic. These occasions contradict her metaphysics, which she has continually professed is based on science. She shows Finn the *Enchiridion* (a book for heroes whose hearts are righteous), using what appears to be a magic crystal ball.[7] When faced with the evil Lich, a powerful wizard, Princess Bubblegum warns that he can cast spells to *"get into your head and control your bod."* It's only special gems that prevent the Lich from having "full control" over them.[8] When she is later possessed by the Lich, she behaves strangely.[9]

---

[5] "Time Sandwich."
[6] "Wizards Only, Fool."
[7] "The Enchiridion!"
[8] "Mortal Folly."
[9] "Mortal Recoil."

It was Princess Bubblegum who recognized that the Flame Princess's unstable "elemental matrix" could burn the world out from the inside, and she was responsible for the Flame Princess being imprisoned by her own father, the Flame King.[10] Princess Bubblegum battles a witch for Marceline's teddy bear, but "wins" by simply exchanging her shirt for it.[11] Marceline drains Princess Bubblegum's blood, yet the "spoon of prosperity" restores her back to normal.[12]

These few instances contradict but do not discredit the sharp distinction that is drawn between science and magic in *Adventure Time*. Princess Bubblegum's metaphysical position is firm: magic does not exist. Rather, science is the only way to understand how the world works and explain what we see and experience.

Taking the Easy Way Out

Finn is surrounded by both science and magic, and he appears to accept and use both without question. But it's his attitude toward using each, and how he expresses his preference for one over the other, that tell us what he thinks of the world and how it works. Finn's metaphysics is that, although science exists in the Land of Ooo, magic is the preferred method of understanding the world and acting within it. Finn's preference for magic over science is demonstrated repeatedly, and this preference affects how he behaves.

Finn's constant companion is his adoptive brother Jake the Dog. Jake is referred to as "magical," and his power is obvious: he can shrink or stretch his body, and even shape-shift on command. In their adventures, it's Jake's magical ability that rescues Finn from disaster on more than one occasion. Magic typically saves Finn; science doesn't.

Finn had a crush on Princess Bubblegum, but she had always refused to reciprocate. She felt that Finn was too young and immature for her. *"Such a silly boy."*[13] Finn pined over his unrequited love for Princess Bubblegum, and later fell for the

---

[10] "Burning Low."
[11] "Sky Witch."
[12] "Red Starved."
[13] "Too Young"; also "Incendium," "King Worm," and "Too Old."

Flame Princess, who can barely control her anger and her flame power.[14] Finn had romantic success with the emotionally unstable girl who has magical powers, but not with the level-headed girl who lives by science. Finn's love life over the course of the series symbolizes his preference for magic over science.

Wanting to impress Princess Bubblegum with a scientific speech at her barbecue, Finn decides that he needs to become smarter. A trip to the library fails. Jake suggests, *"Oh, let's just solve this thing with magic."* Finn objects to this and counters *"No, that's the easy way out."* Jake takes Finn's observation and flips the script. *"Yeah, that's the easy way out!"* Finn then agrees, and he and Jake acquire the magical Glasses of Nerdicon. The magical glasses do make Finn smarter (*"I understand everything"*), albeit with disastrous results.[15] Paradoxically, in his quest to become smarter, magic helps Finn achieve his goal; science does not.

There are numerous examples of Finn relying on others with magical powers, or on spells and amulets, in order to accomplish his goals. Finn uses a magical spell to open a portal to the Nightosphere.[16] Finn and the Flame Princess successfully explore a dungeon by repeatedly relying on her flame powers to overcome obstacles and to protect them from danger.[17] Magical words bring Finn and Lady Rainicorn to the demon Kee-Oth's lair in order to save Jake.[18]

Although both science and magic are seen as ways of viewing and controlling the world, and expressing our will and desires, there's a significant difference. With science, we observe the world, make educated guesses about how it works, and conduct experiments (or at least continue to observe) in order to confirm or disprove our ideas about the world. Ideas that are based on science have a special characteristic known as "falsifiability." If your ideas about the world are wrong, they will eventually be shown to be wrong. Reality is the ultimate spell-checker.

---

[14] "Incendium."
[15] "The Real You."
[16] "It Came from the Nightosphere."
[17] "Vault of Bones."
[18] "The Pit."

And science based on ideas that truly reflect how the world works can result in technology that allows us to control the world! Magic, on the other hand, merely promises us the ability to control our world by using special words or special objects. Abracadabra! Hocus-pocus! Say the right words, or wave a magic wand, and all your wishes will come true!

Although Finn lives in a world of both science and magic, and has access to and makes regular use of both, he consistently prefers magic. Finn doesn't really care about how the world works, nor does he care about the conflict that exists between these two views. He only cares about getting what he wants, when he wants it. Finn has no respect for science and what it can teach about how the world works. Magic requires no thought or understanding, and it's the shortest path from will and desire to gratification in the Land of Ooo.

Magic is the metaphysics of immaturity; and, given that Finn sees and uses both, preferring magic over science is an expression of willful ignorance about how the world works. Finn's metaphysics—that magic is more useful and relevant than science—stands in sharp contrast to Princess Bubblegum's more mature view of how the world works. (No wonder they couldn't hook up. It was all a philosophical disagreement over metaphysics. It had nothing to do with their age difference!)

Episode B: Irresponsibly Responsible!

Finn may well be a headstrong and rambunctious thirteen-year-old boy who prefers magic over science, but at least he's all hero. But seriously, what thirteen-year-old boy hasn't dreamed of being a hero and saving the day, and the princess? Finn explains how he decided to become a hero when he shares the story of how, as a baby, he went potty (or "boom boom") on a large leaf, and fell backward onto it. Lying there, helpless, he cried for a day. *"But no one came to help me. That day, I vowed to help anyone in need, no matter how small their problem."*[19]

This looks like a noble decision based on empathy. But at times it does seem as though there's more to Finn's being a hero than his alleged desire to help people and act by a code of

---

[19] "Memories of Boom Boom Mountain."

honor. He seems to really like the hero role. He likes it so much, we have to wonder if he's driven not so much by empathy as by a desire to have adventures—as would any thirteen-year-old boy. He appears driven to act not merely because of his proclaimed empathy for others, but more to satisfy his own needs for action and adventure. We consistently see Finn rushing into danger without any forethought or consideration of the consequences.

Fighting the Bucket Knight in the Dungeon of the Crystal Eye, he can't believe that he ends up knocked to the ground, badly bruised. *"Oww . . . I rode the knuckle train? But . . . I . . . I'm in my element!"*[20] When asked if he wants magic powers "for absolutely free," Finn yells *"Heck yeah!"* Later, when asked if he's ready to take the Wizard's Pledge, his eagerness stuns the Bufo, who proclaim in unison *"My word, I've never met someone so irresponsibly responsible."*[21] Finn has even "worn" Jake as a second skin, running around wildly, using Jake's magical powers, and proclaiming *"I feel unstoppable! Raaaa!"*[22]

But regardless of the reason, he takes his hero responsibilities seriously—perhaps too seriously. *"A hero always helps someone in need,"* he reminds Jake.[23] Finn defends his actions as resulting from his obligations as a hero, even when it means suffering humiliation in someone else's place. *"I couldn't watch that old man suffer, Jake. My code of honor wouldn't allow it."* When Jake suggests they just leave, Finn replies *"I can't. As a hero, I'm bound by my . . ."* But Marceline whisks him away before he can finish his sentence. Bound by his inflexible code of honor, Finn is forced to become Marceline's henchman and help her feed.[24] When it becomes apparent that they have to stop the Flame Princess from destroying the Goblin Kingdom, Jake asks *"Finn! What's more important? Your love for that screwball dame, or being a hero and saving the lives of innocent goblin folk?"* Finn confirms, *"Being a hero."*[25]

[20] "Dungeon."
[21] "Wizard."
[22] "Jake Suit."
[23] "Freak City."
[24] "Henchman."
[25] "Hot to the Touch."

C-Ooo-exist

We saw that the Land of Ooo is one where science and magic co-exist. We also saw how science and magic differ. Science requires that we be rational, that we try to actively understand the world, and to take steps to verify our understanding. Magic only requires that we say special words, or use a special object, like an amulet, to control our world. No *understanding* is required.

We have come to understand Finn's metaphysics—the way he views how the world works. Finn prefers magic to science. As long as there is magic, especially Jake's, to back him up, he believes that he will win! Magic allows Finn to be as reckless and adventurous as he is. Relying on Jake's magical abilities, and on any other magic he finds, magnifies Finn's will, but it doesn't help him behave ethically. With magic on his side, he can do as he pleases, without having to consider how his actions affect other people.

We saw how Finn's behavior is not as altruistic and empathic as he would like us—or himself—to believe. He jumps into situations for which he has no ethical responsibility. He knows that he can't help everyone, but he continues to get involved. *"Ahhh! Everyone wants different things! And some of them want stuff that's exactly the thing the others don't want."* When Jake asks him what he wants, Finn replies *"What I want is to help anyone in need, so everyone is happy!"*[26] But that can never be.

Finn doesn't think through to the consequences of his actions, and he doesn't consider whether his actions might be extreme. His sense of duty is so inflexible that it often has unforeseen consequences. And by helping when not asked to, or in situations for which he is not responsible, he prevents others from growing and becoming independent, from learning how to be able to help themselves.

If it weren't for the way that Finn views the world—that magic is more important than science, and that magic will always be available to help him prevail—he wouldn't be so foolhardy and immature. And Finn's immaturity is a form of willful ignorance. Because of this, his altruism often becomes

---

[26] "Memories of Boom Boom Mountain."

misguided, and this reinforces his desire to take the easy way out. Had he preferred science, like Princess Bubblegum, Finn would have been careful in selecting when to become involved and which course of action to take. Why? Because he would be invested in *understanding* why things are the way they are.

As long as Finn relies on the "easy way out" he never really has to understand, and just jumps in and imposes his own ethical beliefs on others! Remember how badly things went with Donny the grass ogre? Had Finn taken the time to observe and analyze, he might have realized that Donny was actually helping to protect the House People. But he didn't; he jumped right in, and everything went to cabbage!

If Finn was a bit more willing to take the hard way, the scientific way, he would be more mature in his behavior, and he would also learn from his adventures. But, for now, he's going to keep running into situations without really thinking about them. And let's be honest, we kind of love him for it. Two verses from the song played over the closing credits capture his Finn-losophy perfectly: *"We can wander through the forest / And do so as we please."* And: *"Maybe by next summer / We won't have changed our tune."* And you know that Finn won't change his tune. He will always be that thirteen-year-old boy who believes in magic, and that he can do as he pleases, in his heart, at the very least.

There are a few occasions where we do see Finn mature a bit from his experiences. He learns that the ultimate weapon against evil is love—or *"liking someone a lot."*[27] He also learns that the real treasure in life is friendship.[28] So, there is some hope that Finn can grow ethically. But Finn's ethical development is currently pretty stagnant. The metaphor of the "Mystery Train" best describes Finn's current ethical state. We see Finn on a train that is going around on a circular track. As he progresses from one train car to the next, he fights never-ending battles against all kinds of monsters, and he wins prizes upon defeating them. But that's all that ever happens. The battles are never-ending, and he wins all of his battles![29]

---

[27] "Mortal Folly."
[28] "What Was Missing."
[29] "Mystery Train."

Instead of viewing the world through science, through a rational and mature viewpoint, Finn views the world as one of instant gratification with no long-term negative consequences. With science, we make mistakes, but that's how we learn. With magic, all that matters is what we want—right now. Jake explains the meaning of Life to Beemo. *"If you get everything you want the minute you want it, what's the point of living?"*[30] But that's exactly how Finn lives his life—in the childlike present.

Adventure Time teaches us an important lesson: our view of how the world works—our metaphysics—influences our behavior. It's better to have a metaphysics that gives us a clearer, more realistic picture of how the world works than one that simply caters to our desire for how the world *should* work. This can be tough, because it requires us to set aside our egos and accept a lot that we might rather not accept about the world. But doing this leads us to behavior that is more mature, and more ethical.

We see many examples in *Adventure Time* of how Finn ultimately chooses the "easy way out," which results in Finn making mistakes. Magic, and magical thinking, supports the "easy way out"; science doesn't. This connection between metaphysics and ethics has implications for *our* future, as it does for Finn. Our current view of the world may make it impossible for us to grow ethically—as it does for Finn. We should take time to reflect on how we view the world, our place in it, and how our view makes us behave toward other people.

Let's avoid the trap of relying on a way of viewing the world that seduces us with choosing the easy way out. After all, most of us don't have a magical dog to save our buns when we don't think things through. . . .

---

[30] "Box Prince."

2
Poetical! The Art-Scier Wars in Ooo

DANIEL LEONARD

I can see it now . . . thousands of banana guards pouring down the streets of the Candy Kingdom. Each one, glazed eyes pointed forward, moves in precise lockstep with thousands of his fellow soldiers. File after file marches on with spears shouldered menacingly. The denizens of the kingdom look on. Some yell with patriotic fervor, others shiver with fear, but all are required to watch and celebrate the "Fourth Ripe"—"That time when a new kingdom of peace and order is brought to the land of Ooo."

The ground quakes as the soldiers pass through the candy gates. Princess Bubblegum looks on, smiling, and thinks to herself . . . "All of them smart enough to follow orders, none smart enough to question them." A new era dawns in the land of Ooo . . .

Okay, so we haven't seen PB go completely power-crazy yet. But seriously, what's the deal with Princess Bubblegum? She seemed like any other science-loving head of state: straight-laced, pink, and soft in the center. But lately, the more we've chewed on it, the sourer she's become.

Donked-up stuff about PB:

- **She's hundreds of years old.**

- **She almost suffocated the Flame Princess.**

- **Goliad, the immortal Sphinx she made from her own DNA, tried to destroy its opponents and take over the world.**

- She's watching the whole Candy Kingdom through security cameras labeled BGCCTV.

- Her amulet makes her "the biggest cheese in creation."

- She can create and destroy Candy life.

- She sabotaged Finn's escape plans and knocked him unconscious to carry out her own plan, which involved letting James die, when a colonization mission failed.

- Speaking of which . . . colonization? What gives?

Has Princess Bubblegum been Ooo's final boss all along?

Yes and no. On one four-fingered hand, PB may be turning into a fascist dictator bent on expanding her control and maintaining order at all costs. On the other, she truly wants what's best for her kingdom. After all, her scientific research and inventions have often come to the rescue of her subjects, not to mention Finn and Jake. Bubblegum's attitude toward the world isn't purely good or purely bad in itself. It just needs another attitude to push against it: Finn's.

Where Princess Bubblegum is a scientist, Finn the Human is an artist—not because of his sick rhymes ("I can punch all your buns . . . I will punch you for fun"), but because of his passion for life and his willingness to try anything. To thrive, Ooo needs the interplay of their two approaches. If Finn stays true to himself, he could prevent PB from starting a Second Great Mushroom War. He'd be just like his "son," Stormo, the Sphinx with Finn's DNA who's locked Goliad in an eternal psychic conflict that keeps the peace. Maybe Finn will even help build a new kind of civilization.

How Do You Think about Technology?

Martin Heidegger (1889–1976) picked the wrong side in the twentieth century's Mushroom War. After the Germans lost World War II, he retreated to a hut in the mountains, which he called, creatively enough, "die Hütte" (yup, "the hut"). He spent his days thinking long and hard about the frames of mind people—or candyfolk—can have and how they affect society. A few years later, in 1946, he published an essay ("What Are Poets

For?") on how his country's "destitute time" had been caused by an imbalance between two frames of mind, which he calls "technology" and "poetry."

He doesn't mean "computers" and "sonnets," exactly; Heidegger is referring to the mindsets *behind* things like Beemo's circuitry and Marceline's bodacious lyrics. Ooo faces the same problem as mid-century Germany: an unprecedented spread ("mushrooming"?) of technological thinking. To set it back on track, poetry needs to catch up.

Here's what I mean by technological thinking and poetic thinking. . . . Try this thought experiment: look around you. What do you see? Walls? How would you describe them? Take a second; say what they are—aloud, if you can. (And don't use the word "walls.") . . . Okay . . . so what did you say? If instead of "tall rectangles," you said "neighbor-keeper-outers," then you're living in a "technological mode." In this "mode," in this way of thinking, we look at the things around us as *stuff* we could use—as tools, fuel, or raw material for serving our aims. This viewpoint is great for solving problems that stand in the way of getting what we want.

In "Five Short Graybles," Peebles creates the perfect sandwich by spinning a cow on a centrifuge and combining a jellyfish and a balloon. Where others saw "marine lifeform," PB—thinking technologically—saw "recipe ingredient." Building gizmos, applying scientific method, and rotating cattle are all ways of altering what's around us so that it serves a purpose. But what if the purpose is evil?

Why Think when You Can Destroy Stuff Instead?

Typical low-IQ robots don't question the purpose they serve. Often, neither do we; at those times, we live in the technological mode. This mode has no values of its own except efficiency and usefulness. This means that some devices we usually call "technology" don't participate fully in this mode. Intelligent robots, for instance, like the Gumball Guardians and Neptr, sometimes second-guess their programmed motives. On the flipside, people, when they're at their most technological, can act with a machine's unthinking allegiance to any plan, even a rauncheous one.

When the Ice King finds out about a glitch in the universal source code ("A Glitch Is a Glitch"), he's willing to exploit it to get a date with Princess Bubblegum. He doesn't care that the glitch will delete everything else in the universe as long as it gets him to Tier 2 with P-Bubs.

Compare his behavior with Rattleballs's selfless choice to serve the Princess even if it means his own destruction—compaction into a cube—because he has "found peace" ("Rattleballs"). Any person can enter the technological mode, and any self-aware machine can exit it.

Once we start fitting things into a system and imposing an order on them, it gets hard to stop. When Finn gets the idea to try out romantic pairings on toy versions of his friends, he spends sixteen weeks in his pajamas nudging them into dates and breakups against their will—all in the name of "chemistry" experiments ("All the Little People"). Outside of Ooo, many of us feel compelled to check Facebook twenty times a day just to keep up with Facebook; we end up serving the tool, not the other way around. The technological mode "wants" to be used everywhere and for everything.

Letting a computer take over your world for a while can be okay, like when Finn and Jake enter Beemo's game ("Guardians of Sunshine"). But what if we live technologically for too long without taking a break? If we forget there's more to life than the game, we won't stop playing it. And the better the game, the more likely we'll forget. When Finn spends years aboard the Dungeon Train, he no longer sees any good reason to go home ("Dungeon Train").

We can get so caught up in turning the world into raw material for our designs that we forget that things are more than what they're made of. We're just as vulnerable to this in virtual worlds, thanks to sandbox games like Grand Theft Auto. Such games let us treat objects and characters in odd and destructive ways, even rewarding us for it—with no real-world consequences. So the technological mode disregards our ordinary values; it considers *how* to make use of things, not what they're used *for*.

Beemo and the Mushroom Bomb are both useful devices: each serves its intended purpose. The fact that one befriends heroes and the other ends worlds is irrelevant to how effective they are. That fact is highly relevant, though, to the goodness of their effects. Doing evil efficiently makes it more evil, not more good! Technology tempts us to think otherwise—to value effectiveness for its own sake, regardless of what it achieves. And it can collapse our systems of value even further. Through technology's lens, we tend to see things as lacking any value in themselves—except, that is, for our own values and purposes, our own selves. Thinking technologically makes a rift between you and all else, as if you were Glob and the world existed to serve your will.

Lich Play a Game

But wait! Don't go Amish just yet: sometimes evil technology in Heidegger's sense doesn't need gadgets and electricity at all. The most consistently technological character in *Adventure Time* is its arch-villain, the Lich. A child of the Mushroom Bomb, the Lich sets his aims entirely in line with technology's tendencies; he wants nothing other than "the extinction of all life."

PB values things based on how they might help her protect her kingdom, but the Lich's aim *is* to devalue all things. Try to imagine him, for instance, chatting with a friend, enjoying a walk together by a lake. Nope! His only pleasure is in controlling and destroying everything that isn't him. If he can do so through abusive means, so much the better. He possesses Peebs, wears Billy's skin, and tricks Finn into breaking the Enchiridion, all in service of an attempted Ooolocaust ("The Lich").

There's a paradox here. The more systematically the Lich ignores others' wills—for instance, their desire to survive—in pursuit of his own, the more he surrenders his will to the impersonal "will" of technology. If he's completely an embodiment of self-assertion (which logically leads to other-destruction—"Look out for Number One"), then he's interchangeable with any other villain defined by that single trait.

By being so willing to sacrifice others to his plans for domination, the Lich has let his will become purely negative. He's empty; he's lost anything we could call a self. He's possessed by possessiveness. To quote a famous *Enchiridion*: "Those who try to make their life secure will lose it."[1] The more control we try

---

[1] Luke 17:33a.

to have, the less aware of everything we become! But, like the Lich, we can become so busy trying to own everything, to control it, that we lose sight of what really matters.

Poetry, Poetry, Make Yourself Adventurey

The poetic mode is risky business. Instead of placing your will at the center of the universe, it places your will at stake—to give up control. This is what Heidegger calls "the venture"—as in "Ad-venture Time." To be poetic is to be open to what each new day brings. It's to be up for anything, to value all you encounter for its own sake, and to be in tune with the greater purpose of Life. It's to be, in a word, *exuberant*. A certain character comes to mind. . . .

PRINCESS BUBBLEGUM: See this book?

FINN: Yeah, I see it!

PRINCESS BUBBLEGUM: It's called the *Enchiridion*. It's a book meant only for heroes whose hearts are righteous.

FINN: Shmow-zow!

PRINCESS BUBBLEGUM: The book lies at the top of Mount Cragdor, guarded by a manly minotaur. It's waiting for a truly righteous hero to claim it!

FINN: Do you think I've got the goods, Bubblegum? 'Cause I am *into this stuff!*

PRINCESS BUBBLEGUM: Yeah, I know. And yes, I do.

FINN: Then off I go! [*Finn jumps out of a high tower window*]

Being poetic doesn't require you to end every chat by flinging yourself through the nearest wall-hole, but it does mean throwing your "self"—the idea that you're completely your own—out the window. Finn's identity as a hero is based on saving Ooo, not on getting what he wants. Saving Ooo doesn't just mean rescuing kidnapped princesses; it also means reinforcing the true value of the things and people in Ooo apart from how any one person wants to use them. Finn does this by identifying so passionately with those he serves that he feels their losses and gains as his own.

Remember the song he recited in "Donny"? "Empathy, empathy, put yourself in the place of me." Maybe that's why Finn's always wearing a bear hat. Animals exist in harmony with all of Nature; they can't do otherwise. When a boy refuses to bend his surroundings to his will and wears an animal's unselfconscious, non-abusive mindset as a *choice*, that's something special: a human with a capital H.

Living in poetic harmony with Nature means accepting it as it is, even its dark side. Fact: all living things will inevitably die. Those living in the technological mode can't handle this, because it means their will is limited and the most crucial aspect of themselves is outside of their control. They ignore this fact and instead seek to cure all diseases, mechanically prolong life (like Moseph, Beemo's millenarian inventor who's replaced all but his skin with artificial parts), or simply deceive themselves into thinking their power will last.

What use is it to think about the dead? Those living in the poetic mode affirm all beings, even those that have passed on, and give freely of themselves, knowing that nothing they have is a permanent possession anyway. Finn shows this side of being a poet when he risks his own life to save someone else's soul by engaging in a musical battle with Death ("Death in Bloom"). He proves that the poetic way of accepting Nature isn't a passive head-nod; it requires struggle. Death keeps time, and the battle is a kind of concert.

The struggle is work, and it makes what we call a "work" of art. Poetry does more than just "compare thee to a summer's day" or measure out life with coffee spoons; it's the kind of work that underlies all meaningful artistic creation. Art refreshes our sense of reality. A painting of Finn's shoes would help us to see them not for what they do, but for what they are: black, sturdy, unified items that take up space, have weight, and hold together on their own, even when we're not looking.

Heidegger says that art is "the setting-itself-into-work of truth." The artist makes a thing we can perceive, a work—a sculpture, a dance, an action-adventure-romantic-comedy movie—that helps us perceive everything else more clearly. Marceline's songs clue us into the reality of her emotions. By writing the songs, Marceline even gives her emotions a new kind of reality; they become more definite and more vibrant by being put into lyrics.

Artistic creation has the power to change reality itself. In "Rainy Day Daydream," Finn suffers the effects of Jake's imagined lava, poison fountains, and snakes, even though he can't see them. Our noggins might not be as potent as Jake's, but still, when we set out to imagine something new or bring an artwork into the world, we don't know exactly how it will turn out. The process forces us to give up some control over our lives, stay open to changing our plans, discover new possibilities, then see what happens next; that's the "venture."

So, art is a way to break free of the technological way of protecting our goals from outside influence. It's the opposite of imposing our will on the world. Art lets us ordinary folks join Finn in saying "Yes!" to the universe.

Magic: The Guntering

Adventure Time has its fair share of Magic Men, Tree Witches, and Abracadaniels. And in the conflict between technology and poetry, magic has a special role. The widespread presence of magic in Ooo seems to be the result of the Mushroom War—the fallout of humanity's abandonment of poetry and complete obedience to the technological mode. Some things we'd usually think of as magical—Shoko's slug-like body, Susan Strong's ultra-brawn, the zombified Goo Monsters, the Lich—all turn out to be products of nuclear radiation. But there's plenty of real magic in Ooo, too, from Marceline's red-sucking to Jake's shape-shifting.

Magic is a kind of halfway point between the poetic and technological modes. Like technology, magic can be an extremely effective way to get what we want; it can satisfy our desire to control the world, like when Gunter uses a Demonic Wishing Eye to conquer Ooo ("Reign of Gunters"). But like poetry, magic can have unexpected consequences and can't be fully controlled by any one person. Magic makes Ooo a place where anything can happen. The spread of magic, then, might be the universe's way of preparing a place for poetry; by letting Finn grow up in a magical world, Ooo makes him more open to new possibilities than his human ancestors and more devoted to preserving the wonderful things around him.

But while Finn's learning to venture, technology—the gadgets and circuits kind—is reaching a level where a Mushroom-type attempt at conquest could happen again. In Season Five, Princess Bubblegum:

- **uses a robotic exploration vehicle to scout out new lands ("James");**
- **installs sleeping gas in the Gumball Guardians due to "an increased chance of threat" ("Sky Witch");**
- **wears an invisibility device and performs experiments on Flame Princess to model her "elemental matrix," hoping to suppress her emotions through science ("Earth and Water"); and**
- **makes an android clone of herself, which she gives a synthetic soul because it's "easier to manipulate" ("The Suitor").**

It's too soon to say for sure that she's a National Ice Cream Socialist, but her ends-justify-means side is definitely getting creepy. If anyone's going to keep her in check, it's Finn, the Poet Laureate of Ooo: the one who's so impressed by the inherent value of his land's things and people that he pursues their needs and goals before his own.

Finn's life is his art. If it's a masterpiece that moves PB and the rest of Ooo to loosen their tight grasp of their own aims for the sake of others'—to take the bold risk of thinking poetically—then it might be the start of a new era for the world: *an Adventure Time.*

3
Power and Parenthood in the Land of Ooo

DAVID CABALLEROS

Surrounding Finn and Jake's expedition, goo monsters drool thick green pus in anticipation of eating a fleshy and writhing meal. There is no hope. Every attempt to escape from certain death has been sabotaged. The transport can't save them; our heroes will soon know the cold, radioactive embrace of creatures that are not quite alive and not quite dead—all because a traitor has foiled every desperate plan to get out alive. Now, our heroes lie there, unconscious, easy pickings for the mass of pustulant monsters. The transport will not keep them out for much longer.

Finn opens his eyes for what must be the last time. He sees before him what appears to be an obnoxiously happy, annoyingly nice, vanilla wafer.

"Sure thing, Princess!"

Then James, with his goofy and somewhat dull-witted smile, breaks off a piece of his head, handing it to the princess. He salutes his fearless leader, and with happy "byong!" drops down towards a fate worse than death.

Then Finn, to his surprise, opens his eyes again. Alive, he finds himself being carried away, while he watches James torn apart, piece by piece, alone in a remarkably heroic and painful demise. James died there in that hole without even his lucky coin to protect him while his "friends" ran off to safety. —The friends who James had not long before gifted with his lucky coin in an honest wish that it would bring them home safely.

. . . Not long after, Princess Bubblegum pins a medal on the chest of a new "James" who she has cloned from a piece of the old one. Finn and Jake cannot help but cry in each other's arms, the vision of

James's sacrifice still vivid in their minds. Jake takes enough time from his tears to hand James his "lucky" coin.

"Here's your coin, James."

But the new James doesn't understand the significance of the coin any more than he can remember being sent to his death by the ruler he trusted to care for all of them. The ruler who sabotaged their transport because . . . well, she calculated the risk, and decided that foiling Finn's plans and sending James off to die was the best option.

Princess Bubblegum is my favorite character from *Adventure Time*. And it's not just because she's made out of bubblegum. Princess Bubblegum is the all-powerful nigh-immortal god-tyrant of the Candy Kingdom! And that's pretty awesome. Princess Bubblegum is (as her name graciously points out) a princess, and like most princesses, she holds political power and authority over a kingdom.

The question is though, is her power and authority legitimate? But before you grab your pitchforks and decide to help overthrow her, consider how much like a parent Princess Bubblegum is. Just because she has power, doesn't mean she's a tyrant . . . well, hopefully not.

The political power Princess Bubblegum has is strongly tied to the idea of parenthood. This connection between parenthood and political power is found even in our own political systems. PB's kind of power has its origins, back in the day, in family ties like when tribal leaders were considered everyone's elder and medieval hierarchical ties made the king basically parent and protector of a country. Today, some countries still identify presidents as "parents" of their countries or refer to the motherland or the fatherland.

Another place where the power of parenthood manifests is in religion. Wasn't Zeus the father of many gods, as was Odin? And the Judeo-Christian God is generally considered a father and creator to all human beings. There are political and traditional reasons why the symbols of parenthood are used; mainly, they still manage to shape the way politics work and how we view power structures. Princess Bubblegum and many of the leaders in Ooo are referred to as heroes or villains *specifically because* of the way they act as parents to others in the show.

Finn Came Out of a Cabbage

Traditionally, parents have almost absolute power over their children, even in free democratic countries parents are tyrants and despots in relation to their children. This is not to say that parents abuse their powers or that children should or even could have a say on how they are raised. It perhaps should be taken as fact that children are dependent on their parents and, until they are able to be independent, they are very much incapable of taking care of themselves or choosing how they should be raised; like baby Finn when he was found by his adoptive dog parents, he was alone and defenseless.

For the sake of our conversation let's say that good parents are those who protect their children, who respect and support their children, or at least attempt to. A bad parent represents the opposite; reckless endangerment, outright attempts to harm their child, or continuous attempts to corrupt them. No matter if a parent is good or bad, they still have power over their children up to a point. But should governments have this kind of parental power? Doesn't PB treat the candy people like her kids? She lies to them when she thinks they can't handle the truth, manipulates them so they will do what's in their best interest, and punishes them when they misbehave!

Shouldn't independent reasonable citizens be able to choose their own lifestyles and be able to make their own choices completely free of any government influence? I would hazard to say that most of us would say, "Yes." Maybe most of us believe that that is how the governments are actually run. But, if you think about it, our governments make decisions for all of us, often without even asking for our consent. Governments often require universal vaccination and early education, for example. You can't ditch school, unlike Finn and Jake *most of us had to go to class.* Our government decides, automatically to make us citizens (or not) when we're born in the country, and it forces us to follow laws that were created long before we were even born.

Many of these state decisions stop affecting people by the time they turn eighteen and can choose to move away from a country or vote against regulations that limit their personal liberties. But most people don't really question these decisions or their inherited political systems in any meaningful way or try to fight them. Maybe we, like the candy people and many of the inhabitants of Ooo, should ask if Princess Bubblegum or our own government should have the kind of power we let them have!

A Society of Functional Cannibals

Princess Bubblegum is the reigning monarch in charge of the Candy Kingdom. Beyond that she appears to be the only authority figure in the kingdom, outside of the hilariously ineffective banana guards who are, in the end, her underlings. This "princess" bears all the marks of a political leader, but the question is, is she a legitimate political leader?

It's hard to say that Princess Bubblegum isn't an effective leader since she does in fact rule and protect a peaceful and apparently prosperous kingdom of helpless creatures who would be little more than tasty snacks for those outside of her borders. Seriously, they explode when they get scared, for crying out loud! She rules her kingdom with little more than the help of a teenager, a magic dog, a legion of the aforementioned totally useless bananas, and her created Gumball Guardians (which to tell the truth are totally badass). But still, does she have a legitimate claim to political authority?

This question has remained a key facet of political philosophy: who has claim to legitimate political authority and by extension power, and why? Princess Bubblegum seems like a proper ruler so why would anyone doubt that she is one, I mean, the title is in her name and everything! Thomas Hobbes (1588–1679) thought that a legitimate ruler was one who provided adequate protection to those he ruled over, even if his subjects suffered under him; in this sense it appears that Princess Bubblegum is a legitimate ruler. But shouldn't there be more? Shouldn't we demand more from our authorities?

Princess Bubblegum seems to have come into power over eight hundred years ago and has remained in power for most of that time. Under her steady guidance, the Candy Kingdom has become an advanced modern society with needs far beyond just being protected by their pink monarch. Maybe at the beginning, as Hobbes thought, PB only needed to provide her people with protection, but as the millennia have passed, they have found they need other things too, like say, indoor plumbing (maybe), rules for owning property, access to medical care, schools, roads, and firefighters.

Over all this time it seems that PB's power base has never really shifted while she has remained in power. There was no democratic process, no attempt to gain legitimacy through the will of the people, and any rebellion, as that of the Cookie "Princess," was quickly put down. Few have challenged Bubblegum's tyranny or her authority and any who have are promptly put in prison. Like when Tree Trunks and Mr. Pig reject Bubblegum's authority to marry them and are unfairly thrown in prison for siding with the "One True King of Ooo" (that braggart!).

One explanation why Princess Bubblegum is so powerful is that she is a parental figure to all candy citizens. In the aptly named episode "You Made Me," the Earl of Lemongrab put it best, "You made me . . . you are my Glob." Princess Bubblegum is the creator of the Candy Kingdom as well as the possible creator of all its citizens. The Gumball Guardians who were the most powerful defense of the Candy Kingdom and her creations call her Mother and live to serve her. To PB, all candy people are candy biomass that can be made at will, cloned, and sacrificed, like James. As she said to Finn, "With this sample of James I can clone a new one. He's candy, you are not, I can't make another you."

What about Rattleballs? Once her creations started to think for themselves and became dangerous, she didn't think twice before destroying them even when they still followed her instructions to the letter. The link between parenthood and political power is what keeps Princess Bubblegum in power; it's what makes her a "legitimate" ruler, an all-powerful authority beyond any limitations, the veritable God of all candy flesh. Yet this connection between parenthood and power might be her undoing. . . . If Princess Bubblegum continues to put the candy people in danger at her convenience, we might see Princess Bubblegum become one of the bad guys—or is she that already?

So, He's Like the Bad Guy, Right?

The Ice King at the beginning of the show seemed to fit the definition of a villain perfectly: a crazy old guy obsessed with kidnapping princesses, with an immoderate amount of ice magic and no real redeeming features. But lately he has changed from a constant villain to a lot less than that, maybe more of an insistent child-like annoyance that will sometimes help the heroes out. What changed had a lot less to do with the Ice King himself than with how he was perceived by others. It all started when we learned of the Ice King s greatest secret, he once wore glasses.

The Ice King was once called Simon Petrikov, and he was human. This by itself is uninteresting but the fact that he was once sane and that he changed so much in spite of himself gives reason to pity him. But that's not the only reason for the change; after that the Ice King was still a "villain." It was not until Marceline revealed another part of the Ice King's past, or rather Simon's past, that he fully transforms. It's when we learn that Simon protected Marceline and acted like a parent that he changes from a villain to less so in the eyes of others in Ooo.

If it was parenthood or guardianship which made the Ice King "good" it was his eventual march into madness and forgetting and abandoning Marceline which made him "evil." It was the crown that drove him stark raving mad that caused him to forget; still it was only the crown that gave him the power to defend Marceline. This might mean that the power of the crown which corrupted him was not what made him evil but rather it was his abandoning Marceline and forfeiting parenthood which classified him as a bad guy.

Princess Bubblegum might be on a similar path. The Ice King gained back his humanity when we were shown that he had been a good parent but Princes Bubblegum has shown signs of becoming a bad parent. If she doesn't correct her ways she might end up on the same track as Simon was, the way to the dark side.

The Fire Kingdom Is All Deceitful and Shakespeare

There are few objectively evil characters in *Adventure Time*, but for the Flame King, that's one of his defining character traits and the one that eventually leads to his downfall. The Flame King seems to understand himself and all the citizens of his kingdom as evil, and since the main method of advancement in the Fire Kingdom is murdering or forcefully deposing your family, we might be forced to agree. But the Flame King was not just evil, he was a bad parent! Flame Princess suffered a lot at the hands of the Flame King, starting with when she was born and the Flame King had her wander the wilderness in hopes she would die since she was prophesied to become more powerful than he and to take over the Fire Kingdom. Later, when pressured by Princess Bubblegum, he resorted to keeping her contained, in isolation in a giant lantern where she witnessed the horrors of the Flame Court.

Flame King is an example of a bad parent who loses power and his crown directly because he is a bad parent. His mistreatment of Flame Princess directly results in his losing power. Flame Princess takes over the Fire Kingdom, deposing her father, creating an "honest" kingdom, and fulfilling the prophecy that prompted the Flame King to attempt to kill her when she was born and incarcerate her when that failed.

The fact that she took over shows how the power of a parent can fail if he's seen as a bad parent—a parallel with governments that can fail should they abandon their duties to their citizens. Both in Ooo and in our world the merits of power can be measured in similar ways as the merits of parenthood. A good parent like a good leader deserves our support, while a bad leader, like a bad parent, might be universally censured.

Yo, Man, Don't Eat Those

Another evil character in *Adventure Time* is Hunson Abadeer, the demon ruler of the Nightosphere, Lord of Evil, and the father of Marceline the Vampire Queen. His evil shows quickly through his actions whenever he appears; during his first appearance he attempts to steal all the souls in Ooo. His evil reflects on his parenting; he apparently abandoned Marceline in the human world, making her fend for herself as a child, stole Marceline's bass guitar axe and called it a lute, pushed her to become evil, allowing her to be possessed by chaotic evil magic, and, worst of all, ate Marceline's fries, which were obviously hers.

While his acts of evil label him a villain and his parenting skills obviously need some work, he still claims to love Marceline and might be just attempting to raise her in the way he believes is best according to the ways of the Nightosphere. The Nightosphere is a different dimension from Ooo and this discrepancy might be enough to justify his retaining his huge power while Marceline in Ooo is completely justified in resisting him. Marceline in this point is rebellious against her father but is still seen as completely justified even when her biggest complaint against him revolves around his eating her fries. Marceline's and Flame Princess's rebellions against their parents are seen as justified because they serve a greater good: their "evil" parents must be stopped and any rebelling or power-grab that works against them is seen as a greater good.

You Know You Want Those Bumps

Lumpy Space Princess, being a hot mess, shows us a different side to this paradigm with unjustified rebellion. When she disobeys her parents and completely misinterprets their attempt to help her, she ends up homeless, even though the fight was about her living alone in the first place. She leaves Lumpy Space and wanders Ooo, being forced to attempt to eat bark and create a refuge out of acorns. She later finds help with a pack of wolves, but only for a short time before drama starts and she needs to leave them or be eaten.

Finally, she becomes a villain herself for a short time, terrorizing a small village and stealing the villagers' food. Only when she realizes that her parents were right and decides to go back to them does she find redemption. Lumpy Space Princess's failure to recognize her parents as a legitimate authority and her unjustified rebellion only led her to disaster and unhappiness.

The ties between parenthood, power, and authority in Ooo might not cover all power relationships but they do serve to reflect some ways our current political systems are run. Princess Bubblegum can reflect the ways a state claims authority and power from tacit consent and the dangers of neglecting the needs of the citizens. The Ice King can show how states that may have real and legitimate claims exist are misunderstood but our perspective of them can change. The Flame Princess and Marceline can teach us about justifiable resistance to a state or country when it fails to protect its citizens, when it infringes on their rights, or when it actively works against their best interest.

Lastly Lumpy Space Princess represents how sometimes it's better to live within a regulated state that may seem slightly oppressive than outside of it, and reveals how rebellion against legitimate authority might lead to unmitigated disasters.

Adventure Time seems to reflect many of the values that our modern societies value and the political systems that we have created to prop them up, serving both the functions of relatable entertainment and indoctrination. It's our duty as watchers and citizens in our societies to consider, as the end credits roll, whether those values and ideas are really what we want.

4
Who Governs Ooo?

BEN GALE AND ADAM BARKMAN

First came the Great Mushroom War. Then, the mushroom bomb. The world shattered into a deep, dark green and skull-shaped souls howled across the land. After that, life was different. Bits of debris, smashed electronics, and destroyed cars litter the landscape. Entire skyscrapers and highways, collapsed and overgrown, can be seen across the horizon. The civilizations that existed before the Great Mushroom War were much like ours. When the mushroom bomb dropped and the landscapes were decimated, nations and rulers ceased to exist. The world became a blank slate, upon which the few survivors could write. The inhabitants of Ooo stood on the threshold of a brave new world, one in which they were free from any past society or government, and could create whatever world they chose....

But what if they don't always have an easy and free choice? What if Marceline's dad wants to come from the Nightosphere and destroy everyone? They would be screwed if they didn't have Finn and Jake, or Princess Bubblegum, or even the Ice King to protect their people from destruction. This blank slate with no government is great, but it leaves a lot of room for bad things to happen. And even though Finn, Jake, Bubblegum, and the Ice King have flaws, they are still in positions of power because their people don't want other rulers instead. No one wants the Lich, or the Lord of Evil to be in charge. So how did they end up choosing Princess Bubblegum or the Ice King, or even that weird, murderous Forest Wizard to be in charge?

The Tabul-Ooo Rasa

The "state of nature" is a concept that we've kicked around since the Middle Ages. The ancients hinted at the horrors of anarchy and man without government—Plato talked about these men becoming like werewolves, ungoverned and dangerous. But no one actually began to ask what humans were like before laws were put into place and governments were established. It wasn't until the Enlightenment that Thomas Hobbes (1588–1679) began to talk explicitly of a "state of nature," which he considered "nasty, brutish, and short." And even with government, Hobbes thought things still often sucked, as governments were established through fear and violence.

John Locke (1632–1704), born almost fifty years later, imagined a different, more egalitarian world where people made social contracts with each other to establish law. And Jean-Jacques Rousseau (1712–1778), on the cusp of the French Revolution, saw the state of nature as one free from ownership and property. These thinkers were the fathers of Liberalism, one of the most influential ideas of the last three hundred years. And in the land of Ooo, we see these philosophers' ideas at work as the characters in *Adventure Time* try to carve out their civilizations from war-ravaged, magically mutated, and candy-filled land of Ooo.

In Ooo, after the Great Mushroom War, we get to see how these ideas actually work together to create our own world and government. What we see is the world cleared of government, and then the fighting, politicking, and adventuring that leads to new world orders and governments. The question that really matters to the people of Ooo, is pretty obvious. . . . "Were they better off in the state of nature, without government, or are these new monarchies, dictatorships, and potential democracies the right way to go?"

Freeeeeeeedom!

"Liberalism" is a political theory that focuses on individual rights and freedoms. It charges governing bodies like Princess Bubblegum with protecting people's rights and freedoms. Early on, this protection often was accomplished by a smaller government; any larger governments would take away more power and freedom from the individuals. Liberalism distinguished itself from the previous theories by having the well-being of the citizens as its primary focus: the government existed by them and for them. Earlier theories had this relationship reversed, where the citizens existed to be ruled over by their governments, often claiming a God-given right to rule. Many of the early Liberal philosophers rooted their theories in a Christian theology, but moved away from the "divine right of kings" by exploring the "state of nature."

What was this state of nature? It was the way that people lived before they had any society—No Bubblegum, no Finn and Jake, just a whole bunch of candies running around without anyone in charge. The political philosophers of the Enlightenment saw themselves as constantly on the edge of great discoveries. Political discussion centered on the basic rules of governing, as if they were as clear as following a recipe for making spaghetti. Philosophers agreed on a general concept of natural law: rights and wrongs were built in to our very existence and could be found through reason. With a foundation like natural law, they thought, there must be a recipe of government built in to us, it just needed to be found.

This idea of built-in rules can be seen in Finn and Jake's adventures, as they constantly make decisions over right and wrong based on gut reactions. They don't need to ask if a giant terrorizing a village is a good or bad thing. They do what they can to help those weaker than them, and try to stop unfair treatment. This is instinctive; they never wonder if trying to hook up a giant snail, or punching the Ice King in the face is the right thing to do.

To imagine what a government should look like, each philosopher began with trying to figure out how the state of nature actually looked. Was it a mess of ogres, giants, and Gunters, trying to kill every person in sight? Or was it a walk in the park? In the world they thought of, there were certain problems that naturally came up, and governments, they believed, were created in the hope of solving them.

Ooo is post-apocalyptic, with (we think) only one living human. This makes it the perfect playground for Hobbes, Locke, and Rousseau. The land of Ooo is an untouched state of nature for each of these philosophers, and in Ooo we see how Liberalism, in its many forms can take hold and flourish, or, occasionally, flounder.

The Forest Wizard Can Kill Whomever He Wants

For Thomas Hobbes, the state of nature was "solitary, poor, nasty, brutish, and short": people are free, equal, and naturally self-interested. Everyone is equal in that they are all able to kill another; free in that they very well may do so without any particular restraints. If two people want the same thing, they fight for it; the natural escalation is to war over the same things. The state of nature for Hobbes was a fearful war of all, against all. To sum up this state of nature: life sucks, and people are jerks. Like being stuck beside a baby on a ten-hour flight, this state is something that people would do almost anything to avoid.

But this mess of anarchy is hard to break out of. It doesn't just happen with a simple agreement. Hobbes pointed out that people are unlikely to hold to their agreement the moment that something more advantageous pops up. This is where the government comes in. Out of this mess of anarchy, a social contract arises that has fear at its core. People give up their rights and freedoms, and raise up a "Leviathan" (a giant monster, meaning political authority) to rule. Really, this agreement is about the most basic right of self-preservation. Candies, lumpy space people, or even vampires are all trying their best not to get eaten, squished, and terrorized.

In raising up a government that will demand allegiance and punish any failures harshly, people no longer need to fear each other, and, now, only have to fear one—the Leviathan. This Leviathan is a government made up of the collective will of all who are under it, bound together by fear. Through fear of punishment for breaking their contract, peace is kept—since peaceful means are much preferable to going to war, peace is in everyone's best interest.

In the episode "Storytelling," Finn is nearly killed by the forest animals and their Leviathan, the Forest Wizard. The animals are angry, and don't understand what Finn's trying to do, namely save Jake by telling him a crazy story. All they know is that he's been picking fights, wrecking Boobafina's relationships, disturbing the peace, and making a general nuisance of himself. They get fed up enough that the Forest Wizard, with the help of the forest animals, stops the terror by locking Finn in a cage and nearly killing him.

The ability to destroy people who try to fall back into a state of nature is exactly why a Leviathan exists. Regardless of whether the forest animals believe the wizard is a jerkface or not, he is in charge, and is the one who brings the punishment. The wizard has the power to kill, and the other forest creatures respect it. The wizard would probably treat any of the other forest creatures the same way if they were acting like Finn. But, the wizard also does his best to act fairly. Just rulers often last longer than tyrants.

But even though the Forest Wizard has a crazy amount of power (he can freakin' kill people!), he still needs to have some idea of natural law. According to Hobbes, natural law prohibits us from harming ourselves and includes our right to fight for ourselves. Natural law also suggests that a peaceful solution is best when you are trying to preserve your own life simply as a matter of practicality—peaceful solutions don't involve you putting yourself in danger quite the same way that going to war does. The Leviathan is moderated by self-interest. If those who are under him are discontented, fearful, and abused enough that they are willing to risk death to overthrow him, then he won't last long. But, he can't be nice enough that there is no fear of crossing him. Push the forest animals too far as a tyrant, or fail to protect them by being too nice, and they will get a new Leviathan to take the Forest Wizard's place.

As for what a Leviathan looked like, Hobbes argues that the Leviathan can take one of three forms: a democracy, in which the people set up legislation to govern themselves, an oligarchy, in which a few people take power and rule, or a monarchy, in which a single person commands the people. Of these, Hobbes thinks a monarchy is best because it leaves the least room for infighting at the top, and allows for a strong head with little arguing over decisions. The Forest Wizard, though he may listen to the opinions of the forest creatures, ultimately is a monarch, and doesn't share the decision-making process with anyone.

Hobbes in many ways is considered the father of liberalism, because he centered his theory around the people; governments (Leviathans) are still put in place by the people, and must serve the people's purpose. The Leviathan is made up of the people's consent; he is kept in check by the people. The Leviathan may determine the laws of his country, but he still has practical limits. When the Goblin King Xergiok becomes too tyrannical, spanking everyone he possibly can, he causes enough terror over his subjects that they allow Finn and Jake to kick him out and take over. If a Leviathan abuses the people too much, fails to keep them safe, or generally acts like an insufferable ass, then they will rise up and install a new Leviathan who will rule them better. The Leviathan depends on the people being at least somewhat happy with life to stay in charge.

Why Bubblegum and Ice King Are Good, and Lemongrab Is Bad

To John Locke, the state of nature was one of equality. Unlike Hobbes, who was a bit of a downer, Locke thought that people, at their most basic, have the right to life, liberty, and property, but don't have any right to cause harm to themselves or another, unless it is a matter of survival. This state of nature is governed by the overarching law of nature, which is reason. As Locke says, "Every man has a right to punish the offender, and be executioner of the law of nature."[1] Besides the right of punishment, every person has the right to seek reparations from the party that caused them harm—every kidnapped princess has the right to kick the Ice King in the shin. When an agreement is made, both people take it upon themselves to uphold their word and hold the other to account if they fail to honor the agreement. When Finn and Jake promise to deliver the royal tarts, they make that agreement with Princess Bubblegum, who does her best to make sure they carry it out (by threatening them with her death).

The problem this raises is that people may mess up when they are dishing out punishment. Someone could have an attachment that influences their reason, such as friendship or love; they could also be too hurt from the situation to clearly reason, and go overboard with their revenge. This injustice causes people to break away from the natural law that they are to abide by—when they give up natural law, they give up reason, and cease to be people, only animals that must be put down, or non-talking candy that must be eaten. Because of this

---

[1] *Second Treatise of Government.*

potential to screw things up royally, Locke proposes civil societies formed by a social contract as the solution to this problem of the state of nature.

The state of nature lacks three distinct things:

1. **Established codes of law.**

2. **A public and fair judge.**

and

3. **The power to carry out a sentence.**

In order to gain these three things and escape the state of nature people give up their right to do whatever they want, and their right to get revenge. These are the requirements of moving past a state of nature to achieve a safe civil society. The lack of freedom simply means that they now have to live under laws that are enforced by an impartial ruling power. The ruling power can take the form of a democracy, an oligarchy, or a monarchy, but the end result is that the problems of the state of nature are patched up by making a social contract.

Under this contract, each person gives up their rights of revenge and submits to the laws and rulers. For example, when the Ice King pisses off pretty much the entire Candy Kingdom by generally being a toolbox, none of the candy people take revenge. Instead, they let the Princess Bubblegum give the orders, and decide how to punish him.

The Candy Kingdom, with Princess Bubblegum as the ruler, fulfills Locke's theory of civil government formed by a social contract. All of the candy people gives up their right to take judicial matters into their own hands, and instead let their ruler, Princess Bubblegum (who often appoints Finn and Jake to help) deal with things. Whether it's protecting them from a horde of candy zombies, or from Susan Strong's fish people, Princess Bubblegum is the monarch in charge of the Candy Kingdom and is expected to keep everyone safe. She sets up laws that limit behavior, like making it illegal to eat candies that talk, and has taken upon herself the roles of judge and executioner, using Finn and Jake to work under her in acting on behalf of the candy people. When Princess Bubblegum, Finn, and Jake deal with the Lich, they are fulfilling their part of

Locke's social contract, and keeping the civil society together. When they stop Susan Strong and her people from eating everyone, or causing them to explode with fear, Finn and Jake are fulfilling the agreement.

In the Earl of Lemongrab fiasco, we see Locke's theories distance themselves from Hobbes's more clearly. Princess Bubblegum is not a Leviathan, determining the rules on a whim, only moderated by fear of the candy people rising up. Instead, she is a monarch ruling with the consent of the people in the form of a social contract; the agreement, and the laws that surround it mean that she must be of a certain age to rule. When the Earl of Lemongrab comes to take over, she bows to the laws of the land and lets him. Even when the Earl turns out to be a terrible ruler and, for the good of the candy people, needs to be deposed, she still makes sure that she is eighteen years old again before she retakes the throne.

We also see Locke's theories at work in the Ice Kingdom. The Ice King establishes law, forbidding trespassing, setting up marriage rites, and giving the penguins the right to vote. He also works for the preservation of the Ice Kingdom and its inhabitants by helping to stop the Lich with Finn and Jake. Though he may not be the best ruler, he still holds the power of retribution, and since he seems to maintain the rule, the penguins must be in favor of the social contract they have agreed to—keeping him in power.

The City of Thieves and the Problems of Property

Locke and Hobbes both have some lovely ideas about how governments stop chaos from coming out of a state of nature, but what if this state of nature isn't so bad? What if governments don't solve anything?

For Jean-Jacques Rousseau, the state of nature was the brightest, happiest place. He is famous for beginning his book, *The Social Contract,* with the phrase "Man is born free, but is everywhere in chains." Rousseau's state of nature is absolutely free, with no repressive governments, no dominating hierarchies, and there are no artificial needs, such as shoes (or giant snail shells for slugs). Rousseau saw these artificial needs as the result of setting up repressive societies that did not have absolute freedom as their core value. The state of nature does not have law, property, or some sense of moral inequality, and so, there is no desire to oppress or restrict another's freedom. But what about Princess Bubblegum, and her Lockean Candy Kingdom? Is it rubbish that has corrupted the beautiful state of anarchy by imposing rules and coercing people to give up their freedom?

Had Rousseau been born two hundred years later, he would have been the first hippie in line for Woodstock (and, given some of his later theories, probably the first one to find out that the brown acid was bad). He is much like Tree Trunks: a mixture of naivety, optimism, and recklessness.

Rousseau argued that ultimately, at our core, we as people are good, and, when we are not influenced to act otherwise by restrictions on our freedom and livelihood, then we continue in our good and uncorrupted nature. The state of nature existed in a time before rationality and morality, in a very simple way, before it was corrupted by civil societies.

If we take Rousseau's account seriously, Finn and Jake exist in a state of nature. They are free to do whatever they want; they have no obligations beyond their desires for sleep, food, and "smoochin'." They're motivated by their own self-preservation, and are compassionate in their responses to other people's hardships. We never see them rely on others for the basic necessities of life. They are carefree, happy, healthy, and living as Rousseau could only dream.

This is where Rousseau differs from Locke and Hobbes: he does not see the state of nature as something to fight. Instead, we should try to retain those principles of freedom, in a more complex world than the state of nature that they came from. Property came about when someone put a fence around a tree, said "this is mine," and no one tried to take it from him. This is where the goodness of nature began to break down.

We see this in the episode "City of Thieves." Property is a nearly meaningless thing because of the inequality that came from the differences between the haves and the have-nots. This corrupts even Finn and Jake, the innocent ones without need. The acquisition of property, as Rousseau said, can be the beginning of corruption.

Moral inequality happened when we began to improve our ability to meet our basic needs, and started working with others in increasingly complex survival methods. Society became more complex and we became more dependent on it (imagine living

without a cell phone once you've owned one for a few years).
Moral inequality sprang up as people became less independent
and free, and people with more stuff began to oppress people with
less. This reduces us to bandits, thieves, and rapscallions, all
fighting a sort of class struggle. Those in the land of Ooo without
royal tarts, for example, are constantly trying to steal them. Their
struggle is between the haves and the have-nots, caused by the
creation of property and a corruption of the state of nature.

What Happened?

So, Thomas Hobbes, John Locke, and Jean-Jacques Rousseau
each contributed to the creation of the theory of Liberalism.
Their ideas had a significant influence on Western European
political thought throughout the 1600s and 1700s. The French
Revolution was particularly influenced by Rousseau, and his
excessively romantic and idealistic theories of the state of
nature. This didn't go terribly well for the French, bringing in
Napoleon and a massive war. The ideas of Liberalism also took
root in America; John Locke was probably the biggest influence
on the US Declaration of Independence and Constitution.
Locke's base of "life, liberty, and property" was amended to
"Life, Liberty, and the Pursuit of Happiness" becoming an
incredibly famous document.

The growth of Liberalism was by no means a clean process.
Like the Mushroom War that brought about the current governments in the land of Ooo, a great many wars and tyrannies
took place before something functional and stable was created
with Liberalism. But now, the thought of a government established without a respect for human rights is unthinkable.
Hobbes argued for the necessity of the government caring
about its citizens, and Locke and Rousseau took it a step further, hammering out the language of rights.

In the aftermath of the Second World War, the United
Nations issued a Universal Declaration of Human Rights, bind-
ing all of humanity under an idea of freedom that was birthed
by Hobbes, Locke, and Rousseau. It's these essential rights that
keep the land of Ooo functioning, more or less. Without them,
we'd have zombie candies running amok, penguins oppressing
people, and Susan Strong and the Hyoomans happily munch-
ing away on the populace. Sweet!

5
Should Simon Have Saved Marceline?

MATTHEW MONTOYA

They run. Street after street, blind turn after blind turn, they run. But nothing stops the approaching horde. The monsters won't stop. The forms of the things sputter and shift as their mutated bodies seethe with hunger. The few humans not killed immediately by the bomb were either mutated into those . . . monsters . . . or eaten by them. Glowing green pustulance oozes from their eyes, mouths, and noses, if you can call them that. And there, cornered, no street left to run to, are a middle-aged man and a little girl with pointy teeth. They are about to die. Desperate, the man tosses the little girl into a nearby car, closing the door. She presses her hands and face against the glass window, watching, helpless. The monsters close in on him. There's no choice. The crown at his hip calls to him. It sings of power.

Muffled, he hears a voice. "You promised, Simon!"

The man can already feel himself torn by the rush of magic as he grabs the crown. The last vestiges of his identity become clouded and lost in a stream of ice and torrential frost. The Ice King places his crown on his head.

Making Your Way in the World Today Takes Everything You've Got

The Ice King is one of my favorite characters, if not my favorite character. He's a memorably humorous villain with more hilarious moments than I can even keep track of. How can you not laugh as this "evil" man loves on a room full of penguins, and, then, as they all try to lick his tears away out of love for their "evil" master, he disciplines one for being on a no salt diet? Or when he comes out dressed up like Marceline singing to Gunter a new rendition of Marceline's song in which the "Gunt Gunts his Gunter's fries," and Gunter goes starry-eyed out of admiration. I always lose it laughing.[1]

The Ice King's antics are always different and hilarious. His constant search for love and the kidnapping of princesses from Princess Bubblegum to Hotdog Princess, despite her smell, has made him a lovable contrast to Finn and Jake's constant acts of heroism. He's undoubtedly a villain, but he is a relatable and loveable one. He is a villain that our hearts can reach out to and sympathize with. After all, aren't we all a bit quirky?

While I love the Ice King, it seemed, at first, that he was a one-note character. He would go from episode to episode simply coming up with new ways to kidnap princesses. He was never a very deep character and he lacked a real background or motivation. But just when I was beginning to fear that this might be the case, I was blown away with the revelation that the Ice King used to be a normal human being.

The Ice King used to be a man named Simon Petrikov, and he was one of the few survivors of the Great Mushroom War, the cataclysmic event that mutated the world we know to the magical land of Ooo. The trials and choices that Simon had to endure in this post-apocalyptic wasteland are, in my opinion, some of the deepest and most tragic moments of the show. It was his history as Simon that showed me that the Ice King was more than I had previously been led to believe.

The string of events that transformed him from peaceful and caring Simon to the insane and lonely Ice King are extremely tragic. My friends and I honestly had tears brought to our eyes as our feelings had been punched in their metaphorical stomachs. We learned that within the post-apocalyptic wasteland caused by the Great Mushroom War Simon found a lost and crying little girl named Marceline. This is the same Marceline that we know as the vampire bass player who loves hanging out with our heroes, Finn and Jake.

In their travels together Simon and Marceline grew very close. They bonded and formed a loving father-daughter relationship. Unfortunately, their loving relationship was doomed to fail as Simon was determined to protect Marceline from all

---

[1] "I Remember You."

of the evolving toxic horrors of this post-apocalyptic world. Simon's only means of protecting Marceline was to wear a magical crown that granted him powers over ice and storms. The inescapable horror of this is that we must watch as the crown corrupts his mind. It warps and changes him to the point that he's no longer the same man, but he endured all of it in order to save Marceline. In all honesty, would you not do the same? A true hero would do anything to save a child, right?

Was this right for Simon? Was it right for him to sacrifice his own sanity for that of a child's life? Normally we would say that saving a child is the morally acceptable thing to do, but is it still morally acceptable when an effect of saving the child is giving your mind over to evil? Simon knew the danger of using the crown, but he chose to do it anyway. He knew that he would no longer be the same man, and that he could potentially pose a threat to the very child he was looking to protect. But Simon believed that the choice to save her at the potential risk was an acceptable choice, and I'm inclined to agree with him . . . for good reason. Hold on to your minds, we are about to get *mathematical*!

To Save Marceline or Save Simon's Sanity?

To solve this moral dilemma we must devote ourselves like Beemo, the sentient little computer, to finding the answers. We must pry and search until we reach a satisfying conclusion. The first thing we must do is look at the doctrine of double effect and how it affects our beloved Simon and Marcy.

The doctrine of double effect was first expressed by Thomas Aquinas (1225–1274). We can see what it means by looking at a situation where your choice will produce the intended positive effect as well as an unintentional negative effect. Aquinas uses the idea of double effect to justify the unintentional negative effects, such as the death of another, as a possible result in a moment of self-defense.[2] This is considered a double effect because the intended result was meant to be positive, but allowed for a negative result to also occur as a side-effect.

A big problem with the doctrine of double effect is telling when a negative outcome is intended out of a desire for harm

---

[2] In Part 2 of *Summa Theologica*.

or as a foreseen, yet unfortunate, side effect. The situation with Simon and Marceline is no different as Simon not only regrets that his decision will make Marceline cry, but he foresees that this will happen and still chooses to carry out the action. The question is whether or not Simon's action can be justified by the doctrine of double effect.

Simon had to do what he could to survive in the wastes, and his life was only further complicated when he met eight-year-old Marceline. She was young and afraid, as any child would be. Simon met her crying in the ruined rubble of a city street, and helped calm her down with a stuffed animal, which she has kept to this day. Simon essentially adopted her and took care of her as though she was his own daughter. Sadly, the act of taking care of a child was made even more difficult when the world had been so severely altered by a mutagenic bomb.

Throughout their travels, Simon and Marceline had to look out for and care for each other. They helped each other laugh and find hope in the world. We saw as Simon made jokes to cheer her up when she was sad, and he even pantomimed being in a TV show to keep her childhood alive in the mutagenic hellscape.

Simon and Marcy had to brave the harsh weather of the world and avoid the newly emerging monsters and creatures that were beginning to walk the Earth. They had no weapons, and no combat skills. The only thing they did have was Simon's crown and the magical powers that it gave him. Unfortunately, there was a very large drawback to using the magical crown.

Whenever Simon would put on the crown, he would become a completely different person. He was loud, cackling, and obsessed with himself—the complete opposite of Simon. In fact, he was so different that he frightened young Marceline. Sadly, he realized that this undesired change was necessary if he was going to protect her, but even he feared what he might become in order to save Marceline's life.

Simon and Marceline Sing a Ballad

In the episode "I Remember You," it's revealed to Marceline just how much Simon feared what he would become due to the effects of the crown. Marceline discovers notes that Simon left her before he lost his mind, turning him into the Ice King. The two of them then perform the notes as a song and what they sing is as follows:

> Marceline, is it just you and me in the wreckage of the world? That must be so confusing for a little girl. And I know you're going to need me here with you. But I'm losing myself and I'm afraid you're going to lose me too. This magic keeps me alive but it's making me crazy, and I need to save you but who's going to save me? Please forgive me for whatever I do when I don't remember you.

We can see in these notes just how certain Simon was that he would soon be forgetting Marceline and that he would possibly perform evil acts in the future.

Tragically, Simon was left with two choices. He could choose to save himself and commit one evil action by letting a child die, or he could choose to save the child and *possibly* commit multiple evil actions as a result. These were the two choices that Simon was left with, and the doctrine of double effect would actually prefer the latter as the evil actions he feared are only possible ones. There was no certainty that he would commit evil actions. The doctrine is only concerned with the immediate negative effects not with the far off future implications of an action.

The fact is that the only immediate action Simon permitted in order to save Marceline's life was the consequence of making the child cry. The doctrine would find this to be an acceptable exchange as the positive effect of saving her life far outweighed the negative outcome of her broken heart. Any negative consequence that came from this point on is not applicable to his choice to wear the crown. Only the immediate, or somewhat immediate, consequences of an action are applicable to the doctrine of double effect.

The Theft of Jake's Everything Burrito

The philosopher Immanuel Kant (1724–1804) said that all of our moral actions should be motivated by our duty to help others—something which Finn and Jake would agree with. It was this idea of duty that helped Kant to come up with the idea of the "Categorical Imperative." The Categorical Imperative is a rule that allows for us to decide if performing a certain action is ethical or not ethical, which is why it is useful to apply it to Simon's dilemma.

Kant argues that the Categorical Imperative is essential for moral choice. It is formulated in the statement, "So act that the maxim of thy deed may stand as universal law." In other words, you act morally when you follow a rule that can be applied to anyone at any time or place. It must be acceptable for everyone to follow this rule, not just one person or a select few.

Suppose that Jake is cooking himself a breakfast fit for a hero, and today he has decided to make himself an Everything Burrito. This burrito is the most delicious burrito filled with all the amazing tastes one could muster. Jake loves his burrito. It is large, delicious, and he has spent a very long time preparing it. This is something that he has been looking forward to all morning. He even woke up bright and early to begin cooking it.

Finn, exhausted from monster slaying, slept in and does not have the time to make himself breakfast before embarking on his newest adventure. Finn has to make a choice. He can steal Jake's burrito and eat it himself, or he can simply wait until lunch to eat. Finn decides to judge the situation according to the Categorical Imperative.

Finn asks himself, "Would it be acceptable for everyone to steal?" He imagines a universe in which moral law allows for everyone to steal. This would allow for the Ice King to steal anything he wanted from others, including princesses from their kingdoms! The candy people in the Candy Kingdom could steal from one another without a second thought. There would be no consequence and everyone would be allowed to steal from everyone else. It would be as bad as the City of Thieves!

Now, while that sucks, this isn't what makes stealing wrong, according to Kant. Kant would point out that if everyone's stealing, then the idea of stealing falls apart! How can we have an idea of "property" when we know everything's going to be stolen all the time? So if we make it universal that stealing is okay, stealing becomes an illogical idea, because stealing can only take place in a world in which we can actually own stuff . . . *and we can't own stuff in a world in which everything is always being stolen!*

So Finn decides that by allowing stealing to be morally acceptable on the universal scale it creates an illogical situation where everyone always steals from everyone else. This means that the Categorical Imperative has shown stealing to be immoral. And this, sadly, means that Finn will have to skip breakfast today while Jake eats his amazing Everything Burrito because Finn can't make an exception to the rule of stealing just for himself. If he applies it to everyone, the whole thing falls apart, and if he says it's okay *just for him* he isn't playing very fair at all. . . .

We can apply the Categorical Imperative to the situation with Simon and Marceline. Simon was attempting to determine if he should save the life of a child despite the fear that doing so would cause him to lose his sanity and possibly perform future evil acts. Simon questioned if it was acceptable to let Marceline, die in order to save himself.

With the Categorical Imperative, we have to also ask if the rule, "I should use others just to get what I want" can be universalizable? Certainly, letting little kids die to save ourselves falls under the "taking care of my needs at the expense of the needs of others" category! And we are often encouraged to put ourselves before others. . . . But think about it, if we *all* are following the rule, "It is good to use people *just* to get what I want" (like letting children die) that means others will use *us* just to get what they want too! But that makes no sense, because we made the rule in the first place so that we could get what we want! And being used (often to the point of harm) is *not* what any of us want! So if we make "use other people a rule" the whole rule falls apart, again! So, Simon, if he is going to follow Kant's recommendation, *has* to try to help Marcy because he can't ignore her needs just to take care of himself since none of us, rationally, want to live in a world where everyone is taking advantage of us!

Drowning Candy People in Fountains

There's at least one more way to defend Simon's choice to go insane rather than let Marcy die. Utilitarianism is the idea that a moral choice is one that helps to improve utility, or happiness.

"Act utilitarianism" argues that an action is only morally acceptable if that action is the one that produces the most utility (roughly defined as "happiness"). Choosing an action that produces anything less than the greatest happiness is immoral according to act utilitarianism. The problem with act utilitarianism is that often in the decision making process there's not enough time to calculate all of the consequences of our actions.

Finn is walking past a fountain in the center of the Candy Kingdom on his way to deliver very important plans to Princess Bubblegum. He's in a rush because Bubblegum told him that these plans must be delivered to her as quickly as possible because they hold the secret to saving the world from the Lich forever. While walking past the fountain he observes a candy child drowning. The child looks to be a three-year-old candy cane named Carl. Finn can either continue on his way to deliver these extremely important plans and ignore Carl, or his can save Carl and risk ruining the documents on which the plans are written and be late.

Act utilitarianism would ask Finn to take the time to decide whether saving Carl or delivering the plans would create the most utility—in other words, which action would cause the greatest total happiness in the world?

Finn's situation has a time limit! Finn may not have the time to add up all of the possible happiness. But if we ignore this difficulty, we see that Finn still has to calculate whether delivering the plans or saving Carl will create the most happiness overall.

By delivering the plans to Princess Bubblegum Finn would be saving all of Ooo from the Lich. Countless lives would be saved! On the other hand, saving the candy child named Carl creates happiness for Carl and his parents as they would not have to suffer the sorrow of his death. The utility in this situation is limited to three people initially, with room to grow as time passes. For act utilitarianism, leaving the child to die and taking the plans to Princess Bubblegum is the action that produces the greatest immediate happiness. Saving Carl's life would be immoral according to act utilitarianism.

Rule utilitarianism takes a step beyond act utilitarianism. Rule utilitarianism says that the action that's morally right is the one that, as a general rule, produces the greatest happiness. So yes, sometimes it might save the world to let a child drown, but as a general rule, it doesn't. So we can develop rules *before* problems arise that help us decide what to do like, "Murder is wrong" and "Stealing is bad" because, in general, murder and stealing create a great deal of unhappiness, even if in a few very unusual situations they create more happiness. These already determined rules help Finn to decide almost immediately which action is moral.

Rule utilitarianism would argue that both the plans and the candy child named Carl are important and performing either would produce a great deal of happiness, but saving Carl is what takes priority because the rules value saving a child's life. This means that Finn would be morally correct in saving Carl's life despite the fact that delivering the plans to Princess Bubblegum would produce more utility overall. So what does this mean for Marcy?

The Happiness of a Vampire Child

If we look at Simon's choice using act utilitarianism we must take into consideration all the happiness that was created or taken away from that choice. While this is essentially impossible to do in the moment, we are able to do it as we are looking back on Simon's choice from the future.

We know that by saving Marceline, Simon has increased the happines of Finn and Jake (well Finn at least) as they now have a new friend with whom they can hang out, play music, and shoot hoops. The happiness of Marceline's father is increased, as he is able to continue his evil efforts to attempt to make Marceline the new ruler of his kingdom in the Nightosphere. Even Marceline's happiness is increased due to Simon's choice.

Marceline was and still is saddened by the loss of her friend Simon, but over the years she has moved on with her life. She has created new friends, experienced romantic relationships, and come to terms with Simon's change. Marcy has danced in the Fire Kingdom, ridden giant gold fish, and discovered untold mysteries in the Land of Ooo. And, as seen in the episode "Simon and Marcy," she has come to some terms with Simon's new and eccentric mindset as the Ice King. Her loss makes her sad, but she also, because she lived, has been able to experience a great deal of happiness, not to mention adventure!

When looking at Simon's choice through the lens of rule utilitarianism it's even easier to determine that his choice was moral. As we saw above when talking about the Categorical Imperative, our society has determined that saving children when they're in danger is our duty. It's essentially a rule of our society. This means that when met with the choice of saving Marceline or himself, rule utilitarianism would dictate that Simon save Marceline as that is what the rules of our society have already decided. Simon's choice is once again shown to have been the moral one.

Simon and Marcy, Together Forever

Looking at these three theories, we have seen evidence that shows how Simon's choice to save Marceline is a moral choice. The doctrine of double effect shows that it was morally acceptable for Simon to sacrifice himself as the negative consequence of Marceline's sorrow is outweighed by the positive outcome of saving her life. The Categorical Imperative also supports that saving Marceline's life is moral because a world in which it is universally accepted to sacrifice children is illogical. Finally, utilitarianism agrees that saving Marceline would not only produce the largest utility but is also supported by the rules of our society.

Ethics is debatable. No one theory is universally accepted. Because of this, we can't just assume that Simon's actions are morally correct. By looking at three different ethical theories, we're able to come to a general agreement that saving Marceline is the ethical choice.

Ethics is never completely clear and these theories are not perfect, but they do give us a common basis for looking at how we live our lives. The ethics of any situation is always questionable, but most people do not take the time to analyze the morality of a choice as many of our choices are in the moment.

Simon's no different as he chose to sacrifice himself for the innocence of a child that he loved. This choice was not really one of contemplation or even a hard choice for Simon. He was worried about what would happen after the consequences of his choice took full effect, but the choice to save Marceline was never in question for Simon. He acted from what he believed and *felt* was right.

Simon felt that sacrificing himself to save Marceline was the moral thing to do. Whether this choice is from a source of duty, appeal to utility, or something else entirely is for only Simon to know. It was his choice to make, and according to the three theories analyzed here, it was a morally righteous one.

We all face choices like this every day. And like Simon, we are, in some ways even faced with whether or not we should choose to let children die (say in underdeveloped nations, sweat shops, or abusive homes). The kinds of choices that we do make are about what's right and wrong within our social interactions with one another.

We don't always have the time to question or think about what is the right thing to do. We can only go with our gut reaction and what we believe is the right choice. By looking at these systems, we can see how making the right choice is never easy, but we can see that Simon was right in making his choice to save Marceline. The Ice King might be a villain to some people, but to me, and I'm sure Marceline, Simon Petrikov is the greatest hero the Land of Ooo has ever known.

6
Games Vampires Play

TRIP McCROSSIN

Turn down the lights… grab a flashlight.

… and a blanket …

There are monsters—very, very creepy monsters—that lurk in the dark. They can fly, turn invisible, and they are super strong . . . and they love the color red. They need that color to survive, and they'll do anything to get it. Funny thing . . . isn't red the color of your blood? It wouldn't be that hard to suck it out, would it? . . . Not hard at all for those creatures.

What kind of monster is it? You know . . . vampires, of course! Laugh if you want, but they could be hiding behind any corner, just waiting for the lights to go out. And then, there's nothing that you can do to stop it! It'll just slither right up to you, and before you know it . . . CHOMP . . . you're vampire food! Don't believe me?

I heard of a vampire that haunted . . . or I should say hunted . . . in this very place. Centuries ago, her lust for red drove her to go on a murderous rampage. Powered by darkness and hate, the vampire killed everyone in her path. As she waded through the carnage that she had wrought, the vampire smashed their skulls just for the fun of it. She didn't even have to bite their necks; she could hypnotize her victims with her eyes and they would lie down before her, offering themselves to her on their own! Then, using her magic, the vampire would feed off of the helpless folk, hunched over her victims, breathing in their vaporized blood mist.

That's the tale of the Vampire Queen. Or so I'm told. I heard it from a very reliable source . . .

Okay, okay, maybe Marceline isn't that bad with her kickin' bass skills and her soft spot for Finn and Jake. But Marceline has done some pretty bad stuff. I have to give her credit, though; hanging around Finn seems to remind her what it means to be a better person.

They boys are pretty terrified of Marceline at first, as she kicks then out of their house and tries to drain Jake of his blood, but it doesn't take long for Finn to have a change of heart, and Jake does too, eventually.[1] The boys come to see her as having the potential for evil, but also a tendency to avoid inflicting evil by sustaining herself with shades of red, rather than blood. In this, Marceline's in the good company of a variety of popular-culture reflections of vampires and other demons—the *Twilight*, *Underworld*, and *True Blood* stories, for instance. But Marceline is cooler than the rest of them, and it isn't just because she has a pretty kick-ass grunge rock thing going on and doesn't sparkle (thank Glob).

When people who are potentially very bad resist their capability to be bad, we tend to be pleased, relieved, and even appreciative. We may find what bad behavior they *do* display not so bad after all, in light of what could have been worse. It helps, though, if we see some remorse, or at least regret. And that might really be a problem. Finn and Jake have come to trust Marceline, but does she show enough regret for her past evils? The evil she has done might be forgivable, but only if she is ashamed, right? And Marceline isn't very good at that sometimes, or even just showing care in general. Remember when her dad was rampaging around eating souls? Marceline was pretty preoccupied just trying to get her ax back . . . *while her father killed a lot of innocent people!* Maybe Finn and Jake are wrong . . . maybe Marceline is a monster.

Temper, Temper

In "Evicted!," once Marceline has successfully turned Finn and Jake out of their tree house, they find and remodel a cave

---

[1] Finn's change of heart occurs in "Henchman," the second episode in the story line, and Jake's in "Go With Me," its fourth. The intervening third episode is "It Came from the Nightosphere."

as their new home, only to have her turn up to claim *it* as well. Finn again gives in, as Jake urges: "Vampires will *kill* you, remember."

But things go even worse this time. "I'm gonna let you keep this cave," Finn chides, "but *only* because *Jake* is my home, and he's way better than all *your* homes com*bined!*" "You're right," she retorts. "I guess I'll take him *too* . . . bite him a little, maybe turn him into a zombie." This, Finn *won't* allow.

"Let go of Jake!" he cries. "Make me," Marceline answers back, which he does by knocking Jake from her grasp. Now she's really mad, and morphs into giant-bat-monster form. Finn's not discouraged, but also no match for her, ultimately. As she closes in on him, Jake summons the courage to fly to Finn's defense. He succeeds, but is bitten in the process, Marceline appearing to suck the life entirely out of him, throwing his withered carcass contemptuously to the cave floor. Enraged, Finn lunges for her, with a right hook that she admits "actually hurt," which finally coaxes her out of her rage and monstrous form. She glides Finn to the cave floor, laughing, and, to his embarrassment, kisses him on the cheek.

Finn is confused. "Why didn't you just kill me?" "'Cause that was *fun*," Marceline answers, as if it was *so* obvious, "I haven't fought like that in *years*." Equally confusing, to Finn and also to Marceline, Jake has survived unharmed: "Before she bit me, I used my powers to shrink all my guts into my thumb." Marceline decides that Finn and Jake are "pretty hard core," and allows them, in the end, to return to the tree house.

So Finn and Jake are alive and well, and having won Marceline's approval, they've also won their old home back. We're relieved, and perhaps we're also inclined to forget, or at least forgive, Marceline's earlier behavior. Unfortunately, this includes having fully intended to kill, or at least harm, them both. Okay, and sure, she's returned Finn and Jake to their home (somewhat graciously, given that it did belong to her), but she also long ago abandoned it. Doesn't reclaiming it in the first place seem a little mean-spirited and wrong? Either way, in both cases—trying to kill the boys and trying to evict them—she shows no remorse or regret, which *has* to trouble us. Dude, . . . she just tried to *kill* Jake! That doesn't seem like something you just laugh off, but Finn does. . . .

Vampires Just Wanna Have Fun

In "Henchman," we open with Marceline watching Finn and Jake horsing around on a dinosaur skeleton. As she does, we hear her utter a "hmm," which tells us that seeing them has given her an idea. We cut, then, to Finn and Jake observing *her*, abusing her elderly henchman. When he pleads for compassionate release, they watch her amuse herself instead by abusing him further. Jake's petrified, but Finn resolves to free the henchman. "If it isn't my favorite little goody two-shoes," she quips, as if she's been expecting him. "How're ya gonna pull *that* off," she challenges, "*hero?*" Finn, always brave, tells her, "I'll do what I have to do . . . I'll even take his place!"

As Marceline's new henchman Finn is required to do all kind of things that *seem* evil, at first, but really, aren't bad at all! Finn learns that Marceline is "not how she seems," but "a radical dame who likes to play games!" It was all an elaborate practical joke, as it turns out, which even the former henchman was in on. "Dang, man," Marceline jokes, "I didn't think you'd ever catch on!"

Where does this leave us? Well, practical jokes can be annoying, yes, sometimes in the extreme, but they're not typically *evil*, we think. We might have thought that abusing the former henchman, even for the sake of the overall fun of pranking Finn, might certainly qualify as evil, but in the end we find that he was actually just Marceline's "old diving buddy." And there may not be enough harm involved in turning an elderly pianist's red bow tie white, even if against his will, especially if he ends up liking it better that way. But there's also no evidence that he's another "old diving buddy." So we have to assume that he is truly terrified at first by the prospect of being dinner. Finn is just as truly horrified to be forced to help feed the pianist to Marceline. So this "harmless" fun really isn't harmless at all. The pianist terror is real, as is Finn's fear and anguish. And worse, Marceline again lacks any obvious remorse or regret after the fact.

Not to mention, Jake is never really let in on the joke and spends the whole time thinking he has to save his friend from an evil vampire. Sure, in the end Finn and Marceline make Jake think he's saved the day, but to do it, Finn lies to Jake. Isn't there something pretty crappy about putting Finn in the position of deceiving his best friend? And in the end, again, we get no remorse or regret from Marceline for being part of the scheme.

Daddy Dearest

In "It Came from the Nightosphere," we open with Finn helping Marceline record a song, deeply personal in nature, about
ill treatment she suffered as a young girl at the hands of her
dad, Hunson Abadeer. The ill treatment in question is relatively
trivial—eating her french fries—but the song is heartfelt, and
Finn is moved, and so we are too. Finn is so moved that he finds
out how to summon her dad and does so, to his and Marceline's
horror. After all, "Dad" also goes by the name "Lord of Evil."

Once in Ooo, Abadeer doesn't spend much time with his
daughter. He chastises her, takes the ax she turned into a bass
(a family heirloom) and then leaves to go on a killing rampage,
"sucking up all the souls in Ooo." Finn, with Marceline's
grumpy help, tries to defeat Abadeer, so they release the stolen
souls, and return him to the Nightosphere. Finn's positively
beside himself, mortified to have "unleashed evil on Ooo!," and
determined to right the wrong. Marceline, on the other hand,
is more selfishly motivated. "I'm only coming with you," she
moans, "to get my bass back," though later she admits that she
also wanted to return Dad to the Nightosphere because it's so
"emotionally exhausting" to have him around. She just doesn't
seem appropriately concerned with thwarting Dad's nasty
business.

What might make this more acceptable, for some, is how
messed up Marceline's relationship with her Dad is. At a key
moment, in response to Finn's complaint that their "co-ordinated" effort is maybe not so co-ordinated, she admits, "I just
want my dad to care about me." Okay, fair enough. Her pain
does seem deep and genuine, and we're bound to ask whether
it somehow justifies her actions. But Dad's out and about sucking up souls, so, however unloved she feels, maybe she could
muster a bit more enthusiasm for stopping him. Seriously,
helping people not lose their souls should be more important
than any of her own personal emotional stuff. This is all made
worse when, once she gets her bass back, Marceline up and
leaves Finn to fend for himself.

Finn appears to be out of moves. He knows that the only
thing that will allow him to attack successfully, free the captive
souls, and banish the Lord of Evil back to the Nightosphere is
Marceline's voice. But he can't convince her to stay, and so

plays instead the recording of the "fry song" he helped her to make early. The ruse works, and in the midst of the resulting father-daughter reconciliation, Finn attacks, the souls are freed, and Dad's once again banished.

Finn and Marceline collapse to the ground, physically and emotionally exhausted. All is well again, as they stare up at the sky and watch the freed souls drift about as they migrate back to their bodies. But again, we've got no hint from Marceline of remorse or regret for having abandoned Finn. So far, there really isn't a whole lot of reason for Finn to trust Marceline. He's a good guy, right?, and young, he's probably a bit motivated by her vampiric wiles. But what about Jake?

Is That a Small Dog in Your Pocket, or Are You Just Happy to See Me?

What must Jake think of this? How, in this light, can he be heading for a change of heart about Marceline? But hold on — where *is* Jake? In times of trouble, Jake is always at Finn's side, but he's gone during the whole soul-sucking fiasco! I mean, think about it, Jake comes to view Marceline as a friend too, eventually. But how can we even wonder how Marceline's behavior in all of this can be moving him toward a change of heart toward her, if he's nowhere to be found?

"What's with that pocket on your shirt?" Marceline asks. We hear this and notice for the first time what we should have noticed before. Finn's normally plain blue shirt has a new pocket, visibly and inexpertly stitched on for the occasion. "Oh," he replies, "Jake's in here."

So Jake *has* been at Finn's side the whole time. He was just too frightened of Marceline, we assume, to accompany him to the earlier recording session except covertly, shrunk down to pocket size—and still too frightened later on, to emerge and join in Finn's struggle with her dad. But we have to wonder: from the safety of Finn's pocket, how can he not have been at least *listening in*? And if he was listening, he must trust Marceline even less. On the one hand, he has no clue what's going on because he's too scared, and on the other, he knows what's going on, and it still too scared. So what possibly could cause Jake to change his mind about Marceline . . . especially since she hasn't done much to demonstrate he was wrong?

When he eventually reveals his change of heart regarding Marceline, Jake explains that his "fear was based on *ignorance*." His newfound courage must be based, then, on some newfound wisdom—he's "been learning a lot about vampires lately." But what precisely has he learned? We can speculate about what's not laid out in available episodes—say, how Jake might have hit the books, researched vampires, how they feed, the conventional wisdom that since they're no longer human, they lack the normal moral resistance that humans have to killing little boys and their dogs. But what we *know* from available episodes, and in particular the one at hand, is what Jake has learned about Marceline *specifically*, from the safety of Finn's pocket.

That means that the ignorance he cites is ignorance of what "mitigating factors" can explain the bad things that people who act badly do, which can make them seem less bad, or at least less easy to condemn. The only thing that makes sense is that Jake *was* listening in and he also noticed how messed up, how crazy dysfunctional Marceline's relationship with her dad is.

After all, what Jake's learned is that her *dad* is the *Lord of Evil*. And if that's not bad enough, judging from her mournful "fry song," he treated her *really badly* as a child. And worse still, Marceline's *really old*, and so has suffered the resulting hurt and resentment for a *really long time*. So maybe, Jake learns that he should consider being friends with Marceline, because her bad actions are not just the result of her choices, but also a result of things that happened outside of her control, things from her past and childhood. It's kind of like when a friend has a really annoying habit that you finally yell at them about, and then you learn it's something they do because they were abused as a kid. It's one of those, "Oh, crap, sorry . . . I didn't know, Bro" moments.

But still, . . . something nags at me. Okay, Marceline comes with some serious family baggage, but she still doesn't seem to show much regret or shame for trying to kill our heroes, ditching Finn to fight a monster alone or letting millions die at her father's mouth-orifice thing . . . Even if there is reason to *understand* why Marceline is the way she is, doesn't she have to show remorse for us to forgive her? Isn't that the difference, say, between two criminals who were both abused as kids, but only one regrets the life of crime? We understand why both are messed up, but we only forgive the one who recognizes it's wrong and wishes to do better!

A Spoonful of Prosperity Makes the Blood Flow Again?

Okay, how about this example? Remember when Finn, Jake, and Marceline are exploring the underground Sand City where Princess Bubblegum has sent them to retrieve the mysterious "spoon of prosperity?"[2] Jake's made a mistake that's trapped them in the Sand City, and then another mistake that deprives Marceline of ways of feeding other than sucking blood—human *or* canine!

The episode is taken up with Jake's and Finn's efforts to try to feed Marceline's need for red before she loses control and feeds off our heroes. And it does seem, for a little while, that Marceline really does want to avoid killing her friends. But all the boys' efforts fail, and they are saved just in the nick of time when PB comes to the rescue, literally on a gigantic tunneling sand worm. Marceline latches onto PB and drains her instead. "Thanks, Bonnie," Marceline says, using one of the derisive nicknames she has for the princess. "That's enough low-grade red to get me home, at least." Then, with no hesitation, she adds, "Come on, guys, let's go," only adding to our amazement at her lack of regret and remorse for putting PB in danger, not to mention her general lack of concern for the princess's well-being. The same is not true for Finn and Jake, who were visibly horrified at the princess's being bitten, in general and instead of them. "Are you all right, PB?" Finn frets. Clearly she's not, but has enough life left to ask, "Did you get the spoon of prosperity?"

The spoon of prosperity, as it turns out, will sustain someone in need (like PB!) if only they can press the spoon to the tip of their nose and let it hang there unsupported. Those of us who've tried this trick with a regular old spoon know that it's not as easy as it sounds, and perhaps this is appropriate for a trick that will literally save your life. Be this as it may, it's an impressive bit of magic, and it rescues the princess. "Peeps will

---

[2] "Red Starved."

never starve," the princess coos, "in my eternal empire." And the magic lulls us again, it seems, into thoughts of all being well that ends well, and so on, and we are inclined yet again to forget, or at least forgive, Marceline's bad behavior. Except, *again*, we're missing any regret or remorse on *her* part, which, yet again, has to trouble us.

Finn and Jake have learned a lot about Marceline, and, through them, we have as well. Over time, we've come to learn more about Marceline's childhood shortly after the Mushroom War, about her beloved protector, Simon, before he became the Ice King . . . and then forgot her. All of this helps to fill out a picture of someone who, as vampire, may have moral standards different from conventional human ones, but who also resists acting in immoral, doing so only when necessary...or when it's *really* fun and not *overly* harmful. What's troubling about her story, though, is what also sets her apart from related "good vampire" storylines like *Twilight*, *Underworld*, and *True Blood*. Marceline lacks the ability to regret—or simply chooses not to regret—the behavior she knows does harm, sometimes even to her friends!

In most vampire stories, Marceline would be one of the "bad" vampires, encouraging her goody good, "sparkly," friends to just cut lose, have some fun, and occasionally, if the situation demands, do something naughty. But this is what's weird: Marceline is one of the good guys in *Adventure Time*, or at the very least, the good guys seem to treat her like she's good. And it isn't like Finn and Jake *don't know* she does evil now and then, because a lot of the crappy stuff she does, *she does to them!* Maybe Marceline is just kind of like that uncle that you have to invite to the holidays—you know the one I mean . . . yeah, he's gonna break some stuff, but he means well, and the kids enjoy playing with him, and he's got funny stories from the crazy life he's led. . . . You just have to keep him away from sucking down too much blood, . . . I mean wine. . . .

Marceline's storyline presents us with a serious choice. Should we accept her as she is, without further condemnation? Or should we prefer that she be more like her kin elsewhere in popular culture, acting all depressed and whiny (or at least a bit regretful) about their mistakes? It's worth thinking about. After all, that will tells us how we should think about and treat people who sometimes do bad things in our own lives, like good ol' Uncle . . .

II

Glob Said the Word and It Was "Cabbage!"

7
Dude. Stop. Saying.
All This. Crazy. Nonsense.

NICOLAS MICHAUD

The adventure has been harrowing. The boys have narrowly defeated a disgusting wall of flesh, deadly sign zombies, and a brutal brain beast. They are tired and, to be honest, more than a little annoyed. They had entered the Evil Forest to help Tree Trunks. But they can't sheathe their weapons for more than a second before Tree Trunks finds another way to put herself in mortal danger. Finally, though, things are going the adventurers' way. After a nightmarish journey made only worse by Tree Trunks's own naivety, the three friends will emerge victorious. They've found the Crystal Gem Apple atop a mushroom-shaped tree. The crystal guardian protecting the mystical item is helpless to stop Tree Trunks from eating the apple— the boys have figured out his weakness. He must mimic his opponents, and the boys aren't fighting; they are putting on make-up and prancing about helplessly. Happily, while the boys distract the foe, Tree Trunks takes a well-deserved bite of her prize
  . . . and explodes.
  The boys, and even the guardian, look on in horror.
  [Cut scene.]
  [Roll Credits.]

And so began my introduction to *Adventure Time*. I looked over at my smug friend sitting on the couch and chastised him, using some language not quite appropriate for children's TV. "Really, dude? *That is what you wanted me to see?* This show is <insert expletive here> up!" I was told it would get better. And in a sense this is true. We do learn, for example, that Tree Trunks isn't dead. Rather, she's been transformed into a nearly all-powerful god who later tries to kill the boys. And that seems to be much of the way *Adventure Time* works. The things that make no sense in one episode are explained thirty episodes later.

But that doesn't change the fact that the episode after Tree Trunks explodes, no one talks about losing her. When things happen in the land of Ooo, the characters tend to take them, no matter how insane, with a pretty casual attitude—and move on. For a long time, I found this fact very frustrating. I mean, she just *exploded*! They aren't going to deal with that in the next episode at all??? It seems like everyone in Ooo is pretty comfortable living in a very random world. Yes, sometimes, we get explanations, . . . albeit a season later. *Adventure Time,* though, doesn't pretend that everything needs to make sense. Sometimes we find out why things happen, and sometimes the world is just filled with magic and nonsense. I think that's why adults who have only seen an episode or two can be pretty critical of the show: "But it's so weird and crazy."

The funny thing, though, is that *Adventure Time* mimics our real world far more than we would like to realize. Yes, sometimes we get explanations for the amazing and random things that happen around us, but often we have no clue what's going on and just move forward without comment.

This Place Is Weird

Here's what I mean: our own world is far crazier than we realize. Really, everything just seems pretty stable and sensible because of our size and perspective. The fact is, though, that—like in the land of Ooo—seemingly random and crazy things are happening all around us and *in us* all the time.

If we were as small as an electron, all of the stuff that seems so solid to us like buildings, and bricks, and candy would actually reveal itself to be made of stuff that is whizzing around at unbelievable speeds. The stuff, the matter, which makes up everything around us is made up of constantly shifting particles that never touch, spin around constantly, and speed past each other in what might be random ways. And if we were as large and long-lived as the sun, we wouldn't see the universe as a stable and sensible thing. Everything around us would be spinning, bubbling, and bursting constantly.

Pick the most stable object in the world, and if you really look at it, closely (like with a mathematical super microscope), you'll realize two things: 1. that "solid" object is mostly empty space, and 2. that stable object is more like a boiling pot of water than anything solid. It's like the world of Ooo is just a bit more in touch with the truth of that reality than we are.

It's easy to kind of blow off *Adventure Time* as nonsense because it allows randomness and weirdness into its world, in the extreme. Some of us might defend our beloved show by arguing that it isn't really that random, because so much of it is tied together if you watch enough episodes. But what I'm saying is that *Adventure Time* is mimicking the way the world actually is, particularly because the world really is random, totally crazy, and lacking explanation. I think the creators do this on purpose. You can't watch the show for long before you realize that Pendleton Ward and his team are creating a world that is purposefully playing with questions about the nature of time, space, and reality. They are doing *metaphysics* (the study of the nature of reality), and they are doing it *really* well.

Don't Deny My Science!

"But Nick," you might reply, "How can you say they are doing this so well when science is constantly improving and giving us all kinds of useful explanations for the world? The world isn't random. It follows a series of physical and mathematical laws that we can use to help us understand the world." You might also point out, "*And* because those laws are so reliable, we can use them to predict things like when stars will explode, when Haley's comet will appear, and even, with the right data, the way human beings will act." Fair enough. But I'm going to lay all of my cards on the table. I've decided to play from my Card Wars deck, "David Hume" (1711–1776). BAM. I win!

Oh, you want me to explain why . . . fine, fine, fair enough. Let me backtrack a bit. When we explain the world, we use different kinds of reasoning to do so. One kind is called *deductive* reasoning. This kind of reasoning is very mathematical. Basically, it's the lock-tight reasoning we use when we say, "If A happens, then B will happen. A has happened; therefore B must have happened." For example, what if we know something like, "If Jake gets hungry, he will become a jerk." Well then, if that statement is true, the next time we see Jake get hungry, we know to expect he'll be a jerk. That's almost the way the laws of physics seem to work. They are pretty lock-tight. How do we know a Crystal Gem Apple will fall to the ground? Well, we know, "If I drop it, it will fall." Then, all we have to do is drop it.

Here's the problem. How do we know that first statement is true? For example, how do we know that Jake will be a jerk if he gets hungry? I guess we might say we know from observation. We've *seen* Jake get all jerky whenever he gets hungry. So we can start making predictions. Maybe Princess Bubblegum can examine Jake and give us some sort of explanation like, "When Jake's cells are low on sugar, his brain gets less energy, and so his neurons start firing in an unusual way." But, really, this doesn't explain Jake's *anger*, the feeling. We can see that his brain responds differently when he's low on sugar, but how does that explain his becoming a jerk? In other words, how does specific neurons firing equal jerkiness? PB's explanation, like any scientific explanation, can show us how things work, but doesn't, if you keep looking closer and closer, answer why they work *that* way, instead of some other way.

Let's take a simple example that we're all comfortable with—magnetism. We know that magnets attract. Well, at first, that may seem magical. But scientists aren't big fans of magic (as we learn from Princess Bubblegum) and they want better reasons for why things are happening. So they examine the magnets and they see that the atoms in the magnets align a certain way. To make a long story short, that alignment causes the exchange of particles called photons. When those photons are being switched back and forth between two objects, they move toward each other. In fact, from what we can tell, all of the forces in the universe are caused by the exchange of certain particles. Like gravity is caused by the exchange of a particle called the *graviton* . . . we think, in all probability. Okay, great, so PB has given us the explanation. Magnetism isn't magic; it's the exchange of photons. Done. Right? But wait . . . why does exchanging particles make things attract each other?

That's where the scientist has to struggle a bit. PB might say something like, "Well, when particles are exchanged, that causes a force, and that force brings the particles together." But if we're honest, we have to admit that we don't understand why the particles create that force. What the heck's going on here?

This isn't to say that science is doing a bad job. Science is awesome. The problem is that science relies on a very deductive world. But you can always ask a question about the first statement, like a little kid: "Why?"

Take the famous "Matter and energy can't be created or destroyed" law (known as the first law of thermodynamics). We use that law to make all kinds of predictions about the world, to help us build stuff, and blow stuff up. But if we ask, *"Why can't matter be created nor destroyed?"* PB would be at a bit of a loss. Basically, what it comes down to is, *we've never seen it created or destroyed so we kind of assume.* Okay, okay, I admit there is A LOT of brilliant math that goes into proving the truth of that law as well. But all it will take is one observation, one *good* observation, of that law not holding, and we will have to reconsider that law, and figure a way to deal with this new information, and reconsider our math. That might be science's greatest strength . . . rather than assume truths, scientists try to challenge them, even their favorite laws.

Just Let Science Do the Work

The strength of science, in many ways, is its ability to make predictions. PB makes not just an observation, but *many* and from that she can infer a law. Every time Jake gets hungry, he turns into a jerk. We see that happen over and over again. So now we can make an experiment: "Okay, let's deny Jake food and see what happens." If he turns into a jerk, we have confirmation, and our prediction has come true! We do that a few thousand more times (poor Jake), and we have a "law" on our hands. But every good scientist knows these laws are technically not laws the way we would like to think of them. They are theories. Don't get me wrong, they aren't theories the way most of us think of theories—like guesses. No. No. NO! Scientific theories are tested and tested and tested all over the world thousands of times, and to be a "law" or "theory" means that there has never been a single case of the tests showing a different result. There's a lot of strength behind this. But this doesn't change the fact that even our most super-strong scientific theories rest on *observation.*

This is where David Hume comes in. Hume pointed out that our examination of the world really isn't deductive so much as it is *inductive—we infer truths of the world from observation.*

Induction is great. It is what helps me know that if I keep poking bears with my sword they get angry and try to kill me, so I'd better not poke bears. It's also what helps me predict the fact that the Ice King is probably going to try to kidnap a princess . . . because every time we meet the cabbage-head he tries to cart off an innocent princess victim. But, notice, the key word is "probably." Induction is probabilistic. It can never give us a "law." It lets us say, "Okay, every time I've tried this, this has been my result. So I'm going to say it will *probably* happen again." Sound familiar? This is exactly how science works! The only difference (and it's a very important difference) is that when scientists use induction, they have tried it thousands and thousands of times, *always* getting the same result. And so when they say, "It will probably happen," there is a very good chance they're right! Not to mention there is a butt load of mathematics to back them up.

Really, what we're seeing, though, is that our predictions about the world hinge on our observations of the world. And that's not a bad thing, and certainly not an attack on science. The fact that science is inductive, at its core, rather than deductive, is why we can trust science. If science were truly deductive, then scientists could just assert laws, and we would just assume they were true. Instead, scientists point out to the world and say, "See, we can *observe* the fact that the theory is correct." The one thing that's really missing is that final metaphysical piece. Maybe the scientist is right—gravity is a law, or damn close to it—but *why* does the exchange of gravitons cause the change that we see? Why does the firing of neurons make Jake jerky? And why can matter and energy be neither created nor destroyed (probably)? And the scientist can only look more closely and say, "Well, because atoms have these properties," or, "Because the universe follows this mathematical law." But why??? Why *those* laws? Why those properties? Why? Why? Why? Why?! Sorry, I think I need a sandwich!

This Random Pattern Generator . . . So Clever

Okay, so here's the deal. We're being a bit hard on PB and science in general. Science is awesome and we really should listen more closely to scientists rather than just picking the theories we like and ignoring the ones we don't. After all, you never see a bunch of people start screaming at each other over gravity. We are all more than happy to let scientists tell us about gravity (despite the fact that we can't even find the darned graviton!), but evolution? Well, we'll argue about that and ignore scientific experts.

Our tendency to ignore science when we don't like the conclusion (as is the case with climate change) is not what I'm advocating. Science does have a difficulty, though, and it isn't evolution or global warming. The problem that Hume pointed out was that we make assumptions about *causality* when we observe the world. We *assume* when we see two things next to each other, that they will keep being connected.

Remember that Crystal Gem Apple? If you didn't know it turns you into an evil godlike entity, would you have eaten it? After seeing Tree Trunks explode, I think the last thing I would do is eat that apple! And I only saw it happen once! But what if that was just a random occurrence? What if it only happens to elephant-basketball things (or whatever she is)? What if it was just because the sun wasn't shining in the forest that day? We don't know!

Human beings are pattern-makers. We like to think that we're finding cause and effect in the world, that we're finding patterns, but I think we are actually *creating* the patterns. We are just so arrogant that we assume that the patterns we make are true of the nature of reality. It's kind of like looking up at the sky and seeing clouds. We might see Finn in the clouds, or maybe we see Gunter in the clouds. And we can get pretty annoyed if other people don't see what we see. "Look, how can you not see it? The little wings are right *there!*" But really, that's a pattern we made. Our brain makes the cloud into something we see as Gunter. Our brain likes to connect the dots, but dots can be connected in many different ways. We tend just to connect the dots in ways that make sense to us and help us survive.

So, as is especially the case with bad things, we connect the dots to be careful. If someone eats an apple and explodes, I won't be eating that kind of apple. We're so preoccupied with pattern-making that we even do it unreasonably sometimes! Don't we have a tendency to say things like, "Oh, no, I don't chew bubblegum because this one time when I was five I was jumping rope while blowing a bubble and an eagle saw it and dive-bombed me, and I ran away but the jump rope caught in a tree branch, and I tripped and skinned my knee—so that's why I'll never chew bubblegum again . . ." (You mean that never happened to *you?* Weird.)

You get my point. We make predictions of cause and effect just because we see things happen together. We assume that because "A" happens before "B," there must be a connection between them. "When I let go of the apple it falls, so there must be a causal connection." We feel even more supported in this belief if it keeps happening over and over again. Certainly, that's what science relies on. But what Hume asks us is, "Where is the actual *connection?*" We can do all the math, and assert all of the physical laws we want, but we can't find the actual connection between the two things. We can never say for sure that the next time I let go of an apple that it wouldn't fly up. Maybe there will be a reason, like God changing the laws of physics, or a little UFO sucking upward with its abductor ray, but either way, we don't know *for sure* that the future will be like the past. In fact, it often isn't. But our predictions of the future rely on our assumption that the future will mimic the past in a predictable way.

Why do we think the future will be like the past? It might just be because things seem very stable and regular from our perspective. But we're very mistaken about that. The world of the very tiny, the quantum world, is so random and crazy as to drive philosophers nuts. I like to think that scientists have better reason to assume that the future will be like the past, because they're discovering the basic framework of how the universe works. But if they, and we, are honest, what we really mean is they are discovering the framework for how the universe *tends* to work and *seems* to work. At any given moment, we might discover that the causal connections we think connect events are completely wrong. Certainly, it's happened in the past. It's not unusual for us to develop a whole theory of how the world works, do a bunch of mathematics to support it, and then discover that we were completely wrong.

You Kids Better Stop Donkin' Around!

Think of how we once assumed that the Earth's the center of the universe. It's not like everyone just assumed that without doing some science and math. There was *tons* of mathematics that scientists did to support that conclusion. They could use that math and the physics they developed to make predictions about planets and stars. And what they saw made observational sense! They could *see* the universe moving around the unmoving world. And then Copernicus and Galileo came along and turned the world on its head. *Almost literally! AND THEN* what's funny is Newton and Einstein came along and pointed out that location and motion are relative and (technically speaking) it isn't inaccurate to say that the universe is moving around the Earth—it just makes the math much more complex and annoying. Not to mention the explanation is a bit less sensible.

But that's the problem. It's the same problem when have when we reject *Adventure Time* for being a bit loopy. We want things to make sense, but "making sense" really means "makes sense to me from what I know about the world." But what we know about the world is often wrong. To go back to that first point, we know the world to be stable, solid, and predictable, but really all that stable stuff is made of stuff that is constantly moving, and shifting, and is mostly empty space.

So maybe that's the real problem. We're trying to find laws of physics and laws of causality that *make sense to us*. And by that we mean stable, and rational, without random events. We want those laws to explain a world that we see as consistent and solid—but it isn't. It might be that the people of Ooo are in a far better position to actually figure out the nature of reality. They come from a world that has random stuff happen all the time, they know the world isn't stable or solid, and so they don't try to force it to make sense that way.

In other words, maybe that's why Finn and Jake were horrified—but not really surprised—when Tree Trunks exploded. When the boys try to make sense of the world, they don't try to smuggle in consistent laws of physics that help explain a solid and stable universe. They don't assume that the future will be like the past. So, *to them*, making sense doesn't require that they have this constant concept of "causes always leading to effects." The world that they see every day (which makes sense to them because they see it every day) has random occurrences all the time. We have no idea how to deal with those kinds of things, because the world we grew up in seems to be so regular and constant that we assume "regular and constant" means "sensible."

What I mean is only this: when we look closely at the uni-verse, scientists are now realizing that there is a lot of randomness in it—stuff that sounds crazy, like virtual particle pairs appearing and disappearing for no reason, particles affecting each other across the universe without touching, even particles arriving places *before* they left! And this drives scientists crazy. In fact, Einstein couldn't stand it. He said once, "God does not play dice with the universe!" This crazy randomness of the universe is something that the rest of us ignore. But at least the scientists are trying to figure it out. The worry is that as long as we expect the universe to make sense in the way we assume sense should be—stable, constant, and causal, then we may never understand the universe, because it is none of those things!

The funny part is that all that randomness wouldn't bug us all so much if we lived in a world like Ooo. Well, to be more specific, we do live in a world like Ooo, but because of our size and perspective, we're only just are starting to realize it—but it may only be young minds, those to whom shows like *Adventure Time* make sense, who can really accept and understand the true nature of reality.

8

Ice King Blues

GREG LITTMANN

I can't just beat up the Ice King for nothing. That's against my alignment.

—FINN

It's dark and quiet in the Ice Kingdom. The shadows of Finn and Jake are seen skulking about. Our heroes narrowly avoid detection by Guard Penguins wielding Ice Axes.

"Our secret mission to capture the Ice King is underway. Though I probably shouldn't say stuff like that out loud," Finn tells his friend.

The Ice King, unaware of his danger, is dejectedly playing a puzzle on his bed. Life is lonely in his ice-cold realm. He rises to the sound of his doorbell, annoyed. He opens the door to zap whoever has intruded on his depression, but no one is there. Looking down, the Ice King sees an ever-so-tempting can of peanut brittle. Opening it, Ice King's brief moment of happiness is dashed when Jake springs out of the can and grabs his crown.

"Oahh! Finn, you have destroyed my faith in canned peanut brittle!" the Ice King laments.

As the boys quickly wrap up the Ice King and begin to cart him back to the Candy Kingdom, Jake wonders why they have captured the often-tormented wizard. Finn's reply is vague, only knowing that they are following Princess Bubblegum's orders. But the boys aren't sure they're doing the right thing—after all doesn't the Ice King have to be guilty of <u>something</u> to earn this kind of abuse? He must be responsible for some crime, right? . . . right???

For Finn and Jake, the battle against evil is never-ending. As freelance heroes, they punch, kick, and hack their way through the trouble-makers of Ooo. Though they often show mercy, they often *don't*. Instead, they respond with punishment that is swift and harsh. Monsters are decapitated, thieves pummeled and old men beaten up. Testifying to his worthiness to receive the hero's handbook, the *Enchiridion*, Finn announces, "I'll slay anything evil. That's my deal."

As the Ice King observes, "The way things work is, first, I transgress your meaningless rules and then you maliciously persecute me!" to which Finn replies "That makes sense. You do bad stuff, we punish you." The wicked are not even safe at home. In the tradition of roleplaying games like *Dungeons and Dragons* and computer games like *World of Warcraft*, Finn happily invades the lairs of evil monsters to kill the inhabitants and take their valuables.

The harsh attitude Finn and Jake often show toward the evil is in stark contrast to their attitude towards everyone else. The pair devote their lives to helping people and generally refuse to harm innocents. Finn refuses to slaughter an ant because it isn't evil, but "neutral," even though killing the ant is a condition of receiving the *Enchiridion*. Yet Jake is delighted to learn that his father prophesied that he would hurt "everybody who is evil." Finn goes so far as to dose tarts with poison that will leave any thief paralyzed for life, an act that makes hanging someone for stealing a loaf of bread seem like an act of mercy. How is a devotion to doing what is right compatible with such rough treatment of evil folk?

To ask this question is not to criticize Pendleton Ward and the other writers of *Adventure Time*. Characters who always do exactly what they should are both boring and unrealistic, so it is a strength of the show that Finn and Jake are not perfect. Rather, considering Finn and Jake can help us to consider our own behavior. In our own, pre-apocalyptic world, we too must decide how to deal with wrongdoers. Like Finn and Jake, we punish them, or look for other ways to change their behavior. Like Finn and Jake, we often suspend sympathy for them that we would feel for innocent folk in the same position. For instance, for most of us, the thought of going to prison is nightmarish, but few people lose sleep over prison conditions endured by the guilty. The usual justification offered for this attitude is that wrongdoers are to blame for what they did, having had a free choice between good and evil—and choosing evil.

But, here's the deal, *Adventure Time* can help us to recognize that there is *no such thing* as free will. This means that we must drastically reconsider the way we treat wrongdoers. *Adventure Time* can help us to explore the issue of whether free will exists precisely because of all of the strange, surreal situations that arise in the show. *Adventure Time* is a collection of "thought experiments,"—ways to consider a problem from many perspectives and, as you'll see, is *very* rich ground for investigating free will, which, I'm just sayin' . . . you don't have. . . .

I Can't Help It! Flesh Is Delicious!

Starchy the donut, recently resurrected after dying and becoming a cannibal zombie, clamps his doughy mouth greedily around Finn's leg. "Starchy, you're not a zombie!" Finn reminds him, but the carnivorous pastry replies "I can't help it! Flesh is delicious!" Finn wants Starchy to stop eating him, but to Starchy's mind, he has no choice. The taste of human meat is so yummy to him, that it is overwhelming. Humans are too scrumptious for it to be *possible* for him to resist snarfing them. Perhaps he's right.

Determinism is the view that everything that happens *had to* happen, given previous events and the laws of nature. Nothing ever occurs by chance, with the possible exception of the big bang that produced the universe. The roll of dice may seem to be random, but dice move in accordance with the laws of physics like any other object, so if physics is deterministic, there is nothing random about it. If you knew exactly what position the dice were in when they started to roll and how much force was applied, you could calculate what the roll will be. Your brain is more complex than dice, but no less bound by the laws of nature. If the laws of nature are deterministic, then your brain operates by following the laws of physics!

If we think about it this way, human beings are akin to machines made of meat, doing whatever they are constructed to do and nothing else. If determinism is true, then at the big bang, everything about your life, including every choice you make, was determined before you were even born. Even when you are being driven by your own desires, you're being directed by forces that are beyond your control, since people don't get to choose what their desires will be. Finn didn't choose to want a life of adventure—he just wants it. Likewise, Jake didn't choose to feel passionate about food, *Card Wars*, and Lady Rainicorn, and the Lich didn't choose to crave the extinction of all life. Such things are beyond our control. Even when we strive to resist our desires, we do so because we have other, equally unchosen, desires that are more powerful. When Finn faces his fear of the ocean to save a trapped Jake, he does so because he wants to help Jake more than he wants to avoid the water.

This sounds cruddy and a bit crazy, I know. But think about it like this. All determinism really means is that the past causes or "determines" the future. The past causes the future, yes? When you chose to eat a super-burrito, you did it because, in the past, you were hungry. Once you've eaten the burrito you aren't hungry anymore, so you stop eating and you burp. So, long story short, we can say, "You burped because you were hungry." Your hunger caused the eating that caused the burping.

The problem is simple, then. We can't change the past; it's beyond our control. And, everything that's happening right now is happening because of the past (you're reading this book because you saw it in a bookstore, you went to the bookstore because you wanted coffee, you wanted coffee because you are addicted to the awesomeness that is caffeine . . .). *In other words, since the future is caused by the past, and we can't change the past, we can't change the future!* The future is caused by all the stuff that has come before it, which has already happened!

Hard and Soft Determinism

I'm not mean. I'm a thousand years old, and I just lost track of my moral code.

—MARCELINE

Determinism threatens our standard moral judgments, and it's easy to see why. Finn frequently judges people innocent of wrongdoing because they were forced to act as they did. And Finn's decision to forgive people who were forced to do evil seems right. For instance, Finn doesn't blame his hero Billy for stealing the *Enchiridion*, because Billy was possessed by the Lich. Nor does he blame Ghost Princess for haunting him, once she explains that she's "doomed to haunt this mortal plane" until she finds out how she died.

"Hard Determinism" is the view that determinism is true, and because of it, we have no free will. It's easy to see why a determinist might deny free will. If how we will act is completely controlled by outside factors, as Billy is when possessed by the Lich, then it seems natural to say that we *aren't* in control. Yet not all determinists are hard determinists. "Soft Determinism" is the theory that determinism is true, but compatible with the existence of free will. People are considered to be free under soft determinism as long as they're doing what they want, even if what they want is determined by outside factors. Here, we can hold Billy and the Ghost Princess innocent, since Billy didn't *want* to steal the Enchiridion and the Ghost Princess didn't *want* to haunt people. Yet we can still hold the Lich and other such malicious villains guilty, since the mean things they do are exactly what they *want* to do.

But, it isn't obvious that people are acting freely whenever they are doing what they want. Finn frequently judges people innocent even when they're doing what they want, *if* what they want is the product of outside interference. For instance, he shows no guilt for all the inappropriate hugging he engaged in as a hug wolf. Instead, he accepts Jake's explanation that, having been hugged by a hug wolf, he had no control over his actions: "Every night, hug wolves must go out and hug people to satisfy their insatiable craving for hugs. . . . Oh no, the hug lust has already taken over your brain!"

Similarly, Finn doesn't blame Marceline when she puts on her father's magic amulet and immediately becomes a sadistic demon, dishing out "weird punishment" to the citizens of the Nightosphere. He explains: "That amulet's controlling Marceline." If the amulet is controlling Marcy, it isn't doing so by forcing her to act against her will, but by making her *want* evil things. When Finn objects to Marcy's dad that being an evil administrator isn't what she wants, he answers, "That's balderdash, Baby. The wearer of the amulet is filled with chaotic evil."

It seems that Finn is right to forgive Marcy, even though she was doing what she wanted to *while wearing the amulet*. Yet if he forgives Marcy, he should also forgive the Ice King, whose situation differs only in how long he has been cursed. The Ice King was once a kind and generous man named Simon Petrokov. He protected Marcy when she was a helpless little girl in the wake of the apocalyptic "mushroom wars" that destroyed human civilization. He wore the magical Ice Crown first out of curiosity, then in order to protect Marcy with the ice powers it gives him. However, the Ice Crown slowly corrupts the one who wears it. Every time Simon donned the crown, he slid a little closer to becoming the evil Ice King. A poem of Simon's is discovered were he expresses his helplessness to resist: "I'm losing myself and I'm afraid that you're going to lose me too. . . . This magic keeps me alive, but it's making me crazy. . . . I swear it wasn't me, it was the crown."

There isn't even anything specific about Simon that makes him susceptible to the crown's corruption. In an alternative universe, Finn wears the crown and holds out for less time than Simon before losing control, announcing, "The crown! It compels me to—ice up everything!" and "I am too dangerous to be around. Leave me." It seems then that the Ice King is wicked through no fault of his own.

Finn does feel some compassion for the Ice King and it seems to be motivated, at least in part, by his understanding that the crown corrupted him. After viewing a video that reveals the Ice King's backstory, Finn and Jake decide to invite him around every year to socialize, in what Shelby the worm describes as "a fleeting moment of empathy for the biggest weirdo in Ooo." Finn cannot stand the idea of punishing anyone, even the Ice King, wrongfully. When the Ice King is imprisoned though he's done nothing evil lately, Finn takes the Ice King's place in prison rather than allowing the injustice to stand. He explains: "I can't just beat up the Ice King for nothing. That's against my alignment." Yet if the Ice King's actions are dictated by his magic crown, then every time he is punished, he's punished for something he had no control over!

Doing What Comes Naturally

Poor Little Dude. He was just doin' it up the only way he knew how. It wasn't his fault he was created evil.

—Finn

We could try to make room for free will by accepting that an action of yours is free if it is motivated by a desire that arises from your own nature, rather than from an outside imposition that is contrary to your nature. This would allow us, for example, to absolve Marcy for tormenting demons and Simon for tormenting princesses, while still blaming Marcy's dad for tormenting demons and the Lich for seeking the destruction of all life. However, this theory also doesn't seem to cover all cases where we wouldn't want to hold someone to blame.

Finn frequently accepts the innocence of even those who are overcome by their natural desires. For instance, he bears no grudge against Marcy for almost sucking out Jake's insides while suffering from "red-starvation." He and Jake accept her explanation that she cannot help herself: "I'm going to go into feral mode. It's not going to be pretty. . . . I won't be able to control myself much longer. I can feel the feeding frenzy coming on." On another occasion, Finn's trademark hat is accidentally brought to malicious life. "My magic imbues anything it touches with an evil spirit, one that craves destruction and chaos," explains an embarrassed wizard. Yet Finn forgives his hat for attacking the Candy People, reasoning "Poor Little Dude. He was just doin' it up the only way he knew how. It wasn't his fault he was created evil."

Again, it seems that Finn is right in not holding Marcy and Little Dude responsible. If they are genuinely controlled by desires that are not of their choosing, then they must genuinely be unfree. Often, though, Finn sees having an imperfect nature as no excuse. He condemns the Lich, even though Bubblegum explains that the Lich acts as he does because "His only desire is to destroy life!" If destruction is all that the Lich desires, then how can the Lich do anything other than destroy? How is he less morally culpable than Little Dude or by Marcy while in feral mode from red-starvation? A similar complaint could be raised by the evil dungeon monsters whose homes Finn so enthusiastically ransacks. If monsters didn't choose to be monsters in the first place, then how can Finn blame them for their monstrous behavior?

Likewise, Finn has little sympathy for Lemongrab, though Lemongrab explicitly points out that he has no control over his own nature. The Earl is alone because of his mean and selfish ways, but insists that it is Bubblegum who is responsible for his actions because it was she who created him the way that he is. Paraphrasing Frankenstein's monster, he shrieks, "I am alone and you made me like this. You made me. You made me. You're my glob!" The only thing Lemongrab *wants* in life is to be a jerk, and he wants to be a jerk because that is how he is constituted. As he tells Bubblegum, "I look into the lemon heart you gave me and see my lemon way to act."

It is later confirmed that Lemongrab doesn't have the emotions that drive compassionate behavior. When Finn and Jake start the heart of the giant lemon Lemonjohn, Lemonjohn announces that he has developed "the feeling of caring unknown to lemons." Finn suggests to Bubblegum that she cure Lemongrab's selfishness the same way, a suggestion she rejects by stating, "Their hearts are fine; they're just *like* this." Bubblegum's response is too quick, though. Perhaps their hearts *are* just fine, but there must still be something in their physical composition that explains why they are "like this."

No Escape in Randomness

Anyway, that's it. There's no other way around, you dummy!

—Talking Bush

So it looks as though we must not be free if determinism is true. But is determinism true? Strictly speaking, no. Our universe is *largely* deterministic. However, according to quantum physics, there are genuinely random events at the level of extremely small particles. Unfortunately though, this randomness isn't enough to allow for human freedom. After all, if you are doing something at random, you *still* aren't controlling your own actions. You have simply become the puppet of random events instead of deterministic ones. Either way, you aren't free.

Deterministic causation and random causation are the only possible ways in which something could be caused to happen. Things either happen for reasons or they happen for no reason. There are no other alternatives. To the degree to which a system isn't deterministic, it is random, and vice versa. Even if magic existed, as it does in Ooo, magic would have to work deterministically except where it works randomly. Likewise, we can't make room for free will by insisting that human beings are non-physical souls, unbound by physical laws. Either souls act as they do because they are determined to act that way, or their actions are undetermined and so random. Either way, we are not free. Not to mention that our bodies still seem bound by physics and determinism. So even if our souls were "free" they couldn't force our bodies to break the laws of physics.

Punishing and Helping the Bad Guys

Be Better!

—The Oculus of Rehabilitation

If I'm right that we aren't free, what are the implications for how we should treat wrongdoers? I don't think that it means that we must not punish wrongdoers. One reason why it might be sensible to imprison them is in order to make sure that they can't keep harming others. In condemning "Princess Cookie," Bubblegum seems to reason along these lines, declaring, "That cookie is a menace. Once the hostages are safe, cookie goes in my dungeon. In my dungeon for his life!" Another reason why it might be sensible to punish wrongdoers is if it has a deterrent effect against future wrongdoing. Finn also seems to reason along these lines as he expels the abusive Goblin King Xergioc from the Goblin Kingdom, hitting the departing monarch in the eye with a rock and shouting, "And stay out, muffin top!" Likewise, Finn tells a little girl who has had her basket stolen in the City of Thieves, "I'm going to get your basket back from whoever took it, and then I'm going to beat my purity into them." Nor does abandoning our belief in free will mean that we should use our own lack of freedom as an excuse not to care about how we treat wrongdoers. You *could* use your nature as an excuse for doing the wrong thing, but you will only do that if you care more about having an excuse for your crappy behavior than you do about doing what is right. If that's the sort of mean person you are, you will act like a jerk whether you have an excuse or not.

Abandoning our belief in free will does mean that we should never use "just deserts" as a reason or excuse for making people suffer. If people are not in control of their actions, they can't be morally blamed for them. That wrongdoers should suffer because they deserve to suffer is an idea that drives the way our society treats wrongdoers. For instance, one of the main factors that leads voters to favor punishment over prevention and rehabilitation is the belief that justice requires it. In the

United States, it is presumably only this belief in deserved suffering that allows voters to tolerate a system that keeps almost one out of every hundred citizens in prison, often in conditions that would cause most of us enormous distress. On the other hand, if we abandon the idea of just retribution, we're able to focus on whichever methods are most useful for bringing about the best results for both society in general and, as far as practical, wrongdoers themselves. Not to mention that when we find ways to rehabilitate criminals (in other words find out the *reasons* why they do what they do and *change* the reasons) crime rates go down! People do what they do because of some physiological or psychological cause, a cause that we could potentially remove. But if we are too busy trying to kick their buns, we won't ever realize it!

Finn and Jake understand that it can be more important to help a wrongdoer than to hurt them. For example, when they learn that Donny the Grass Ogre has been terrorizing the House People, they befriend him and teach him how to get along with others. Finn finds that his hero, Billy, has gone so far as to declare force useless as a tool for opposing evil—"All my life, I've beaten on evil creatures, but new evil keeps popping up. Kicking their butts was a hopeless effort." Finn tries Billy's way, but rightly comes to appreciate that force, and even violence, are necessary for public safety.

Sometimes, for the common good, butts need to be kicked. The problem is that our society has fallen in love with force and punishment. We're obsessed with the idea of giving wrongdoers the suffering that we think they deserve, and turn instinctively to retribution instead of being guided by research into what practices have the best results. Like Xergiac, we have gone spanking crazy. If we would pay something like the same sort of attention to helping and rehabilitating wrongdoers that we do to punishing them, our society would reap tremendous rewards. (Don't take my word for that; check the research for yourself.)

All human beings wear ice crowns that control us, though we wear them on the inside of our skulls, encoded in the structure of our brain. Some of us are cursed so badly that we become Ice Kings, unable to relate in appropriate ways to other people. Moral duty and self-interest alike should urge us to free the Simon Petrokov's underneath, if we can.

9
The Owl and the One-Armed Boy

Liam Miller

In my travels around Ooo, I had the opportunity to speak with many people on many subjects. My most memorable time was when I spent several days (many, many days) having lunch with Finn the Human and Jake the dog. Jake made one of his specialties, an Everything Burrito. Little did I know that a friendly lunch between friends (we're friends, you see) could last as long as it did. The presence of the Everything Burrito should have been a sign. Long as it was, it did give me an opportunity to talk to the guys about many pressing matters.

We spoke of heroism, righteousness, and justice. We struggled with many notions, and some serious gas. In the end, though, we realized that almost every conversation we had was really about free will. . . . After all, can you really be a hero if you aren't truly free? And doesn't justice require that the guilty acted of their own free will? But here's the problem. . . . The Cosmic Owl, as far as I can tell, is the only being who definitely has free will in the Land of Ooo. There could be others out there; maybe everyone has free will. All we can be certain of, though, is the Cosmic Owl.

When I pointed this out to them, Jake said that free will is an illusion anyway. Cinnamon Bun just laughed and said, "Hehe, what?" Finn was pretty quiet on the subject, but he's pretty sure of his ability to choose his own fate. I think he was trying to figure out just what to say. Princess Bubblegum, or 'Peebles' as she totally said I could call her, found my methodology lacking in hard evidence and proceeded to run her own experiments. Apparently, this happens a lot with Peebles.

. . . But seriously, the longer we spoke, the more I realized that even everything they said was pre-determined. It was almost as if it

was all written down for them, long before they ever said it. And then I realized it. I didn't have free will either, . . . and I can prove it.

An Owl that Is Cosmic

Everyone knows about premonition dreams in Ooo. These are mysterious dreams that allow the dreamer to catch a glimpse into their future. There is usually some sort of message, warning or key piece of information in a premonition dream. And every premonition dream has the Cosmic Owl in it. Some premonition dreams are dire, dark, and a bit scary. Some depict the dreamer's death; these are known as croak dreams. Some are very cryptic and it seems impossible to understand them. Others come in stages, often over several nights. But they all have one thing in common; the Cosmic Owl is in all of them. The presence of the Cosmic Owl proves the dreams' authenticity.

The first thing we can take from this is there must be at least one future that exists now. It is widely thought that premonition dreams are unchangeable. The Cosmic Owl shows the dreamer a future that is unavoidable. If this is true, it would mean the future is set. An unavoidable future is a predetermined future—one that's inescapable. This is what we call "Determinism"—the idea that the future is caused by the past. And the only way to make a different future would be to change the past. For example if the future is and has always been predetermined, Simon Petrikov was always destined to find his magical crown and become the Ice King. The only way he wouldn't become the Ice King is if he didn't find the crown, but he did, and we can't change that, so there is no way to prevent him from becoming the Ice King. Determinism leaves very little room for the possibility of free will because free will *requires the ability to choose between many different possible futures.*

Jake has on several occasions advocated for Determinism. His philosophy is one of passive acceptance, especially about croak dreams. But how reliable is his information? If premonition dreams are set in stone, we have some pretty good evidence for an entirely predetermined Ooo. This would mean that every decision anyone makes in Ooo is not really their own, it was always going to be that way. When Finn and Jake go out adventuring, the outcome of their trials are already decided. They just live it. But here's the thing about the Cosmic Owl. *He shows the dreamer their future.* And that makes all the difference.

Croak Dreams and You

When Jake had his croak dream, he was convinced of his fate. "No one can change a croak dream Finn. Not even you." He saw himself floating in the blackness of space, surrounded by twinkling stars. In the distance, he saw a rocket ship and the Banana Man with a glass helmet on his head. Earth was a small blue marble, hanging in place as if suspended in fluid. Jake tried to stretch his arms out to the rocket, but it was too far. He exhaled the last of his air with a whoosh and turned blue. The last thing he saw before he woke up was the flash of the Cosmic Owl filling his vision, proving the validity of his croak dream.

We have to accept that whenever the Cosmic Owl is in a dream, it *definitely is* a premonition dream of some sort. Whenever Finn and Jake talk about these things, this detail is always just a given. It's a part of Ooo. These things just are. But, Jake's dream was set in motion not long after he woke up that day, yet he lived to tell the tale. Either Jake's dream was not a real croak dream, or someone changed the future. But the dream *was* a real croak dream.

Let's look at what changed, that way we'll know who changed it. That morning the Banana Man came to Finn and Jake's house. Apparently, he just wanted to borrow some sugar. The Banana Man left sugarless and Finn and Jake, suitably freaked out, followed him to his home. This is the first point of divergence. Talking to both Finn and Jake about this particular adventure, I think Jake would have gone to the Banana Man's house alone if hadn't dreamed about his death. Jake is pretty chatty and inquisitive. He could easily have gotten into a conversation about anything with the Banana Man (say, rockets?). It's not hard to imagine a scenario where Jake casually turns to Finn and says,

"Hey Finn, I'm gonna go hang with this Banana Man, talk about space and rockets! You in?"

And Finn would reply, just as casually "Nah man, that stuff makes my brain fall asleep. I'm gonna stay here and play with Beemo."

"Hehe, yea. Seeya later buddy!" Jake would say as he waved goodbye. . . .

See, it was *because* of the croak dream that Finn and Jake even knew of the Banana Man. Without the knowledge of the Croak dream, the boys would not have been freaked out by the Banana Man showing up. And Finn wouldn't have felt the need to follow Jake.

Everything else that happened was a direct result of that initial point of divergence. If Jake hadn't had the dream, Finn would not have joined him. But Jake *did* have the dream, so Finn *did* join him. The future shown in Jake's croak dream (Future A) was altered into what actually happened (future B). Like a good murder mystery we are left with a tantalizing who-dunnit, only instead of murder, it's changing the future.

What Is This Singular Doing in This Realm?

In deciding who changed the future, Finn is the obvious choice. Because it is his presence that changes everything. The biggest bit of evidence for this can be found in Jake's croak dream. He's what he tells us about it, "There was a rocket ship, you weren't there, and there was a Banana Man and I ran out of air and in outer space, and isn't that great Finn!" But when the actual event happened there was a significant difference. As Jake put it, "Hey no wait, in the croak dream it was me and Banana Man, but this time you were here too." So there is a difference. And that difference is Finn!

This doesn't mean that Jake's croak dream is in any way wrong. Certainly not. Jake's croak dream was never in space; his dream was of that underground lake. The Earth in the croak dream is the same model Earth Jake saw when he was drowning. The point of all this is that the *only difference* between Jake's croak dream and what actually happened was the presence of Finn the human. Finn was then able to save Jake by allowing Jake to save him from drowning. Pretty math, right? Well, it would be if it were correct.

Finn is the heroic sort, all saving princesses and conquering dungeons. When Jake told him about his croak dream, Finn's natural instinct was to save Jake from his fate. "Jake, your croak dream just gave us the upper hand. We can cheat now! We can cheat Fate." But this is the tricky thing about determinism. Finn believes he's making a choice to save Jake; that he's exercising his free will. But would Finn have ever done anything different? If Finn is all about being a hero (which he is) he would never choose to do something that's not heroic! I'm not saying Finn will always do the right thing, because he doesn't always know what the right thing is. But if he had a choice between saving Cinnamon Bun from an ice golem or helping an ice golem beat up Cinnamon Bun, Finn is definitely going to save CB. Under these conditions, it appears meaningless to talk about Finn's decision to save Cinnamon Bun. We all know he was going to do it all along.

Let's try another example. The Lich is the embodiment of evil in Ooo. He makes Hunson Abadeer look all sweet and cuddly (Don't tell him I said that). Given what we know about him, could the Lich fall in love with Hotdog Princess and settle down to raise a dozen or so Hotdog Knights?

Can you imagine, the Lich and Hotdog Princess, living in that doghouse? No way. That's just something that the Lich could never choose . . . because it just isn't who he is! But if this is the case, it seems like there are at least some things that the Lich is incapable of choosing. All we need now, in order to predict the future perfectly, is exact knowledge of everyone and everything everywhere. A perfectly predictable universe like this doesn't leave very much room for free will at all, not even for great evil like the Lich or great stupidity like the Hotdog Knights.

Even if there's no way of knowing everything, the fact that it's possible to predict the future is enough to question everyone's actions. There is no way to tell if anyone is truly acting freely, or if they're just doing what they always were going to do. This is why I don't think it was Finn who changed the future. Finn was doing *exactly what Finn would do when he found out his friend was in danger.* Given who Finn is, he couldn't do otherwise. *AND* we know, because of the croak dream, that *if Jake didn't tell Finn about the dream, Finn wouldn't have gone with Jake to the ship!* Isn't that proof of just more determinism? Finn went to the ship because of what he knew about the dream. A future where Finn doesn't follow Jake requires changing the past. But the past happened, Jake *did* tell Finn and so Finn followed Jake.

It seems as if we're right back where we started from. We know the future was altered. We know this because the future

Jake saw (Which was accurate based on the presence of the Cosmic Owl) and the actual events that happened were different. So who changed things? Whoooo, indeed. As I've said, the Cosmic Owl is the only being who definitely has free will in the Land of Ooo. Let me tell you why.

Anatomy of an Immortal Bird

The point of divergence, the bit where the timeline changed was when Jake was shown his croak dream. That was the difference. In Jake's croak dream, he had no idea what was going on. When Jake fell into the lake, however, Jake seemed happy and excited. Which I bet messed Finn up. A lot.

So in the vision of the future that Jake saw, he must not have originally seen his croak dream. That's the difference. *Jake saw his croak dream*, because he saw it, he told Finn and Finn didn't leave his side. And it was the Cosmic Owl who showed Jake his croak dream.

The Cosmic Owl's the only person who could have changed the future, so he must have free will. He doesn't seem to be able to physically change it. In fact, he doesn't seem to be able to physically appear at all. The only time we see the Cosmic Owl outside of a dream is in the Time Room. This may be because he exists outside of time, but I can't be sure. This would make sense; it would mean the Cosmic Owl is viewing all of time and space like a giant rug, or map, or dungeon layout. He can see all the events of everything laid out in front of him, where all the treasure is, and he can see potential points where he could change things. Why the Cosmic Owl changes things is a topic for another day, but he does seem to have good intentions.

The other thing we can say about the Cosmic Owl is that he might be all-knowing. Yes, he (as far as I can tell) lives outside of time, has free will and is capable of altering the timeline, but I don't think he could change the future without knowing a lot about everyone. Maybe everything. For instance, Jake's croak dream successfully altered the timeline for the better. There have been other times when the interference of the Cosmic Owl has seemed to either fail to stop something or actually caused the thing to happen, but maybe that was the plan all along.

For example, Finn had a series of premonition dreams about Flame Princess and the Ice King. In order to have the dream several times (to decipher its cryptic messages) Finn repeatedly put Flame Princess and the Ice King in situations where they would fight each other. This inevitably backfired and ended his relationship with Flame Princess. But the message the Cosmic Owl was trying to tell Finn was, "You blew it." three words, signifying the near cataclysmic end of Finn's and Flame Princess's courtship (not to mention the destruction of the Ice Kingdom).

There are two possible reasons for this action. Either the Cosmic Owl tried to warn Finn about doing something stupid, and in doing so accidentally made Finn do something stupid. Or his plan succeeded, and our resident owl is just a bit cruel when it comes to breaking people up. (I would think there are easier ways to end a relationship). Or maybe, just maybe, there was a good reason for Cosmic Owl to want that event to happen . . . like helping the Ice King make friends. After all, when his kingdom is destroyed the boys let him stay with them (out of pretty justifiable guilt). Maybe the Cosmic Owl can see our actions the way we can see a series of dominos. If you knock *this one* over, a whole series of events *will* occur!

But, then again, when I told Jake of my thoughts on this matter he pointed out to me (with a mouthful of burrito) that the Cosmic Owl was trying to say the same thing in all three dreams. He was telling Finn he 'blew it' before he blew it. Maybe the Cosmic Owl is all-knowing, but just not very good at giving bad news. But here's the deal, if the Cosmic Owl knows the future, doesn't that mean Finn and everyone in Ooo doesn't have free will?

As Jake points out, we can't prevent what the Cosmic Owl knows will happen! So if the Cosmic Owl knows that Finn is going to follow Jake, . . . then Finn *will* follow Jake. Even though Finn *feels* like it's his choice (and it is) he can't do other than what the Cosmic Owl knows he's going to do. And the Cosmic Owl knows he's going to do it, likely for two reasons 1. He can see the future and 2. The future is *caused by the past!* So how is Finn really free? And don't we have the same problem if God, . . . I mean Glob . . . knows the future? *How can you be free to make choices if the future is already determined?*

Something we know about Ooo is that the future, or some future, is already set. We know this because of the various beings and objects that can accurately predict or show the future. What we're dealing with here is a world that has a future that is predetermined. But, there is also at least one being capable of changing the future. Generally speaking, determinism and free will aren't that compatible. They're like Abracadaniel and Lumpy Space Princess, you never see them together. There is, however, a compatible type of determinism: *soft* determinism. This would mean that the future is predetermined, but it also allows for instances of free will because free will is more about our ability to cause the future we want than it is about changing the future.

It's Speculation Time!

Finn the Human has no free will. No Singular, as the Cosmic Owl puts it, has free will. This is where we must start if we are to truly get to the bottom of this. Determinism, which is the situation we find ourselves in in Ooo, is the idea that the universe is predetermined. All the decisions anybody makes have already been decided. There is no way to tell if, when we act, we're acting of our own free will or not.

Maybe it doesn't even matter. There is no apparent difference between Jake making the perfect sandwich because he really wanted to or because he was always destined too. Either way Jake wakes up one morning and decides to make a sandwich. Either way, due to his amazing sandwich-making ability he creates something that transcends mere bread and fillings.

But it does matter, to some of us. If Finn defeats all evil in Ooo and becomes the greatest hero of them all, even greater than BILLY (wicked guitar solo), he wants to know if it was his doing or if he was just always destined to be the greatest hero. Our successes (and failures) are more truly ours if we possess a free will. Every dungeon we overcome, every piece of loot we find, even every battle we lose, is worth more when it is because of a decision we made. Yes, even our failures are important in this instance. When we own all our actions, we see we are fully responsible for them. Praise and punishment are no longer dished out at the will of Grod, but because we truly deserve to be praised or punished.

The One-Armed Hero

Think about it like this. . . . A close examination of Finn the Human reveals that it was inevitable that Finn would lose his arm. You might think this is trivial, but I believe it is one of the most important aspects of our hero at this point in his life. For reasons unknown even to the most bearded of wizards, Finn keeps being shown different versions of himself, *all missing his right arm*. In daydreams and worm dreams, alternate realities, parallel dimensions, past lives and in the future—all other versions of Finn the Human are missing their right arm.

It wasn't until recently that Finn began making the connection between all these visions. During our great lunch of the everything burrito, this topic came up, ironically. We had this conversation *before* he lost his arm trying to stop his father! We started talking about Shoko, a past life of Finn's that he recently found out about. Shoko was a one-armed thief who stole something very precious long ago. For the next couple of days Jake and I helped Finn piece together several other distinct occasions where he either had lost his arm or he was shown a version of himself with only one arm. Between, of course, mouthfuls of burrito . . .

When Finn got lost in Jake's pillow fort and ended up in pillow world, he claimed to have lived an entire life. Finn himself has only just recently remembered the experience. He can only ever recall pieces, fragments as if from a dream. But he definitely remembers having lived a long and full life and, at some point, losing his right arm and constructing a prosthetic out of pillows.

The nature of the pillow world is shrouded in a duvet of mystery. Is it an alternate reality, or a world that only existed in Finn's head? What we do know is that it was definitely Finn who lived a life there. Unlike Fiona, Finn cannot meet pillow world Finn because he *is* pillow world Finn.

A somewhat more ambiguous example is Farmworld Finn. When Finn and Jake chased the Lich through a portal to the Time Room, Finn made a wish that the Lich never existed. The result was Farmworld; a world where the mushroom wars never occurred, but where an ice age had covered the planet for four hundred years. In this alternate reality, Finn lived with his parents and younger sibling on the outskirts of a small rural community. Jake in Farmworld was just a normal dog and Finn just a normal boy, with one slight difference. He was missing his right arm and had a crude mechanical one that was little more than a claw.

Finn has no recollection of Farmworld, because Jake ended up changing the world back with his wish. But it's interesting to know that Finn has seen his Farmworld self before. Finn and Jake had a bit of a worm problem at the treehouse at one point. At first the worms were small and cute and only did things like crowd around on Finn's bed, but then things got out of hand. When the King Worm trapped the boys in their own dream to feed off their life energies, Finn saw some pretty weird stuff. The weirdest by far (WAY weirder than the two-mouthed Lady Rainicorn) was a reflection of himself in the mirror that was slightly off. He had a strange face, slightly different clothes and, where his right arm should have been, was a crude mechanical arm that was little more than a claw.

And again we see Finn without his right arm on a train, . . . a dungeon train. From car to car they went, fighting crystal ants, blob monsters, and level bosses. Finn, having recently gone through some "stuff" (girlfriend stuff) lost himself a little in the simple pleasures of dungeon crawling. Much time passed, and Jake got hungry and bored. He stumbled upon a future crystal and was shocked to see a vision of Finn, far into the future, still fighting on the train they were on. And poor Jake? He was there also, old and still hungry and still bored. And guess what Finn Looked like? He looked bad ass, all clad in armor and weapons, . . . *and missing his right arm*. Eventually Finn realized the folly of living in a dungeon train for the rest of his life. When he saw what it was doing to Jake, he changed his fate, and the future crystal reflected that.

All of these stories have a common thread. As Shoko, Finn was a thief who betrayed Princess Bubblegum; Farmworld Finn had the unfortunate fate of becoming the Ice King instead of Simon; pillow world Finn had a quiet and peaceful life, but one where he constantly searched for an exit back to his old life; and dungeon train Finn (from the future) had no real kind of life at all. As Jake said, "Man, this whole train is just butter!" In all of these instances, Finn was shown a version of himself where he was missing his right arm.

Heck, it even happens in Finn's imagination! One time when Finn was meditating with Bubblegum all he could think about was how cool he'd look as a grown-up hero. He imagined he was big and muscular, he wore a legendary sword strapped to his back, a huge white flowing cloak around his neck, *and he had one huge mechanical arm where his right arm used to be.* But this was no ordinary day. Shortly after this, Finn was given a legendary Gauntlet that once belonged to BILLY!!! (wicked guitar solo). Princess Bubblegum gave Finn this sacred weapon to defeat the greatest evil in Ooo, the Lich. For those playing at home, the gauntlet was right handed. While it was ultimately his sweater and not the gauntlet that defeated the Lich, arguably Finn could not have done what he did without the gauntlet. . . . Finn never daydreamed about having only one arm again.

Do You Think I've Got the Goods, Bubblegum? 'Cause I Am into This Stuff!

There's definitely a connection between all these adventures, but as yet this does not add up to Finn having free will. The dungeon train case is an interesting one because this is the only time where Finn directly sees his future outside of a premonition dream. Premonition dreams don't help us here because the Cosmic Owl is involved, and we already know he has free will. When Finn first saw himself as an old man still battling away on the train, all armor clad and missing an arm, he was genuinely excited that that was his future. But eventually, when he saw what would become of Jake he changed his mind and the image in the future crystal changed as well.

An avid determinist, like Jake, would say Finn was always going to change his mind and leave the train; that this example in no way signifies any sort of free will on the part of Finn. But an avid determinist like Jake can't explain objects like the future crystal. Finn was definitely shown *a* future. Then, as a direct result of seeing that future (specifically the future of Jake), Finn changed his mind *and the future crystal changed as well.*

Soft determinism is the theory that there is a predetermined universe; that the future is set. But, that set future is less like a rock golem and more like a snow golem—it's kind of squishy and malleable. The future can be changed. I think we can definitively say the Land of Ooo is a place ruled by soft determinism. We can say this because the future is something we can see through certain objects or be shown by certain people. But this future can be altered.

Whether or not anyone other than the Cosmic Owl has a free will is still a mysterious mystery. While we can say that Finn changed his mind in that dungeon train and that changed the future, we can't say for sure if he was always going to. Soft determinism allows for a changeable future, and allows for free will, but it doesn't guarantee anything.

Consider this. If Finn had not been shown the future crystal, would he have changed his future? Showing Finn the future crystal is what set him on the path to leaving the dungeon train. Yes, the future can be changed. But I just cannot say that Finn chose to do so freely.

The final piece of the puzzle is the right arm of Finn. Possibly the most important appendage in all of Ooo, maybe even of all time. There is no way to know. The one-armed Finns may be unrelated; it might all be coincidence. Or they might be signposts; warnings to Finn to not deviate from his destiny. *Can he deviate from his destiny?* And that brings us back to Jake's croak dream. Everything the boys do, they do because of something. If Finn follows Jake it's because he knows about the dream, and if he doesn't follow him, it's because he doesn't know about it. But just like us, everything Finn does he does for a reason, because of the past (like Jake telling Finn about his dream).

I do think Finn has a destiny; an epic fate meant only for him. But will he *choose* such a fate freely or will it be thrust upon him? Really, that's the difference between hard determinism and soft determinism. Either way, Finn is determined to do as he does, but can we still say he is kind of free if he *chooses* his fate . . . even if the Cosmic Owl knew what choice he would make? That's the problem we all must face.

Are we free because we make choices? Or are we determined because *the choices are caused by forces we can't control or change.* Even if we can't see the future, like the Cosmic Owl, our choices are predictable based on the past. Perhaps they aren't known by Glob, the Cosmic Owl, or Prismo in our world, but we make our choices because of our past . . . and none of us can change the past.

. . . damn burritos.

10
Did Prismo Create the Best Possible World?

Matthew Montoya

Rolling pastures gently unfurl from horizon to horizon. A boy and his faithful dog travel across the land towards Junk Town. The little yellow dog runs around the boy happily. But the boy doesn't laugh. All he can think about is the men harassing his father. Seeing them abuse his family brings something to the surface in the boy; he feels a call to action, a call to violence. The boy is holding something in his hands, something that changed the world once, and will change it again. A chill runs up the boy's spine. In his mechanical right arm, he holds a crown, gold set with red stones
  . . . It seems to pulse with possibilities.

Did you know that according to scientists there is a real possibility that our reality is not the only one? It's even possible that within all of these different realities there are different versions of all of us! When I discovered that there was a possibility that there were multiple realities containing multiple versions of me my jaw hit the floor. In the words of Lumpy Space Princess, it was a truly "Oh my Glob" moment. I had never considered such a possibility before. My mind raced with excitement! The possibility that there were other versions of me, and that each one of them was different from the last, completely blew my mind.

Our heroes, Finn and Jake, are shaped by their world and their interactions, just like we are. From the time we are all born, their futures were shaped by the world around them, this means the people and places within their lives. But what if their world was different? If Ooo was different, wouldn't Finn and Jake be different as well?

In the episodes "Finn the Human" and "Jake the Dog" we saw what the land of Ooo would have been like if the Lich had never been born. We saw Simon Petrikov, aka the Ice King, sacrifice himself to prevent the mutagenic bomb from going off preventing the transformation of Earth into the Land of Ooo. Characters we learned to love never came into being because their ancestors never mutated, and our heroes' lives were so twisted that they would have been better off spending the night in the Nightosphere. This reality is known as Farmworld.

The horrors inflicted by the Lich had no longer occurred in the Farmworld timeline. Instead, Finn and Jake become the horrors that they had once fought to stop, the Ice King and the Lich. The horrors that Ooo had endured to become the beautiful land we know never happened.

But in Farmworld, Finn unleashes the mutagenic horrors, possibly at the cost of our heroes' lives. So, is Farmworld better than the land of Ooo that we'd come to love? You'd best bet your sweet buns it isn't! Farmworld may, at first, seem like a nice place to live because there is no Lemongard, Ice King, or Lich, but it really isn't because all of our heroes end up dying. All of our heroes lives are destroyed through death or tragedy thanks to an almost fate-like unleashing of mutagenic evil.

Multiple World Theory, Lumpy Space, and Farmworld

Which is the best possible world, Farmworld or Ooo? We should start by looking at what a multiverse is and what means for the characters of *Adventure Time*. Currently, we live within a universe, and this universe contains one world, which we live in. A multiverse, on the other hand, is the idea that there are multiple universes—maybe even an infinite number of them! Each of these universes holds their own unique characteristics, and each is at least slightly different from each other in the same way that Farmworld and Ooo are very similar.

All of the different worlds exist within their own universe, and they exist within their own space and time. There are two main ways in which possible worlds can diverge and split off from each other: 1. Through the change of the physical rules of the universe, or 2. Through changes in the history of the universe. But these changes come from the same idea that there is some rule or action that is different that alters future possibilities for that divergent universe.

We can see the first of these in the magnificently curvy world of Lumpy Space Princess, a universe where the rules that govern it are completely different from our own. The physical properties of Lumpy Space are very different from ours. This kind of change, in the rules of the universe, could make it so that up means down and down means up. Or even gravity could no longer exist, friction could become meaningless, a vacuum could support life, and so much more. The laws of physics as we know them would be completely turned on their heads. It is so globbing ridiculous how insane this would make our perception of the universe!

Adventure Time has its own multiverse and rules set along with it, but it is extremely similar to our real world idea of a mulitiverse. Within *Adventure Time*, the multiverse is a large number of independent universes all connected through mystical portals. This allows for completely independent universes to interact with each other. In the episode "The Lich," the *Adventure Time* multiverse is described by Booko:

> At the center of the multiverse is a dimension called the Time Room, believed to be the quasi-corporeal dwelling place of the almighty Prismo. The Time Room is the single dimension that exists outside of time. The Time Room produces time waves that are experienced by other dimensions. Some dimensions have permanent links that allow travel to and fro. Others become linked temporarily by naturally forming Worm Holes. And others can become linked artificially by magical portals, torn open by items of great power.
> <http://adventuretime.wikia.com/wiki/Booko>

So, while it's not known whether Lumpy Space is a part the same universe as the Land of Ooo or if it's another universe that is connected through a portal, it's easy to see how an argument could be made stating that Lumpy Space is another universe because within Lumpy Space the laws of physics are different than the Land of Ooo. I mean, come on! Have you seen those sweet lumps? Still not convinced, huh? Okay, let's take a look at how Lumpy Space is different.

For starters, all of lumpy space is a globby mess! The matter is comprised of some sort of weird lumpy material. There are no sharp angles, but instead the world is gifted with the grace of lumpy curves. Secondly, everything tends to float within the air—It seems like there is no actual earthly ground in lumpy space. Then finally, Lumpy Space hovers over a black hole but isn't sucked in! There are definite changes to the laws of physics. So, while it's not specifically stated that Lumpy Space is another universe it's not hard to imagine that it is, due to how different the physical rules seem to be in lumpy space, not to mention the radically different anatomy of those who live there.

Fiona and Cake Might Exist

Another way universes can diverge is slightly different. These universes will stick to the same rules of physics as our own, and go through many of the same historical events as our own. These universes only break off and diverge from each other at certain points where something, either a choice or action, is different from each other. This allows for a new future set of possibilities to be created. This is typically expressed as having something altered within the universe's timeline.

For example, the world of Fiona and Cake would fall into this category. The laws of physics have stayed the same, but the actions and results of reproduction have changed so that the genders of all the characters have changed. All of the males are now females and vice versa.

This is an example of a different universe in which the world that exists is greatly similar to the one we know and love. The reason for this is that only a small factor has changed, in this case the genders. Everything else has remained essentially the same, such as personalities, but has skewed slightly to compensate for the altered genders. This type of additional universe is much easier to wrap our heads around because it is so similar to the one we know. A universe that is drastically different from our own because the physical qualities of that universe have changed, like with Lumpy Space, is a bit more difficult.

When we look at Farmworld we're looking at a universe that falls into the same category as Fiona and Cake's universe. Farmworld was created by the will of the seemingly omnipotent and generally awesome, if not slightly two-dimensional, being named Prismo when Finn wishes that the Lich never existed. This causes the Farmworld to diverge from Ooo's time-line at a very specific point, the end of the Great Mushroom War. In Farmworld, a lot more than gender is different . . .

Messing Up the Universe

Finn and Jake, having been tricked into opening the portal between universes by the Lich, follow their adversary into the Time Room where Prismo lives. They arrive too late to stop the Lich from wishing for the extinction of all life. Luckily, since our heroes are now in the Time Room they are protected from the Lich's wish because the Time Room exists outside of time within the multiverse.

Prismo offers both Finn and Jake a single wish. The two of them decide to use their wishes to stop the Lich, but Finn says that they have to be careful what they wish for otherwise "the Lich could just jazz it up again."[1] Finn chooses to wish that "the Lich never even ever existed." Finn's wish ends up creating an alternate timeline and world where the Lich never existed called Farmworld.

Farmworld is what the world would have been like had the mutagenic bomb never gone off. Since the bomb never went off, Earth's people remain human. We would think this world would be so much better for our characters. They would never have to go through the horror of the mutagenic apocalypse. But Farmworld, while nice at first glance, is a horrible and tragic world for our amazing heroes.

Leibniz: Ooo versus Farmworld

Gottfried Leibniz (1646–1716) wrote a theory about the best of all possible worlds that lends itself really well to our current question about whether Farmworld is better than Ooo. He wanted to argue that if there's an all-powerful God, which he maintained there was, then this God would be all-knowing, all-powerful, and all-good. This would mean that there would be no way in which God could create a world that existed with evil inside of it unless God created it to be that way. But that would mean that God allowed evil, which would contradict the state-

---

[1] "Finn the Human."

ment that God was both all-powerful and all-good. In *Adventure Time*, we see no such beings other than the Cosmic Owl and Prismo, both of whom are far from perfect.

This problem is known as the Problem of Evil. How is it that an all-powerful and all-good being, such as God, could allow or create a world in which evil was allowed to exist as well? Leibniz attempted to answer this question with his theory about the best of all possible worlds. This is where it gets really lumping complicated.

Leibniz argued that God created the best of all possible worlds because God is omnibenevolent (all-good). He argued that the world must be made with both good and evil because if we did not have evil there would be no way to tell what is good. Since God is omnipotent (all-powerful) and omniscient (all-knowing) then God is able to see, judge, and know about the outcomes for all other possible worlds. This means that God is able to know which worlds allow for more or less evil then the others, and would create the world with the least amount of possible evil, our world.

Prismo the Almighty

Prismo serves as the stand in for that omnipotent being in *Adventure Time*, but he may not be omniscient nor omnibenevolent. He grants everyone one wish and allows for the consequences of that wish to unfold, even if the consequences are horrible. When Finn wishes that the Lich never existed a new universe is created from that wish. All of the events up to the end of the Great Mushroom War appear to be the same as with the timeline where the Land of Ooo exists, but when Simon Petrikov sacrifices himself to prevent the mutagenic bomb from going off this creates a new universe, Farmworld.

Since this world was created by the ever two-dimensional Prismo and not created by an omnibenevolent being, as was the argument from Leibniz, the situation becomes a bit different. Prismo is not acting from a position of benevolence, at least not at first.

After Prismo spends some quality time hanging out with Jake, he decides that he likes Jake and wants Jake's wish to turn out for the better. While Prismo shows Jake all of the negative consequences attached to Finn's wish, he forms a kind of over-attached relationship to Jake. Prismo decides that he wants to help Jake make a wish with no horrible consequence. Prismo even goes so far as to say the wish for Jake before just restoring Ooo to the way it was for his new friend. By having a friendship with Jake, Prismo wants to create the best world for his friend to return to, and because of this Prismo recreates the Land of Ooo.

Seeing how Prismo, our stand-in omnipotent being, decided that Ooo was the best of all possible worlds for Finn and Jake helps us consider Leibniz's idea. As Farmworld was pretty horrible . . .

No More Candy and Jake the Lich

Within Farmworld, we see a world where everyone lives poorly, save for a select few. All of the merchants are struggling to get by and survive. Finn, now missing his arm, and his family are struggling to get by. They're constantly being bullied and harassed by the Destiny Gang, and they have to sell their horse, Bartram.

Farmworld appears to be a land free of monsters, save for an elderly, and very gassy, Marceline whom we shall talk about momentarily. Farmworld is also free of candy people. This means that the majority of the characters we have grown to love in the Land of Ooo no longer exist within Farmworld. Their entire lives have been wiped out thanks to Finn's wish, and in a way this helps to carry on the Lich's desire of extinction in that the Candy people have never come to be.

Since the majority of our characters are either dead or never existed we must look at the ones who are alive to see why Farmworld is not the best of all possible worlds. Characters such as Jake, Marceline, and Choose Goose are completely changed from their "Ooo selves," but are the only ones we can turn to in this messed up world.

Jake is no longer Finn's magical canine step-brother, but is a normal dog. He barks rather than talks, walks on all four legs, and can no longer stretch out long. He's completely normal. This is not the Jake we have grown to love. Then, to kick a magical dog when he is down, the mutagenic bomb goes off and transforms Jake into a new Lich, a fate far worse than the one he experienced in Ooo.

Choose Goose is no longer the rhyming goose who sells adventuring merchandise to our heroes. In Farmworld, he is Choose Bruce. Choose Bruce is a rhyming merchant who sells merchandise to our heroes. Other than his appearance, he is essentially the same character. But tragedy strikes Choose Bruce when the Destiny Gang destroys his shop for helping our heroes out. He is assumed likely dead when the mutagenic bomb goes off at the hands of Finn.

Finally, Marceline's life is obviously worse off in Farmworld than in the Land of Ooo. In the Land of Ooo, Marceline is a young, attractive, sane, and butt-kicking bass player. She has friends, romantic relationships, and a life to call her own. She is happy. But in Farmworld, Marceline is a sad and lonely vampire. She has spent the past thousand years living in a hole in the ground with the dead body of Simon Petrikov. She has also grown old, senile, and has started to hear voices in her time alone. Then her life is ended at the hands of Finn and Jake when the mutagenic bomb goes off and she falls into the pool of mutagenic liquid.

We can see how our beloved characters' lives are much more tragic in the Farmworld reality, but an argument could be made that just as much suffering occurred when the mutagenic bomb went off in the Ooo reality. This would mean that Farmworld only appears worse to us because we have personal connections with these characters who have suffered.

It seems that we cannot judge whether this world is worse from their point of view, as it would be another reality with suffering at a different point in the world's history. But, what about Finn? All of this is a result of his wish to Prismo. He wished for this world as a way to get rid of an evil being. He was attempting to make the world better. Wouldn't Farmworld be better for him at least?

Finn the Human or Finn the Ice King

Finn's life appeared to be better off when we were first introduced to his Farmworld life. He lived in a peaceful countryside. But that doesn't last long. We soon began to see that Finn and his family were extremely poor and were the victims of bullying gangs.

Finn decides he will not be a victim anymore and attempts to fight those who have been making his life miserable. He puts

on the Ice King's crown, and unleashes all the horrible consequences we have discussed up until now. This is what causes
both Finn and Jake to become the villains they have tried to
defeat. Finn has become the new Ice King, and he unknowingly
unleashes the mutagenic bomb. This ends up destroying the
world all over again, kills Marceline, and creates a new Lich by
exposing Jake to the mutagenic horror.

Our heroes' lives are utterly destroyed. They are transformed, possessed, and killed due to the existence of
Farmworld. This is a far more horrible fate than the one they
would have had in the Land of Ooo. They are no longer the
heroes of Ooo, but are its potential destroyers.

A Better World for Finn and Jake

Leibniz would argue that if Prismo is an omnipotent, omniscient, and omnibenevolent God then Farmworld could never
have existed. While not an omnibenevolent being, Prismo does
restore Ooo out of a desire to create a better world for his friend
Jake and all those that Jake cares about. Prismo's good-willed
desire restores Ooo and proves that Farmworld is not the best
possible world for Finn and Jake.

In Ooo, our characters get to play the role of the hero as
opposed to that of the tragic villain. They don't have to suffer
the horrors of being dismembered or transforming into the
Lich and the new Ice King respectively. Even our villains are
better off as they are alive, and they are given the ability to
come to terms with their places within the world.

We can see that Leibniz's theory, with its idea of multiple
worlds, is not an easy one, and it certainly has its critics. Even
though we can't prove that Leibniz's approach is valid we can
still use it to examine possible outcomes within our lives. We
have all wondered if we made the right choices in our lives, and
whether we would have been better off if things had been different. We have all wondered what we would have done differently if we were given a second chance at a certain point within
our lives, but doing this would change our reality in ways that
we could never predict.

This is what happened to Finn and Jake with the creation
of Farmworld. Their lives changed for the worse simply because
they changed one thing. If we went back and altered one part

of our past then our lives could change for the better, or they could change for the worse.

If we want to be heroes like Finn and Jake then we can't dwell on the past since changing it is not a possibility of our universe. All we can do is look to the future and make choices that allow for our universe to grow in a way where we can become the heroes we desire to be.

11
Oh God, Where the Glob Art Thou?

POOM NAMVOL

"*You are Ooo's greatest hero, Finn; no evil can stop you!*"

"*Haha, yeah, I guess that's true. Mathematical!*"

"*Seriously Dude, with all the awesome loot you've won over the years, I don't think even I could stop you. And I'm pretty awesome!*"

"*Yeah, I am pretty math . . . I mean we've slain a lot of monsters. And we've taken all their loot and stuff. I guess I could kill anyone I wanted and take anything I wanted; no one could stop me . . .*"

"*Haha! Yeah, Dude, good thing we only slay monsters, right Finn? . . . Finn?*"

It was then that a shadow passed over Finn's innocent eyes. . . . There were no rules, no consequences: he could do what he wanted, take what he wanted, kill as he wanted. The inhabitants of Ooo cried out for mercy. And the world burned a second time. Melted sugar spilt out into the streets. . . . Caramel.

They called out to Glob. But there was no Answer.

There is no God in *Adventure Time*! . . . Or is there?

I'm not referring to any "god" like Zeus, Thor, Cthulhu, or the Party God (who appears to be the only god the people of Ooo know of). The god I'm talking about is the all-powerful, all-knowing, and all-good "God" of Christianity. That god's doctrines have become one of the most practiced religions of our time. It is said that his judgment on all of our deeds determines whether we go to Heaven or Hell. This god's name finds its way into our daily conversations. After all, how many times do we find ourselves saying, "Oh my God!"? True, there are a few characters in *Adventure Time* whose natures and powers are "godlike," namely Prismo and the Cosmic Owl, but none of them, so far, fit all of the requirements to be like God (basically perfect in every way!)

Instead, the people of Ooo have "Grob Gob Glob Grod"—whom, for the sake of simplicity, I'll just call "Glob." They worship him in church, at least so Finn assumes. They pray to him for everything from a safe, monster-free journey back home to a bride of royal bloodline. They believe he'll tally their deeds after they die. They even exclaim "Oh my Glob!" or "Oh Glob!" every once in a while.

So, Glob is the Oooian equivalent of God. And if the world Finn and his friends live on is either a post-apocalyptic version of ours or a parallel universe to our Earth, it can be assumed that "Glob" is indeed our "God." Funnily, there is a difference, at least it seems between their belief in an almighty Glob who answers their prayers and protects them, and the four faced Martian entity who takes selfies with the Lich.

I can't help but wonder if we suffer a similar cosmic irony. We assume that God is all-powerful, all-good, and all-knowing, but what, if like Glob, God is powerful, but just as fallible as we are (not to mention prone to selfies and vanity) as we are. And for the worst-case scenario: should it turn out God is no more, and the almighty Glob that the people of Ooo put their faith in, is just a senseless word? What if he's too busy taking care of business on Mars to pay attention to the needs and prayers of the people of Ooo? Even worse, it seems entirely possible that the God who is so popular in our world might similarly be busy elsewhere. In fact, couldn't our concept "God" after a thousand years and World War Three, have morphed into the Oooian "Glob?"

In the Beginning Was the Word, and the Word Was "Glob"

First of all, what is it that turned God, the all-knowing, all-powerful, and all-good, into "Glob," a name which, if I may repeat myself, up until now represents no one or nothing physical at all?

Well, we all know that it was the event called the Great Mushroom War that brought an end to the previous civilization of humans and paved the way for the Land of Ooo and its magical inhabitants to come into existence. So, then the

Mushroom War might be responsible for how God changed into Glob too.

You see, "Glob" is used commonly in the age when Finn and Jake live, which is approximately a millennium after the Mushroom War was over. However, in the events that occurred in the short period after the Mushroom War ended, which we see in "Simon and Marcy" and the alternate reality in which the bomb from the Mushroom War never exploded in "Finn the Human" and "Jake the Dog," the word "Glob" is never mentioned, not once! Simon Petrikov and young Marceline didn't pray to Glob for their daily safety, neither did the farmboy Finn Mertens exclaim "Oh my Glob!" when he found the deadly bomb frozen in an underground cave. "Glob" didn't come up in their conversation or monologue because some other word, other religious being, was used instead—"God", maybe?

Of course, it could be other names, like Yod or Brog, or it could be nothing at all. But as evidenced by various remnants of the past civilization throughout Ooo, such as cars, sunken cities, the Korean language, and even the King of Mars—Abe Lincoln, it might not hurt to think that Finn's world used to be ours, or was a parallel world of ours until the Mushroom War broke out. And since people of our world worship God, then Finn's Glob might once have been our God as well.

Aside from blowing up a chunk of Earth's crust and somehow filling the world with magic, literally, what the Great Mushroom War did was wipe out a major part of humanity and mutate many of the survivors, giving them extra organs like glands and fusing their consciousness into inorganic matters such as candy, food, rocks, wood, and fire. Through these survivors, some human cultures, mainly languages, were preserved, but some, like humanity itself, may have been lost forever or transformed through time. How "God" became known as "Glob" is in the latter case.

But that's not all. Over a thousand years, post–Mushroom War Earth has been populated with magical and bizarre creatures, some of which used to be only fictional or mythical. Even Abadeer, the Lord of Evil, the absolute bad guy who's reckoned to be the polar opposite of God, the absolute good guy, appears to be clearly alive and kicking. Yet Glob, formerly known as God, only appears in words but never as a person. It seems that God's existence, should He have existed before the Mushroom

War, has been reduced to Glob. The Mushroom War not only killed mankind; it killed God too.

God Is Dead. What Remains Is Glob!

Okay, so when we say that something is "dead," we mean that it is not alive anymore. But what does that mean for something that is more powerful than mere mortals and supposed to be eternal and infinite?

To answer this, we need to consider the nature of God outside of religious explanations. Don Cupitt suggested in his book *The Time Being* that gods (including our God) "are just what people can be seen to be worshiping" and "have no existence outside our faith and practice." What this could mean is that as long as belief in a god remains intact, and all the rites and rituals in its name or to worship it are performed according to the traditional beliefs, then the god is considered to be "alive." Otherwise, the God is likely forgotten and nonexistent, or, more precisely, "dead," which is what seems to have happened to gods and goddesses from the classic stories about gods and goddesses.

People nowadays don't see the Greek, Roman, or Norse pantheon as religious figures who look after every aspect of our lives. There's no human or livestock sacrificing as an offering to please Zeus or Odin anymore (well that we know of!). The temples of the gods were left in ruins and became tourist attractions. Their stories became lessons in Mythology 101 and have been adapted into games, movies, and popular literature.

A similar yet slightly different fate befell the Christian God in the era of Ooo. Most of His followers might have perished sometime around the Mushroom War along with the majority of humankind. And those who survived, mutated or not, were undoubtedly too busy adjusting to their post-apocalyptic lives and trying to stay alive to concern themselves with preserving culture. In fact, and this has been known to happen on occasion, if things get really bad, people might stop believing in their God and abandon the religious beliefs and practices from their former, glorious time. At the very least, people in a post-apocalyptic state are unlikely to concern themselves with the nit-picky details of worshiping a god. It would be awfully difficult to pray "in the right way" when there are few if any physical churches left, most of the people (including priests and pastors) are dead, and the most of the items needed for "correct practice" like Bibles, rosaries, and prayer manuals are lost or destroyed!

Over the course of a thousand and odd years, like humans, the notion of God could be altered into that of a separate entity. And though the people of Ooo still worship Glob at church the same way Christians do now, I doubt whatever ceremony they perform resembles much of what we see in our current ceremonies. The only living person who may have remembered the original concepts and practices of God in the Christian way is Simon Pretrikov, and his mind and memories have been screwed up by the curse of the Crown of Ice! (Marceline doesn't count because, according to her father, she's not alive to begin with, and being the daughter of the Lord of the Nightosphere herself, I honestly don't think she gives a damn about God or Glob). Having no one left to remember or believe in Him, the forgotten God lost his existence and died off. What the people of Ooo call "Glob" is likely a radically different god born from the remains of the long dead "God."

Thou Shalt Not Kill God

A German dude who happened to be one of the most controversial philosophers of the nineteenth century (and still one to this day) declared God dead. Friedrich Nietzsche (1844–1900) wrote that "God is dead. God remains dead. And we have killed him." He wasn't referring to any god like Cupitt does. Nietzsche was talking about, the all-powerful, all-knowing, and all-good Christian God. Yet Nietzsche claimed God is dead despite having over a billion active followers all over the world. What gave him the guts to pronounce such a controversial statement!?

Well, good ol' Friedrich never made it clear what it is that killed God exactly. It seems like he means that because of the knowledge we have now, the knowledge of science, particularly, we no longer *need* God to explain the world. It can be gathered from his various writings that he meant God doesn't play as important a role in human life as it did in the Biblical or the Medieval Ages. God is no longer the Supreme Almighty up there whose eyes see through every deed and misdeed, and whose wrath makes every mere mortal tremble in fear of eternal damnation.

Rather, God seems like a senile grandfather whom we pay a visit on Sunday, sometimes out of love, but mostly out of a feeling of duty. We half-heartedly beg him for every bit of luck we can muster in a day, and we are more than willing to curse him with the rudest phrases our brains we can come up with. Even God's name loses its sacredness, as evidenced by how much the word "God" shows up in random chitchats, swearing, and exclamations, despite the prohibition in the Ten Commandments demanding that we don't do that! To Nietzsche, and to many of us today, God is but an obsolete "dead" concept, just like those classic myth gods and goddesses.

By combining Cupitt's theory with what we've managed to squeeze out of Nietzsche's famous quote, we have a glimpse of the notion of God before the Great Mushroom War. Surely, how humanity was capable of inventing a weapon of mass destruction so critically lethal that it took almost the entire species of theirs is a blatant sign of mankind's high devotion to sciences and technology, and not giving a heed to God at all. God had been dead before the War broke out, and he remains dead as Glob.

But is He really dead?

Oh, Nature, Nature, Why Art Thou So Godless?

Among different beliefs about God, there is one theory proposing that God resides neither in nor outside the universe; He *is* the universe and everything within it: Sun, Moon, stars, dirt, trees, animals, humans. In short, God is one with nature. This belief system is known as *pantheism*.

Looked at from a non-religious perspective, pantheism is kind of a compromise between traditional religious and natural scientific worldviews. Look at nature; it's one tremendous web of interrelated complex systems working in sync and harmony with each other: the solar system, the ecosystem, even all the organic systems inside every living thing's body. Everything in nature, down to the least atom, is seemingly purposefully designed, and each is good in its own way.

Take the pantheistic view up one level, and we might get an idea of God's state in *Adventure Time*. Glob could be understood as the magical force that's dispersed not only all over the world, but also all over the universe, or even the multiverse, allowing all the magical and bizarre creatures we've encountered throughout the series. As nature in *Adventure Time* is full of miraculous beings and environments, it might not be an absurd idea at all to suggest that the presence of those things is how God or Glob takes form after the Mushroom War ended. In this sense, God has become the whole of nature.

Unfortunately, there are some problems to that idea. If we accept that what the Oooians refer to as "Glob" is actually God materializing in the shape of every surreal life form and scenery, then we have no choice but to accept the parts of nature which seem crazier, creepier, or more awkward than others are also Glob! Like the tribe of naked humanoid inhabitants of the Swamp of Embarrassment in "Blood Under the Skin" who seem to be doing nothing at all but taking showers and getting freaked out every time someone spots them doing so, or the demons in "Return to the Nightosphere" whose certain orifices excrete bananas instead of . . . well, you get the picture. Those things might be good in their own ways, but to think that they could be some forms of God in the physical world? Doesn't that mean that Glob, who is supposed to be good, also exists in evil or seemingly evil forms?

And if you think that's not bad enough, then let's talk about the worst. In *Adventure Time*, evil is evidently inherent to nature; it's part of nature. Of course, some 'evils' in the series were artificially born: the obnoxious, selfish Earl of Lemongrab was created in Frankensteinian style by Princess Bubblegum, and the diabolical, life-abhorring Lich first came into existence out of destructive energy radiating from the Mushroom War bomb.

But there are some "evils" that were naturally born. Gunter, the Ice King's right-hand penguin, Abadeer admits is the most evil thing he's encountered "of all history's greatest monsters." In "Reign of Gunters," this seemingly innocent penguin even stole the Ice King's magic artifact to create an army of replicas and attempted to conquer Ooo. Also, it appears that Hunson Abadeer, the Lord of Evil himself, has always existed, unlike Satan, the Big Bad of Christianity, who was once a creation of God as his finest angel. According to his claim in *The Adventure Time Encyclopedia*, Abadeer doesn't know how he came into being, but he only knows before "the Vast and Ineluctable

Scope" of his memory began that he "existed Forever," and his earliest memory is of him sitting atop a mountain and eating a ham sandwich eons before the Mushroom War began. The credibility of this claim may be doubtful, as the whole *Encyclopedia* was written by Abadeer himself. But given that he's the Lord of Evil, not Lord of Deceit, then it may not hurt to hold him as a reliable source.

Evil seems to be in nature all along, whether before or after the War. This notion alone is enough to make the idea of God being nature tricky, because it would be impossible for evil to be a part of something or someone that's all good. So God or Glob couldn't be nature, and again we come to the conclusion that He is dead. What hope is left for the people of Ooo then?

I suggest that they, as well as we, can put their hope in the only surviving member of the same race who murdered God: Finn the Human.

Who Cares about Glob? We Have Finn Anyway

What does it mean for God to be dead? What effect would His death have on the people who believe in him or used to believe in him?

In his novel *The Brothers Karamazov,* Fyodor Dostoevsky gave his opinion about belief in God through the words of one of the main characters, Dmitri—without God, "all things are permitted." What he meant is that God, or at least the belief in His existence, is deeply linked with many rules and restrictions, like the Ten Commandments and the Seven Deadly Sins; and once God is gone, or people don't care anymore if He really exists or not, then those rules and prohibitions can easily be rejected. People would no longer have to do unto others as they wish to be done unto themselves; people could do whatever they would like to do. Forget the others!

A world like that would be in perfect chaos, wouldn't it? In it men and women with a little bit of conscience left would live in daily fear of getting killed and having their possessions stolen! Honestly speaking, that's not quite different from life in Ooo—when ya'll run into a soul-sucking demon lord, an undead sorcerer whose wish is to exterminate all life, or a cheeky Martian who can turn your body inside out, and this Glob you often dearly pray to seems to have better things to do than respond to prayers!

Dostoevsky's view, though it sounds convincing, has been disputed by a Slovenian philosopher named Slavoj Žižek. Žižek argues that if there is no God, then all things would be prohibited rather than permitted. He explains that although God is dead, as Nietzsche had declared, His shadow, taking the forms of all the moral rules and regulations made under His name, lingers on. Little by little throughout history, those rules and regulations have plunged their roots deep into man's hearts until they stayed firmly there despite the decline in faith in God.

Most people today, whether they believe in God or not, would feel guilty if they stabbed someone to death! This guilt would then force them to behave themselves in ways others want them to! If anything, there might be *more* reason to be "good"—after all if there is no Glob to join in the afterlife, wouldn't we be careful not to waste our lives in prison for breaking the rules?

The land of Ooo, though at times very dangerous, is a place where there is virtually no limit. If you know how to protect yourself, have the guts, and live independently from any kingdom, then you're more than free to travel into the wild, explore dungeons, fight monsters, and loot treasures as much as you like. As the theme song says, *Adventure Time* is filled with "very distant lands" where "the fun will never end." But since life is almost limitless in Ooo, the adventurers are in danger of crossing the line of morality. You could become so addicted to fighting and looting that you end up enjoying stealing and killing others. And as Glob is but a word, you can't expect Him to show up and miraculously stop you. All you can rely on is your self-regulation and the ability to feel guilty.

Finn, being a teenager—an age torn between living to the limit and living responsibly—has to face this same problem with double pressure. No doubt the most influential person in Finn's life is Jake. And as we all see, Jake, while being a good friend and a supportive big brother, is not much of a reliable adult. Sometimes, by following Jake's lead, Finn gets himself into trouble. A good example occurs in the *Marceline and the Scream Queens* comics, where Princess Bubblegum appoints Jake as an interim king of Candy Kingdom while she's accompanying Marceline and her rock band on their tour. Instead of doing the royal deeds, Jake holds the Rule Burning Ceremony which withdraws all the laws of Candy Kingdom, allowing the citizens to act crazy, get naked, and cause havoc as much as they like. They even tie a pig to a tree and dress it up to look like PB! On her return to duty, she has Jake and Finn, as his accomplice, locked up in a dungeon for a month. Quite a valuable lesson for Finn on living outside of the rules.

Finn often comes across situations that tempt him to enjoy himself to the extreme, and he has slowly learned that his lack of self-regulation can do harm to others as well as himself. In "All the Little People," Finn is given, unknowingly from Magic Man, a bag full of miniature versions of many people of Ooo, including himself. He enjoys playing with them so much that he spends sixteen weeks straight obsessed with them, developing a messed-up web of relationships between each of them and watching it go from bad to chaotic. In the end, Finn realizes how much evil he has done to their lives and attempts to apologize to them. And in "Dungeon Train," Finn fights on a train that runs endlessly, with new enemies to fight and cool items to collect. Finn loves the train so much that he decides not to leave, but as soon as he knows Jake will stay on board with him forever out of worry and care for him, he begins to feel sorry for his canine(ish) pal and changes his mind. Just as Žižek's argues, it's guilt that urges Finn to see the need for self-regulation.

As *Adventure Time* is not going to end any time soon, Finn still has a long time to grow up, physically and mentally. And there'll be many more situations where his self-discipline will be tested and given the chance to improve. If Finn continues to keep in mind how important it is to always keep himself in control, he's sure to become a messianic hero for the whole land of Ooo, and whether Glob or God still exists will no longer be of any importance.

An Adventure Time of Our Own in a Globless World

There's a good reason behind choosing a human to be the hero of a show that takes place in a fantasy world teeming with peculiar creatures—because we, human audiences, can easily identify with him. And although *Adventure Time*, being a remarkable piece of art, is apt to be interpreted in many ways, I propose to view the series as a retelling of our real life, of how we can survive in the world where God's existence is still in question.

Just like Finn, each of us encounters adventures in different levels on a daily basis. There are no fire-breathing dragons for us to slay or hidden treasures for us to find, but there are bosses whose fiery rage will burn us alive if we make mistakes in our jobs, and a hefty bonus at the end of the year if we perform outstandingly. We know how our prayers to God often go unheard as much as Ice King's pleas for Glob to give him a princess bride. And most of the time, we realize that good things can happen because of our self-discipline and sympathy towards others, not because of a miracle. In the end, it's always Finn, not Glob, who saves the day.

Okay, so maybe Glob is the four-faced Martian God-brother of Magic Man and doesn't seem all that much like the bearded old man we often talk about. But even so, the important issue is not whether or not God and Glob exist; it's how humans continue to sympathize with each other and be good to each other, regardless of any higher spiritual power. That's how mankind could hope to improve as a whole.

After all, the death of God could lead to the birth of a true Hero.

III

Life Is But a Croak Dream

12

The Paradox of Horror and the Ocean of Fear

MICHAEL J. MUNIZ

In the dark recesses of the mind, a disease known as FEAR feasts upon the souls of those who cannot overcome its power.

—PAT MCHALE

One day you decide to play a game of "Poots on Newts" with your dog. This nice, gentle game is quite appealing—until, that is, you've chased a giant fire-breathing amphibian towards the ocean. You see waves crashing violently on the sand. Your dog continues to chase the boot-thieving Newt into the Ocean as he poots on him. Soon, you realize that this body of water is not a lake, or a well, or a river, or a stream, or puddle. But how can this be? What is this body of water called, the ocean? Meanwhile the giant beast scurries away as your dog returns in joy. But, it isn't until your stomach clenches in crippling fear that you wake up and realize it was all a dream. Your relief lasts only a moment, and, to your horror, you look down to see something dark stirring in your belly . . .

It may have all been a dream, but truthfully, it could have easily been a reality. Here's an extra drop to your sweat: when I describe scenarios from *Adventure Time* as "real" you probably think I mean Pendleton Ward, or the Cartoon Network created it. But no, I mean these are real now. They're real when you watch the shows. And not just in some cutesy bubble-gummy "let's pretend" sense; I mean that in the most important über-mathematical ways you can say, *real*.

The Scary Minds of the Animator People

So, is the Land of Ooo scary? Think about it. Look at all the creatures that inhabit the land: talking dogs with stretchy powers, demonic eye creatures, Martians, lumpy space people, bubblegum princesses, ooze monsters, wolf men, vampires, ice kings, skeletons, demons, fish, little people, rainicorns, dragons, lemon people. and more demons. So why aren't we scared when we see these creatures on TV? It's because they don't look real! In other words, we're depending on how the creators of *Adventure Time* tell their stories. In books, we depend on how the author uses words and plot to tell a story. In the movies, we depend on the director's ability to show us images in a certain order so that a story can both be told and seen. Well, in animated TV shows, we depend on how both the animators and the directors create a fictional world.

We can test the importance of the animator-storyteller by experimenting with a basic fairy tale that almost everybody knows: *Little Red Riding Hood*. What would happen if, say Pendleton Ward wrote his own version of *Little Red Riding Hood*? We would probably get some bizarre tale of a gumdrop princess prancing through the forest of trees where a bunch of fantastic creatures live. By the time Red gets to "Granny's," a heroic Finn has killed a werewolf demon and throws a party. Well that would be great, and maybe we should ask Ward to write the story, but let's be honest, Ward's version wouldn't quite provide us with the same *experience* as the original.

Although it may technically be *Little Red Riding Hood*, in Ward's version we wouldn't get the same experience as we would from a more traditional version that we remember from childhood. There's something very important about *how* a story is told. Even if the story keeps the same basic plot, the way writers, like Pendleton Ward, compose it can radically change our experience.

Consider the Ice King's stories of Fionna and Cake. These are his twisted and insane versions of Finn and Jake's adventures. Even if the basic idea is the same, a hero and her faithful companion travel throughout Ooo saving the day, the person telling the story *matters*. And if the Ice King is writing the episode, we know we'll get more than a different story, we'll get a whole different *experience*. Storytellers are a necessary and important element to experiencing a story. To better understand a story, we should look to how a story is told rather than just at the story itself.

Ooh! It's the Land of Ooo!

I think Princess Bubblegum puts it best when she says, "If my decorpsinator serum works, all the dead candy people will look as young and healthy as you do."[1] It seems that she's implying that we tend to become corpse-like couch potatoes when we watch too much TV, but she could also be talking about animated TV shows themselves. What if the animated programs that we see on TV were actually candy people trapped on the other side of a glass screen? What if the TV is like an aquarium where we are actually mutated people, and the events that are happening right on screen are actually happening? Talk about being a peeping Ice King, huh? Okay, we know that the TV isn't an aquarium (I wouldn't open it up to check!) But just *imagine* for a moment that it was. . . . What if we perceive what happens in *Adventure Time* as real?

Philosophers, film theorists, and psychoanalysts have all added to the idea that movies and animated TV shows are real in some way, shape, or form. Animation storytellers tend to take these theories into consideration and exploit them when making an episode. They know that even if we believe it's all fake, we get drawn in, if they present it right. Think about the idea of the danger our beloved hero Finn faces. Finn is a young teenager. And it seems quite normal to suggest that nobody likes the idea of children in danger. Yet, for Pendleton Ward, putting Finn in danger is a great way to elicit fear in a TV audience. He's done this in just about every episode. By doing that, by placing a child in danger, we get a bit tense, a bit worried. We know it isn't real, but we experience *Adventure Time* as real enough that when heroes we love suffer, we worry!

Think about storytellers. Ward's *Adventure Time* is quite different from say J.K. Rowling's Harry Potter series, or C.S. Lewis's *Chronicles of Narnia*. But, the one element that is guaranteed in all three of these stories, which is mandatory for them to work, is danger towards children. To prove it, ask yourself: Would I still be experiencing the same thrill of adventure

---

[1] "Slumber Party Panic."

if no children were present in any of these stories? Would *Adventure Time* be as awesome and mathematical as it is if Finn was an adult? We're much more comfortable with adults experiencing danger than with kids.

The fact that the adventures we experience in *Adventure Time* are presented through a child, pulls on our heartstrings. We're kind of like Lemonhope. Maybe we don't want to care, and we know on some level that none of it matters, but good storytellers get in our head, make it feel real enough that we *have* to get involved emotionally.

Whoa, That Has to Be True . . . and False

Imagine this. . . . You're undergoing a jury selection survey for a robbery case. The prosecutor asks you whether or not you've ever witnessed a robbery before. Now, if you're like me, you've seen a lot of caper movies where cool robberies take place all the time. So, am I telling the truth when I say to the judge, "Yes your honor, I've seen many robberies. In fact with my experience of watching many robberies, these guys make it look like taking candy from a baby!"

If you did say that you'd probably be escorted to another courtroom and sentenced to do time at a special facility. So even though you've seen robberies on TV, you can't say that you have. But this is where it gets weird. . . . How else, though, do you describe events in a story? If I say, "Finn beat up the Ice King because the Ice King captured a princess, don't you know what I mean? In fact, wouldn't it be pretty odd, if not inaccurate if I turned to you and said, "So Dude, what did you think of that episode when the drawing named "Ice King," that is actually a series of drawings flashed at us really quickly so it looks like movement, looks like it is beat up by another two-dimensional drawing . . . *blab la blab* . . ." ? Doesn't it just seem more accurate to say, "I saw Ice King get his buns beat by Finn"?

Does that mean we can say that we've *actually* seen Finn and Jake, or any other Ooo character? If we say, "No," then why do we tend to get scared, or feel a sense of thrill, when the Lich is terrorizing Finn and Jake? This problem between knowing what's real and feeling what's real is a type of paradox. In other words, if we know it's all fake, all 2D drawings, why do we get excited if we see Finn defeat a monster, feel sad for Marceline and Simon, or worry when Jake has a true dream about his own death? Shouldn't we just shrug our shoulders and say, "But it isn't real, so who cares?" On some level, for us to feel as we do, it has to *feel* real to us! But if it isn't real, then that's a monster of a paradox.

By "paradox" I mean a statement that says something that goes beyond what you'd normally believe. A paradox may appear impossible, but is in fact true. Paradoxes have been around for many years. Some would even say that paradoxes would continue to exits even after the most brutal of mushroom wars. Paradoxes are used all the time to challenge certain viewpoints about certain issues, like can the Ice King and Simon be the same person? It seems as if they are and they aren't, and that tells us a lot about what we mean when we say, "a person."

In the case of stories and reality, the paradox is called, "The Paradox of Fiction." It can be stated as three simple sentences:

1. **People only respond emotionally to what they believe is real.**

2. **People don't believe that fiction is real.**

3. **People respond emotionally to fiction all the time.**

The paradox happens when you realize that the first sentence and the second sentence should add up to a different conclusion. If we only respond to what we think is real, and fiction isn't real, then we *shouldn't* respond emotionally to fiction! And yet, it seems that the third sentence is also true *because we do respond emotionally to fiction.*

This may look like a contradiction, but we're going to have to wade into this ocean of concern in order to get to the heart of the matter and then see how we can escape. Philosophers, who're determined to show that this paradox can be cracked attempt to prove that one of these sentences is false. Other philosophers, usually in the minority, have recognized the paradox and settled on the fact that our emotional responses to fiction are basically irrational (crazy).

The Paradox of Horror

Okay, look at it like this. . . . There are two major types of emotions: active and passive. Passive emotions are instantaneous.

They occur at the moment without any thought. For example, when you're walking across the street and you hear the sound of a loud roar from a big monster truck that speeds by, you jump back and your heart begins to pound. You didn't stop and think; your survival instincts triggered a series of brain events that forced you to jump back and you *feel afraid.* Your fear is momentary, and you didn't start the chain that led to that fear. One minute you're fine, the next, you're heart-thumpingly terrified. But, an active emotion is when you dwell on the thought of a situation for such a long time that the result is an emotion. If you're Finn, the more you dwell on the possible reality of falling into the ocean while battling a fire-breathing amphibian, the more your stomach tightens and starts to grumble, *the more fear you start to experience.*

Now, this is where the paradox comes in. If I am actively dwelling on my fears while watching a thrilling episode of *Adventure Time*, then I will, without a doubt, be afraid during frightening scenes in the episode. So, am I actually afraid of the scene itself, or my thoughts about the potential situation that could arise if the TV show's events were true? Haven't we all at one point or another asked ourselves: What would I do if I were in that situation?

You might think about this with Marceline. If you're a parent and watch her story, you might start to wonder what would happen to your own children if you died. The more you think about that, the more you worry. So it isn't really Marceline's story that worries you at that moment so much as it is a possible situation that could actually happen to your kids. So then the paradox isn't a problem, right? I'm not really believing the scene is real, I'm just afraid of a potential real scene brought to mind by Marceline.

So most people tend to accept that sentence #2 of the paradox, "People don't believe that fiction is real," is true. But there are certain arguments out there that philosophers have given that would have us think differently. This would mean that at least some fiction is seen as real. For example, if I see the *Adventure Time* episode "Business Men" and I know that it is fiction, but I believe that the "Giant Robot" sequence (at the end of the episode) could occur in my hometown of Hialeah, Florida, then it becomes real to me. So unlike the case of my kids being orphaned, this is a situation that feels real to me, but is actually impossible. So, the fiction has become a sort of reality.

Another way to try to resolve the paradox is to argue against sentence #3: "People respond emotionally to fiction all the time (or at least often)." Someone might think that the emotional responses that we have to fiction are in fact not honest—a sort of make-believe emotion. It feels like a genuine emotion, but it is in fact a fake emotion. Some philosophers have gone so far as to say that these are "fictional emotional responses." But what the flip is a fictional emotional response? Apparently, while everything else about my emotions is genuine, because the TV episode (or story) is fictional, I am having a "fictional emotional response." Trying to solve the paradox from this third point leaves us hanging upside by the bubblegum stuck under our shoes when it comes to wondering about what is fictional and what is real.

This leaves us with our acceptance or denial of sentence #1 of the paradox—"People only respond emotionally to what they believe is real." If I've been accepting sentences #2 and #3 of the paradox, I should be able to accept #1.

Let me explain. . . . I don't believe Jake is real. He is a fictitious character. But, I laugh at what Jake does. I become sad or hurt when Jake suffers. Does this mean that my sadness or hurt is not real because I don't believe Jake is real? We have active and passive emotions, remember? Active emotions are rooted in immediate beliefs, like the belief that I am in danger from a car, and passive ones require that my emotions are rooted in brain activity (the more I think about some things, the more afraid I become).

But if I reject sentence #1, that would mean that we have emotional responses to things we don't think are real, but doesn't it seem that our emotions require that we believe something is actually happening (so it's an active emotion), or actually could happen (so it's a passive emotion)? Why would I be afraid if I don't believe it *is* happening and don't believe it *could* happen? If I deny sentence #1 of the paradox, I'm just digging too deep and not finding any bones to back me up. So, it could be quite satisfying to just accept the paradox as it is, and not tinker with it.

The End of the Beginning

So, as Pat McHale would have us believe, "And so fear is forced deep within the soul of a hero. Conquered . . . at least, for now."[2] Controlling fear is like controlling love, there needs to be a real source behind the emotion. If you or I don't believe it's real, then our emotions are not real. In the end, we all believe that what we're seeing on the screen is either actually happening or not. If we accept the paradox of fiction then what we're really saying is that any emotional response to any episode of *Adventure Time* is irrational. So, don't judge me if I'm crying out of sympathy for the Ice King's desperate search for love. Your feelings are just as nonsensical as mine.

In the end, if there is something to take home after all of this, there should be a balance of our beliefs. Just like how Jake balances his time with Finn and Lady Rainicorn, we should balance how our emotions reflect our beliefs. *Adventure Time* is an excellent model of how we should not be afraid of the characters that live in Ooo, or in our belly buttons. But, rather, we should be able to take what's real and see how Finn and Jake, or any other character in Ooo, would respond. What we believe to be real is a reflection of who we are.

[2] "Ocean of Fear."

13
Play Time? Interpretation Time!

MARTY JONES

*T*he screen starts black and you can hear a swirling wind as a dark hill littered with apocalyptic trash materializes on the screen. You're only given a second to take this in because suddenly you're zooming forward, flying over hill and dale, past hissing vampires and kissing penguins. You travel, dizzyingly, over a Technicolor dreamworld of icing and candy people, through the streets and byways of bizarre kingdoms and far-flung realms until you burst through the window of a massive treehouse and snap to a halt in front of our heroes: a talking dog and boy with a big grin. Their fist-pound explodes across the screen with a clap of thunder.

Then there is a strummed ukulele chord and a cherubic voice sings, "Adventure Time / come on, grab your friends . . ."

Adventure Time's opening sequence perfectly captures the spirit of the show. We, the audience, are shown lands and creatures of all kinds across one of the most ecologically diverse worlds imaginable in an epic sweep that resolves on our heroes—heroes who will explore and chart this world for our entertainment and delight during their designated times for *adventure*. The grandeur of the montage is cut down to childlike size with a ukulele and a reminder that the adventurer here is a young boy. The spirit being channeled is a spirit of pure, distilled play—the sort that is characteristic of the joyful, ongoing discovery of the world during childhood.

This love of play puts *Adventure Time* above so many other shows of its kind. *Adventure Time* founds itself on creativity and imagination. The show's achievement is in its sharpening and clarifying the spirit of play that characterizes our younger years without sacrificing either adult sophistication or youthful exuberance. In fact, what *Adventure Time* proves is the importance of play, even dealing with real, even life-threatening, problems.

We Have to Take Play Seriously!

In the most basic way, we might say that play is at the heart of *Adventure Time*. The philosopher Hans-Georg Gadamer believed that play was a clue to understanding how we interpret and understand works of art and written texts. In Gadamer's great work *Truth and Method*, there's a section entirely devoted to *play*. Gadamer argues that play is massively important because it's the "mode of being" of works of art. In other words, *Adventure Time*—because play is so essential to its existence—is a work of art.

Gadamer explains: "Play fulfills its purpose only if the player loses himself in play." This is a perfect starting point. Finn's enthusiasm defines him as a person. Whether he's been called upon to rescue princesses or go questing for the *Enchiridion*, Finn is virtually incapable of doing anything halfheartedly. The only time we see Finn hold back is when he thinks it might be a wrong thing to do, like when Princess Bubblegum told him to guard the Ice King without telling Finn what the Ice King was guilty of. But if Finn believes he's doing the right thing, he goes all in!

Finn's whole-heartedness reminds me of everyday experiences of play. When we *play* a game, one of the first things that *has* to happen is that we commit to it: We endeavor to pick up its rules and subject ourselves to them. As Gadamer puts it, this is the "sacred seriousness" of play. The person who doesn't enter into the limited world of the game and doesn't take its rules seriously is a spoilsport who ruins the game! He banishes the spirit of play; he is left to his lonesome by departing players, who probably call him names as they walk away from the ruined game. But no matter how off the wall a request is made of Finn, he treats his adventures with absolute commitment.

Finn's enthusiasm also reflects the enthusiasm of the show and its creator, Pendleton Ward. *Adventure Time* wears its heart on its sleeve, and nowhere is this clearer than in the first episodes of Season One. In its first run of eleven-minute tales, Finn and Jake find themselves caught up in the Candy Kingdom, Lumpy Space, the Ice Kingdom, the Forest Where Tree Trunks Lives, and Mount Cragdor in pursuit of glory, a cure for the Lumps, protection from the candied undead, a precious stone, and the fabled book of heroes. The pace is rapid; the amount of information disclosed is huge. The excitement does not abate—episode after episode whips by in a rush of creativity. Finn commits to his play, and so does *Adventure Time*. These episodes show us that we can learn a great deal about a person from that commitment, from the way that they play.

Play Is *Real*

Play, in Gadamer's view, allows us to experience a great deal of self-realization. Play isn't just a mindset that Finn takes on when adventure calls him; play draws Finn in, and, as Gadamer says, "fills him with its spirit." Finn is able to "lose himself" in play—even to a point of self-forgetfulness, as when he's possessed with bloodlust and attacks Jake in Season Three's "Morituri Te Salutamus." Play points to a reality that is beyond Finn and he can lose himself in. We get lost in play, and it goes beyond us too.

From the beginning Finn's thrown into a situation where he simply has to act to solve problems. We see our hero placed in a situation where he has to both fully commit and become submerged in a world far greater than he is. When we watch this, we get lost in it too. Remember the first episode? All we know during "Slumber Party Panic" is that Finn is friends with the princess of the candy people, and that she's a scientist, and that because of a mistake she's made in one of her experiments . . . oh, man . . . dead candy people are totally coming back to life with a hunger for candy flesh and Finn has to hold these glucose-crazed zombies off without letting any of the living candy people know what he's doing, while the princess races to find a solution for her faulty formula and by the way, if the candy people get scared enough they explode like popcorn? That's quite a mouthful! But that is all of the information that's given to Finn, and us, *all at once!*

That's a lot of information! But all of it is specific to the situation. Finn jumps in to prevent catastrophe for the candy people, given what he knows. The funny thing is, as Finn races about slamming doors and improvising his own games to distract the Princess's subjects and prevent a premature Candy Apocalypse, he actually shows us a lot about himself and his friends. We see Finn's character, his friendship with Jake, and bits of his and other characters' personalities as they all respond to the situation. All of this happens within the enclosed world of the game. The episode creates for Finn, and for us, rules to follow, rules that direct Finn's energies as he participates in play.

What's happening, then, is that through the play of Finn and other characters in "Slumber Party Panic," the universe of *Adventure Time* is actually being built—or, rather, revealed. Through play, Finn and all of the characters are actually showing us the truth, in shades, of the Land of Ooo.

In what way can we say that there's "truth" to the Land of Ooo? Isn't it, after all, a fictional place? Isn't it really just an imaginary game that Pendleton Ward is playing with us? Sure, but that doesn't mean that Ooo doesn't have its own logic and reality. Plenty of things could slam against that reality and even do damage to it. That's what happens when fans of a television show feel betrayed over a favorite character dying or a turn in a plot that "ruins" the story. These "mistakes" are understood by us as errors made by the writers because we have an idea of the truth of the world of the show. The show has promised us a certain kind of truth about itself and it has promised to follow a certain set of rules. That "truth" can either be built on and brought to further and fuller realization, or contradicted and chipped away.

The "truth" of a game like poker is that everyone takes a turn. If you skip someone's turn, you have violated that rule, which is a fact. But you won't find that rule written in the fabric of the universe. It isn't "true" the way we think of physics as true, and yet, if someone said, "I get to skip your turn" we would be right to say that they were lying *because it isn't true!*

Remember the episode "Morituri Te Salutamus" I mentioned earlier? If Finn had never emerged from the fog of his delusion and remained a psychotic jerk for the rest of the show without hope of recovery, fans would have complained! And they would have been right! They could have said the writers of the show betrayed them by betraying Finn! The writers made him into something that he's not—and they would have crushed the exuberant spirit of the show in the process. So maybe "Finn" isn't real, but, in our play, we can honestly say things like "Finn is a good guy" and if our "real world" writers turn him into a bad guy, they have violated that truth!

So, in the same way, the Land of Ooo has certain truths to it. Rules that the writers could break and we'd all stop watching the show. True, the play of *Adventure Time* shows us that the Land of Ooo has only a few principles. In Finn, Jake, and Princess Bubblegum's world, magic and science co-exist and even combine into a mystical hybrid. Organs become independent agents of love and destruction; a giant ogre can fall to pieces over having his dollar stolen; a tiny elephant can carry a basket of hot buns around—for goodness' sake, the gender of every character can be flipped for a whole episode once a season, and it remains beautifully faithful to the reality of the show because the Land of Ooo is a place where almost anything can happen.

There aren't normal laws of physics to obey, nor an ironclad causal history that would lock Jake into normal dog-dimensions. This is true with the play of children, too. As long as you don't oppose the spirit of the game and violate the rules, you can be a superhero or drink invisible tea with your best friends, Mr. Bear and Mrs. Sprinklewhiskers. You can fly like Lady Rainicorn and drink as much invisible tea as you want. You can probably do both at the same time, even. Stranger things have happened. But you have to let yourself be drawn in, and as any child will tell you, if you don't really *commit* to the invisible tea and take your turn, *"you aren't playing fair!"*

TrOooth

For the truth of the Land of Ooo to be presented through *Adventure Time*, something very basic has to happen: Episodes have to get made. When an episode is completed and made available for viewing, it's complete. Pendleton Ward and his team are finished with it; each eleven-minute story now exists independently of them.

The play of the show still happens, but it's different for us as viewers than it was for the team of writers and illustrators who wrangled it into shapely stories for us. Gadamer calls this completion, this "consummation" of the finished product, the "transformation into structure."

The true being of the story has been achieved by the time it hits episode form. The players—in this case, the creators—have disappeared, and what they were playing at—the episode— remains.

Again and again, *Adventure Time* brings the Land of Ooo into existence. Importantly, it's not our world or an extension of it, but a world unto itself, and it's according to the standards of that world, not ours, that each episode can be judged. We don't complain about *Adventure Time*'s disregard for *our* laws of physics because that complaint just doesn't make sense according to the universe of *Adventure Time*. A complaint like my hypothetical "You ruined Finn by making him into a psychotic jerk!" would be a real concern because it violates the truth *of the show* not because it violates the truth of a Finn in our world.

The important thing here is that we're talking about *recognition*, which is a term usually reserved for something like seeing another human and understanding that she's your mother, or hearing a great crash and knowing that your cat has missed the window sill she was jumping for again. In other words, we're back to facts and realities—questions of truth.

When an episode of *Adventure Time* is completed, it has transformed into structure, which reigns in the wild and free energy of Ooo in order to express that energy in a specific way. Instead of limiting Ooo, this transformation actually fulfills the potential of Ooo.

One episode can never say all there is to say about Ooo, though. For instance, if the show had ended after "Trouble in Lumpy Space" we'd have become acquainted with a handful of characters and two environments that feature in the show, and we could even have said that we had gotten a true picture of Ooo. But the episodic structure, the constant return to Ooo, is essential to what *Adventure Time* is. We get to experience and explore it again and again. And that's because return and repetition are essential to play.

Coming Back Again and Again and . . .

When you've finished a round of a game you love—say, Settlers of Catan, or Diplomacy, or Punch Your Brother in the Shoulder

Real Hard—do you sit back and say, with contentment, "what a great game! Glad to have played it. I'm going to put it up on the shelf forever now, because I'll never need to play it again, seeing as I have already played it once!" Well of course not! Neither does Finn get back from a quest and tell Jake, "Algebraic! That was a good adventure. Guess I'm going to do other things for the rest of my life now." No way!

This is because of the nature of play, which drives both our enthusiasm for our favorite games and Finn's constant adventure-seeking. A game or an adventure isn't something you just do once and consider finished forever. When you say, "So-and-So is a great game," you're not referring to the one time you played it—you're referring to the game that you play time and time again. The sort of being of the game has everything to do with its "becoming and return," as Gadamer would say.

We could even say that play only actually has *being* in becoming and returning. There isn't something fixed that exists when we aren't playing the game except its rules, which are empty by themselves. When we talk about games, we're talking about the experience of playing; the experience that we keep coming back to; the thing we *do*. Think about what you mean when you say "I played a game." That doesn't mean you pulled out the box and sat there staring at it. Playing a game means something more than that, a kind of interaction, an interaction that you can return to every time you take the game out *if you play the game*.

Adventure Time shows us this side of play in a similar way. When I tell my pal Will "I love *Adventure Time!*" the thing I'm telling him I love is the ongoing return of the show, episode to episode, the constant deepening and enriching of its world with each new chapter and every rerun of an old one. Gadamer would connect us here also to the idea of a festival. Consider a state fair, for instance. When you tell someone about how great the fair is, you're telling them about how great *going to the fair* is. It's something you have done, and could do again. It exists as something you go and do.

And just as going to the fair is *participating* in the fair, being present before a work of art—or watching an episode of *Adventure Time*—is participating in it, too. Just like the way Finn is taken up into the spirit of play, losing himself completely in it, we, his audience, are taken up into the show and lose ourselves in it too.

It might be tempting to think of watching the show as a passive activity, but really, this absorption has a seriously positive aspect. In becoming forgetful of ourselves in our love for Finn and Jake, we're given ourselves back in a new way. When we're outside ourselves, we're wholly within something else, you might say. In recognizing the truths of the Land of Ooo that bubble up to the surface during episodes of *Adventure Time*, we also recognize new sides of our own, living reality.

Playing at Interpretation

Adventure Time offers us a beautifully realized world full of life and color, as well as some surprising depths—it has all the vividness of a child's dream, and all of the enthusiasm and rapture as well. Play is clearly at the heart of it all, spurring Finn into discovering new dimensions of himself, his friends, and his world—and here we can come back to Gadamer by connecting play with interpretation.

Consider all the swirling meanings of the universe of *Adventure Time*—everything that's true of the world, true of its characters, true of its internal principles. Now, consider what's true of your own world—your lived reality. Think about where you are sitting right now, what you are doing, and all of the rules and facts that make up your life and world.

So now we have an idea of each world in each hand. In your left palm are a tiny Finn and Jake and Princess Bubblegum and Tree Trunks and Marceline and the Ice King and Gunter(s), and in your right hand you can now see tiny versions of yourself and your family and friends and basically the sum of your life. Now, bring your hands, palms-up, toward one another until they are touching side-by-side.

This is a picture of what Gadamer says happens when we read something. We bring all of our ideas and beliefs and perspectives on the truth—our world—into contact with another fully-formed world of meaning enclosed within its own backdrop. We try to understand the main ideas of the text with the help of our expectations about what those ideas will be. We also try to understand that other world (the world of the text, Gadamer would say) in terms of own ideas and biases and prejudices. If we're reading well, we also try to be open to the world that emerges from the text, which is a world different from our own with its own ideas.

For Gadamer, the experience of reading and interpreting happens right where those two worlds meet. Consider how it happens with *Adventure Time*: Finn and Jake and Tree Trunks, as odd and "out there" as they might seem, are understandable to us because we have ideas already about what a boy is and what a dog is and even what a talking dog or miniature elephant is. When we open up to the show—when we're taken up into the experience of it, time and again, and join in its play as spectator-participants—we see the ways in which our ideas help us understand and imagine Finn or Jake the Dog. We also see how these characters are different from our expectations for them—how there are parts of them that are solid and unyielding. We can try to fit Finn and Jake into our own ideas of what a boy and what a dog are, but the world created for us by the show also forces us to open up to a different kind of possibility.

When we're fully present to the show and participate in its play, we can't help but let our concepts be changed by what we're seeing. Our idea of what an adventurous young boy is changes because we've met Finn. And if we have a faulty idea of who that boy is and what he's about, the character of Finn may very well correct it.

The cool thing is that this process, exactly like play, happens constantly and repeatedly. Every time I create a new understanding by synthesizing my world and Finn's world, I can return to *Adventure Time*, and fuse my world with his once more. As I develop a relationship with the show, its concepts will begin to echo through my own, and I'll begin to see parts of my own world with a tinge of *Adventure Time*'s magic in it.

This action, this kind of *play*, is a process that is essential to human meaning-making. Play, as it emerges and re-emerges in *Adventure Time*, is at work every time we read and interpret someone else's text message, a mom's displeased face, an old schoolteacher's personal blog, the treaty that ended the war of 1812, a significant other's body language, and the pink slip we find in our intra-office mail. Play is a great, ongoing event in human life that makes understanding—and empathy—possible. When we interpret something like *Adventure Time*, if we do it right, we climb into the story, fully commit to it and its rules, and merge it with our own understanding of the world. When that happens, a completely new way of understanding our own lives becomes possible!

The truth of *Adventure Time* is wound up into its playful core. The show is an ongoing expression of the sheer exuberance of self-forgetful play, play that keeps returning to realize itself anew in each new quest and adventure and bid for meaning. This refers us back to our own reality, and helps us see some of the truths about our own lives. In other words "play" isn't the physical game or the show; it's engaging in the game fully and watching the show. When we do that, when we lose ourselves in the meaning we create with others by playing with them, we create whole new worlds of understanding and shared experiences. *Adventure Time* reminds us that play, the act of losing ourselves repeatedly and sharing meaning, is essential to life. That's because when we watch and enjoy *Adventure Time*, we are reminded that play runs through the center of life itself—buoyant, ongoing, and vibrant, it is a golden thread in the loom, and it unites us all.

14

If a Tree Fort Falls in a Forest . . .

ROBERT ARP

You remember this . . .
Season One . . . "Evicted!"

> *Finn and Jake finally win back their treehouse. When they return to it,*
> *they find themselves confronted by King Worm. He demands that the*
> *boys hug him. The gigantic worm hypnotizes them with his gaze. The*
> *boys, mesmerized, approach the king, their arms open for hugs. King*
> *Worm turns his gaze towards us . . . There the episode ends.*

Three seasons Later . . . "King Worm"

> *Finn wakes up to the realization he is the King of Ooo, married to*
> *Princess Bubblegum. He's there, on the candy throne, when his crown*
> *floats to the ceiling . . . there's a **shift** and he finds himself sitting in*
> *the forest with Flame Princess. She changes into Peppermint Butler,*
> *telling Finn he is trapped in a dream. Things **shift** again. Finn and Jake*
> *come to realize that they are in a linked dream, and Finn slashes a*
> *hole in the wall with a sword that becomes a shark. The boys escape*
> *and find themselves in a field with the Ice King. Finn tries to talk with*
> *the mad wizard, but two monsters made of penguins suddenly attack*
> *him. Eventually, as things get weirder and weirder, Finn learns that he*
> *must dream of those things that terrify him the most. By becoming ter-*
> *rified Finn destabilizes the dream, the world **shatters** and Finn con-*
> *fronts the monster that has trapped him . . . King Worm.*

Ever since "King Worm," how can we know what's real in the
Land of Ooo? We know that Finn and Jake escaped from King

Worm but for three seasons we didn't even realize that what had begun with a hypnotism-forced hug in the first season would end with this series of dreams within dreams well into the fourth.

I have to believe that Finn and Jake are right, this time. They have escaped, and they are once again dealing in reality (well as much reality as the Land of Ooo allows for). Because, otherwise, that may mean something pretty horrible for the rest of us. All the things we see, all the things we believe are real, couldn't they be dreams, or hallucinations, or maybe even the mechanizations of an evil and crazy worm-king? Definitely *not!* Right? Well *probably* not . . . okay, well, I hope not . . . *Cabbage.*

Adventure Begins with a Little Trip

You ever check out the website parody of Wikipedia called Uncyclopedia: The Content-Free Encyclopedia? While doing some research for this chapter, I stumbled on Uncyclopedia's entry for *Adventure Time*, where someone wrote: "Pendleton Ward claims to have conceptualized *Adventure Time* when he was tripping very badly." I laughed because the first time my eight-year-old daughter said, "Hey Dad, check this out. It's called *Adventure Time*," I thought the exact same thing after watching the first-season episode, "What Is Life?"

It seems like there's several cartoon shows out there that could easily be entertaining for kids *and* trippers alike, such as *Felix the Cat, Ren and Stimpy, Animaniacs*, and *Teletubbies*, of course. Even many of the lines on *Adventure Time* would seem to make sense only while stoned, as when Finn says in the Season Three episode "Marceline's Closet" that he'll "fly the paper, as an airplane, down the bedroom ladder. It'll triple barrel-roll past the kitchen, open the fridge, and cook some eggs; then eat the eggs and unfold itself as it lays on the carpet in front of Marceline's door." Dude, that's a plan.

Adventure Time reminds me of tripping, which in turn reminds me of the fact that, while tripping, someone has a very active imagination, hallucinates, and can see things that aren't really there. Although I've never tripped, been stoned, wasted, or used any illicit drugs ever (I swear!), I had a bizarre reaction to a painkiller when I was in the hospital once, and I thought someone had stacked pebbles on the bedside stand next to me that I had to eat. From my hallucinogenic perspective, the pebbles were *there*, waiting to be eaten. I called the nurse in to ask her if she saw the pebbles, too, and after laughing a bit, she told me I was "seeing things" that were not there, probably from the painkiller. It was actually Jello on my bedside stand.

Adventure Time and my hallucinogenic hospital experience get me to thinking about the difference between what I perceive to be the case and what really is the case concerning myself, the world around me, and reality in general. But what makes up a person's "reality?" Is reality just my own collection of perceptions and ideas only, or is there a world outside of me? Also, if there is my world of perceptions and a world outside of me, then how, if at all, can I get beyond these perceptions to know if they match up with reality? Further, assuming that there's a reality beyond my perceptions, I want to be sure of my knowledge of that reality. I want to know that my perception of a pebble is in fact a pebble, or that my experience of Jello really is Jello.

When you take a look at the *Adventure Time* stories, you can find a theme that emerges time and time again, namely, the idea that what I *perceive to be* the case is not always what *really is* the case. In "Rainy Day Daydream" where Jake and Finn discover the power of Jake's imagination, Finn highlights the perception-reality distinction by claiming, "Imagination's for turbo-nerds who can't handle how kick-butt reality is." And in "Memory of a Memory" Finn and Jake enter Marceline's mind to awaken her from a sleep spell she had cast on herself, without knowing that they're being tricked by someone from her past.

While being deceived, Finn and Jake think that the perceived deception *is* reality. And it may be the case that all of the adventures in the last half of Season One, all of Seasons Two and Three, and half of Season Four are just a dream. Why? Because at the end of the first-season episode "Evicted!" Finn and Jake were hypnotized by King Worm, and some eighty or so adventures later in the fourth-season episode "King Worm," Finn and Jake finally break out of the hypnotism that King Worm had put them under—Finn and Jake thought that they're experiencing reality for *years*, but they weren't!

I'm Going to Blow Your Minds

It seems obvious that other people, dogs, backpacks, swords, mountains, cartoon shows, TV stations, even mathematical relations like the Pythagorean Theorem, exist "out there" beyond our perceptions of them. Most of us take it for granted that there is a world of things existing outside of our minds, regardless of whether we're perceiving them or not. Also, we think that they would continue to exist whether or not they were perceived by us, or if we ceased to exist.

However, take a moment to think about what you're aware of when you perceive other people, dogs, backpacks, and the like. For example, right now I'm sitting at my computer typing this chapter on a deck overlooking a beach at Lake Michigan. I see the computer screen in front of me, I smell the lake water, I hear the waves crashing on the shore, I feel the tips of my fingers strike the keys of the keypad, and the deck under my feet. And I can close my eyes and form an image or idea of the screen, keypad, deck, lake, and waves. Notice that we can talk about three different kinds of things in this example:

1. **The Perceiver**: there is me, the *perceiver* who has the perceptions and ideas.

2. **The Perception**: there are *my perceptions* of the screen, keypad, deck, lake, and waves that take the forms of the sensations of sight, sound, and feeling, as well as images and ideas.

3. **The Perceived**: there are the *external objects of my perception*, the actual computer and keypad sitting on the table, the lake itself, the hard-wood deck.

In the history of Western philosophy, this three-part distinction can be traced back at least to Plato (427–347 B.C.E.) in his famous work *Republic*, Book VII, where he talks about the "allegory of the cave." In this allegory, Socrates asks his listeners to imagine someone (the perceiver, let's call him "Billy") chained in a cave facing a wall. At first, the only things Billy sees are shadows on a wall in front of him (the perceptions). The shadows are produced as people and other objects move around behind Billy in the firelight (the external objects of perception). But then, imagine that Billy breaks free, turns around to see things in the firelight, and eventually makes his way out of the cave to see things clearly as they really are in the sunlight. Plato points out that Billy's mind would be blown! Imagine what it would be like to realize that the world was much more than just shadows on the wall! The allegory of the cave is supposed to represent the movement from the darkness of ignorance to light of knowledge, but it also can be viewed as a movement from perception to reality.

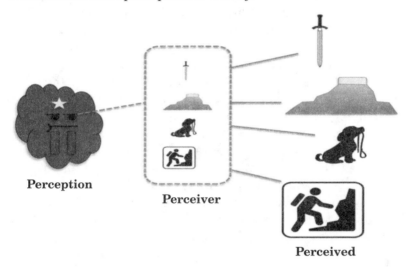

Figure 1: *Lumpy Space Princess the Perceiver, Her Perceptions, and Her Perceived World.*

Consider Figure 1. There is Lumpy Space Princess, who is the perceiver. There are her perceptions, which include her sensations, thoughts, and ideas about people, dogs, swords, backpacks, mountains, and other things. Finally, there are the external objects of her perceptions, which include *actual* people, dogs, swords, backpacks, mountains, and other things out there in the world which her perceptions are supposed to represent.

I Think This House Is a Reflection of Your Sick Brain

But now, there's a problem, given that there's me, my perceptions, and the external objects of my perception. Can I really get beyond my own perceptions? Remember, I think I'm sitting at my desk near Lake Michigan. Am I perceiving the screen, keypad, deck, lake, and waves *themselves* as they really are? Maybe all that I can perceive are my own perceptions?

How can I be sure that the external objects of my perception are really there, or that how they present themselves to me in my perceptions match up with or correspond with how they really are? After all, I can't step outside of my own perceptions and look at myself in relationship to external objects to see if, in fact, my perceptions correspond with these external objects. Am I "locked inside" my own head? Am I locked in a world of my own world of sense perceptions? If so, how do I know that there is even any world out there beyond my perceptions?

This is at least part of how Marceline felt after she awoke from her sleep spell and how Finn and Jake felt after they discovered they were being tricked in Marceline's dream. I know it sounds crazy . . . But think about it like this: What if I'm crazy? Remember my hallucination while in the hospital? I know that I can be mistaken about reality. The world sure *seems* real, but isn't that exactly how someone having a seriously butt-kicking hallucination would feel?

These questions and problems have caused some thinkers to hold philosophical positions known as *epistemological idealism* and *metaphysical antirealism*. Epistemology is the area of philosophy concerned with the sources and justification of knowledge. An epistemological idealist thinks that our perceptions or ideas (*idea*lism) are the only source of knowledge. (I'm talking about *philosophical* idealism, which has nothing to do with the common understanding of idealism meaning being really dedicated to a noble cause!)

Philosophical idealism means that I can never tell if my perceptions really match up with the external objects of my perception. It's as if the perceiver is forever barred from access to the objects of perception. Many characters on *Adventure Time* probably feel this every time one thing morphs into something else, or when a thing *shifts* to reveal what it really is. Metaphysics is the area of philosophy concerned with the nature and principles of what really exists, and a metaphysical antirealist (or the really hardcore metaphysical realist) thinks that there is no real world outside of her perceptions or ideas.

Idealism and antirealism fit together nicely. "After all," reasons the idealist, "all I can ever know are my own perceptions of things as they appear to me." In other words, my own perceptions make up *all of what I can know*. And "after all," reasons the antirealist, "if all I can ever know are my own perceptions of things as they appear to me, and I cannot get outside of myself to see if my perceptions match up with any reality, then my perceptions must be the sum total of my reality." In other words, my own perceptions make up or constitute *all of reality*.

If I were thrust into the Land of Ooo, after a certain amount of time I would start to think like an antirealist! After all, how many times can one person experience reality shifts, shape morphing, and all around mind-rocking surprises before beginning to doubt what is "really" out there?

Epistemological idealism and metaphysical antirealism can be contrasted with *epistemological realism* and *metaphysical realism*. According to an epistemological realist, even though a person has perceptions there must be a world outside that our perceptions represent because, otherwise, we would not have certain perceptions in the first place. Despite the fact that the mind can be very creative in making up all kinds of ideas in imagination—like Jake and Finn do in "Rainy Day Daydream"—there seem to be certain perceptions and ideas that could not have been generated by the perceiver. In other words, there must be some things "out there" that directly cause the representation of our perceptions "in here."

For example, we can see how someone like Pendleton Ward can imagine all kinds of talking animals, sentient video game consoles, grouchy cloud princesses, folklore, and mythological amalgamations of beasts like Lady Rainicorn. People have been doing this for as long as they have been able to tell stories. But, how can the mind generate the idea of a fossilized fern, a Dodo bird, or the Pythagorean Theorem solely from its repertoire of perceptions and ideas? These things seem to have been *discoveries*, not invented constructions of the mind. Remember "Mathematical!" the promotional video (and possible les fest between Princess Bubblegum and Marceline) that featured mathematical objects? It's hard to see that these mathematical objects—although understood, articulated, and explained by minds—were invented *solely* by minds. Rhombus!

This is where epistemological realism and metaphysical realism fit together nicely. If you believe that there is a world of things "out there" that really do exist and would continue to exist whether or not you or anyone perceive them, then you are a metaphysical realist. Consider that according to the theory of evolution, there was a time when human beings, complete with perceptions, didn't exist.

Are we to think, asks the realist, that prior to the evolution of the human mind, there was nothing occurring out there in the world? What are we to make of the fossilized fern? Was there no evolution taking place prior to our perceiving or thinking about the fern or any other fossil? This seems absurd, according to the realist. Didn't the fern exist and fossilize at some point prior to the existence of human minds and their perceptions? And wouldn't the fern still have existed and still have fossilized, even if humans with minds to perceive things never existed? Dodo birds have not outlived our species, but other species likely will, so are we to believe that these other species will cease to exist when we do?

Also, consider this *Adventure Time* twist on an old proverbial question: "If Finn and Jake's Tree Fort falls over in a forest, and no one is around to hear the Tree Fort fall, does it make a sound?" Sound requires a thing *to make* a noise as well as a thing *to hear* the noise. According to a realist, the Tree Fort's crashing to the ground of the forest would produce sound waves whether there was anyone or any thing around to perceive or pick up the sound waves. So technically, the Tree Fort hitting the ground would not make a sound if no one or no thing with the capacity to hear were present. But the slam on the ground still would make air molecules move. That motion could be picked up by a person or thing with a capacity for hearing sounds. The antirealist would have us believe that there would not even be sound waves that are produced from the crashing of the Tree Fort if there were no perceivers in existence.

Realists believe that Pythagoras *discovered* and *formulated* the theorem that $a^2 + b^2 = c^2$ for a right triangle, rather than *wholly invented* it. They also believe that the Theorem would be what it is and exist as what it is regardless of whether it was ever known by any mind. In fact the realist believes that right now, out there in reality, there are all kinds of things waiting to be discovered by the human mind and its perceptions. Despite the fact that the mind can be quite creative in its imaginations, and despite the fact that there can be many different ways of perceiving, there is still some reality out there beyond the mind and its perceptions. To think that "reality" is constituted by the mind and its perceptions, as the antirealist does, seems false, according to the realist.

This NDE is Giving Us Euphoric Altered Awareness!

Most people are epistemological and metaphysical realists—and that includes Jake, Finn, the other characters in *Adventure Time*, and Pendleton Ward himself. Despite the fact that Ward's mind is full of all kinds of perceptions that could be categorized as having been imagined by him, he seems to take it for granted that his perceptions do, at times, accurately represent external objects. The same goes for the characters in *Adventure Time* he and other writers have created throughout the seasons. *That* the stories in *Adventure Time* often feature illusions, hallucinations, and dream sequences indicates that the characters in the show, as well as the writers of the show, advocate straightforward epistemological and metaphysical realism.

While on their adventures in the Land of Ooo, Finn and Jake have moments when they can be mistaken about whether their perceptions represent external objects in the Land of Ooo accurately, but they believe that their perceptions still can accurately represent external objects (insofar as there really are denizens and objects of Ooo). In fact, because Finn and Jake are aware of, and concerned with, the confusion, gross alterations, and crazy logic they perceive in themselves, others, and the world of Ooo, this shows that they think there is an accurate representation to be found in external objects. The confusion, gross alterations, and crazy logic arise from a discrepancy in the relationship between their perceptions and the external objects of their perception existing in Ooo.

Now, we have to be careful here. I am arguing that Jake and Finn *think* or *believe* that there's a real world out there to be discovered, and they think that it can be accurately represented in their perceptions. Whether there is, in fact, an actual world out there is an open question. Obviously, Ooo is not real! But it seems that Jake and Finn, like most of us, take their world for granted and just assume that there is a real world beyond their perceptions. Jake and Finn combine their epistemological realism with their metaphysical realism. They thinks that it's possible for perceptions to represent external objects of perception accurately, and this is so because they believe that there is, in fact, a real world of external objects that exists whether perceived or not. When Jake and Finn are deceived by a person or thing itself as something other than what it is, they believe there is some real person or thing, out there, doing the deceiving.

No One . . . Leaves the Nightosphere!

One unfortunate consequence of holding to idealism and anti-realism is what's known as solipsism. If all you're aware of is your own perceptions, and you are forever barred from knowing whether your perceptions match up with any external objects of your perception, then you can't prove that you're not alone in reality. It is as if you're "locked inside" your own world of perceptions, never knowing whether there is even any world out there beyond the perceptions. Think of what it would be like to be trapped inside Finn's four-dimensional bubbles which are "Beyond Comprehension! Beyond Space! Beyond Time!" ("The Real You").

In the history of Western philosophy the British empiricist, David Hume (1711–1776), figures prominently in suggesting the idea that the mind may be nothing other than a collection of perceptions, and that one may be considered a theater goer, viewing the "perceptions successively making their appearance." Also, in his *Three Dialogues Between Hylas and Philonous*, George Berkeley (1685–1753) seriously entertains the idea that we may be trapped inside of our perceptual reality, with no access to the external world.

Think of Lumpy Space Princess as being locked inside the room of her own mind, kind of like someone trapped inside of a movie theater. Now imagine that there's a movie screen inside of the theater, representing her or anyone's perceptions, that is connected to a movie camera on the outside of the theater that views the outside world. The camera represents a person's five senses.

A perceiver, like Lumpy, only has access to her own perceptions on the movie screen of one's mind. She could never get outside of the room of her own mind to see if her perceptions match up with some external world, let alone whether such a

Figure 2: *Lumpy Space Princess in Her Own Mind.*

world even exists! So, for example, when Finn tells Jake, "I'm hanging the piñatas . . . They are all around you! Smash the piñatas!" in the first-season episode "Slumber Party Panic," there is no way for Jake to know *for sure* whether there are *in fact* piñatas around him to be smashed!

Now, it could be argued that since life can be perceived to be solitary at times, but not at others, indicates that all of life cannot be a series of perceptions with no reality. How could we even know what a perception is if it were not for some reality with which it could be contrasted? Just as one could not even understand what things such as pain, selfishness, or love would be like without understanding their corresponding opposites of pleasure, altruism, or hate, so too, how could one even begin to understand what a perception is if it were not contrasted with reality?

Though I suppose someone could argue that we are just comparing perceptions to each other, after all how do you describe the difference between what you perceive is real, and what is *really* real? Life would just be like a series of dreams, each time I wake up, I wake up into the next dream. And each time, I wouldn't realize I'm in a dream until I woke up into the next one . . . the dream that I am sure, *this time*, is real. I shudder at that thought! I imagine that's what it must be like for Finn and Jake to escape from King Worm's hypnotism. After that, can they ever be sure . . .? Cabbage!

Oh Man, I Imagined My Mom Naked!

A big part of why *Adventure Time* fascinates us has to do with the perception-reality distinction. Our perceptions have enabled us to imagine all kinds of fascinating things and circumstances, and we all love to fantasize, at times. We've all had dreams where we wish we could never wake up. But, we've all had nightmares, too.

When all's said and done, I'm glad that imagination, fantasies, and dreams are contrasted with reality because I agree with Jake that "You gotta focus on what's real, man." Plus, I prefer reality. At least there are fairly reliable constants in reality, and I never have to worry about demon-vampires or friggin' talking dogs, squirrels, and bananas!

Now go sit in the corner and think about your life . . .

15
What's Time Anyhoo?

MARY GREEN AND RONALD S. GREEN

What then is time? If no one asks me, I know: if I wish to explain it to someone who asks, I don't know.

—SAINT AUGUSTINE

After narrowly escaping the destruction of the Land of Ooo at the hands of the Lich, Jake returns to the Time Room to visit his buddies Prismo and the Cosmic Owl. Jake, being the hungry hero that he is, just wanted to enjoy a sandwich and have a nice soak in the hot tub. Little did he know, he was about to get an earful of the true nature of time.

JAKE: Three, two, one, go. We're three nice dudes, havin' fun! We got warm bubble water on our buns! I love this spa, and that's a fact! But if I stay too long, I get a pruny back! [*Joins Prismo and Cosmic Owl in beat boxing.*] *Poooh, haka pah a poooh, haka haka pah, a poooh.*[1]

PRISMO: Have another pickle, Jake. I'm glad you called me to bring you back and hang out.

JAKE: Yeah man, you're still, like, a strong number three on my Cool Guys List. Hey Prismo, man, does your big TV get any more channels besides the monkey paw network?

PRISMO: You call it. Right now, we're sitting in the only room outside of time and space, so even the sky's not the limit.

---

[1] Quoting Jake from "Finn the Human."

Just one more perk of being almighty.

JAKE: Okay. Let's start by having another look at alternate-wish-world-Finn with the nose and all.

PRISMO: I still have that one on the previous channel button. Here it is.

JAKE: Whoa. You know, it's funny, man. Finn once told me he saw the same junked-up stuff in a dream mirror: he had the same one arm, the same mad uglies and everything. But, how could he have seen it way back then, Bro? I mean, he didn't even make that wish till a lot later.

PRISMO: There's no *then* or *now* in the Time Room or anywhere else without the waves sent out from here. The Time Room is at the center of the Multiverse. It's the only place that's outside of time.

JAKE: That's a little freaky. What is this Time Room? No, wait! There's no time anywhere else without the waves sent from this room? I thought time was like a thing . . . you know, like a sandwich, something you have and, like, as you use it up, it kinda disappears.

PRISMO: Well, there are a lot of ways of thinking about time. We'll just call that one "Jake's sandwich theory" of time. But there are other ways of understanding time.

JAKE: Okayyyy, . . . so then, what's time, anyhoo?

PRISMO: Well, it's really hard to understand, even though people have tried. You have your "sandwich theory," but some people have come up with the A-theory of time and others have the B-theory of time.

JAKE: Huh?

PRISMO: Well, look at Finn on the screen. The A-theorists say there is the past, the present, and the future. You saw mad ugly mirror-Finn in the past, you see alternate-wish-world-Finn on the TV in the present, and you will see a jar of pickles from me in the future.

JAKE: I love me some pickles. *Mmmm.*

PRISMO: A-theory is how we ordinarily think of time. It says the past and future are not as real for us as the present and that the past is fixed though the future can change. It's an internal view of time, from your perspective. You've already experienced mirror-Finn, so you think of that as the past. You're watching Finn on TV right now, so it seems like the present. And you're thinking about getting pickles soon, in the future.[2]

JAKE: I *am* thinking about the pickles.

PRISMO: The B-theory of time doesn't mention past or future, or even present. It's different. To the B-theorists the fact that you can remember the past but can't remember the future is just the fault of having a not-so-perfect brain.

JAKE: Wait, Bro . . . You mean I should be able to remember eating this pickle *before* I eat it!?

PRISMO: Well to the B-theorist, you are wrong when you think of the future as less real. It is just as real, and the fact that you can't remember it just is, well, like a brain hiccup . . .The B-theory doesn't explain time in the ordinary way but almost as it would be seen from a Glob-eye perspective: all at once. I can see Finn on TV, mirror-Finn earlier, and you eating pickles later. Kind of like if I show you a bunch of screens on the TV at the same moment, each one showing Finn at a different moment. So if you believe A-theory, you believe that future hasn't happened yet, but if B-theory is right then because of the way you perceive time, it's basically just your brain's fault that you can't remember the future. So the A-theory and the B-theory are very different.

JAKE: Far out. Which theory's right?

PRISMO: Oh, it's not that simple. A-theorists don't all agree with each other, and neither do all B-theorists. For example, from the A-theory came Presentism and the growing block universe.

---

[2] This refers to the tense logic of Arthur N. Prior, expounded in *Past, Present, and Future.*

JAKE: Huuhh?

PRISMO: Two different ideas about linear time. Presentists say only the present exists.[3] The growing block universe says the past is real, and more of the world is coming into existence in the present, growing like new blocks. But they say the future isn't real.[4]

JAKE: Oh, man. Me an' Finn have seen the future a lotta times and usually you're there, too, Cosmic Owl.

COSMIC OWL: Whoo.

JAKE: Didn't *anyone* think they're all real—past, present, and future?

PRISMO: You *know* they did! Remember how I said there are a couple of different kinds of B-theory? One of them, eternalism, says events in the future are already there, and there's no flow of time.

JAKE: That's just like my croak dream, man, when I went up in a rocket with Banana Man. No one can change your croak dream, not even Finn. You just gotta embrace it. You can't stop deatheny.[5]

PRISMO: Well, maybe *you* can't. If you think so, you might like the time theory called four-dimensionalism. It's also a variation on B-theory.

JAKE: Whoa, whoa. Last time I heard "four-dimensional," I was on the being-sucked-in end of a black hole Finn blew with a bubble blower.

PRISMO: Don't worry, this isn't about Finn's kind of 4D stuff where space is a fourth dimension like the other three. In this, the fourth dimension is time. It says that things have three parts, one in the past, one in the present, and one in the future. All three are equally real. They look at it like this: the Jake we see now is not the whole Jake, and neither is the Jake that was in the Time Room chasing the Lich. The Jake chasing the Lich was like the left-headed

---

[3] Dean Zimmerman, "Presentism and the Space-Time Manifold."
[4] Michael Tooley, *Time, Tense, and Causation*.
[5] A quote from "The New Frontier."

side of the Ancient Psychic Tandem War Elephant.

JAKE: Ancient Psychic Tandem War Elephant! Let's make a wish!

PRISMO: Remember, wishes always have those ironic unexpected consequences . . . Anyway, if the Jake chasing the Lich was like the left-headed side of the Ancient Psychic Tandem War Elephant, the Jake here now is like its right-headed side. It's both the Ancient Psychic Tandem War Elephant, but as many pieces stretched across the fourth dimension of time.

JAKE: Right on! Sitting in the Time Room like this, that does seem kinda right. It's like a bunch of times are happenin' and different versions of the same time are all going on at once. Your pad is pretty neat man. But, what's up with the Time Room?

PRISMO: Booko explained it about as well as the Multiverse can be explained.

JAKE: Huh? What'd Booko say about the Multiverse?

PRISMO: Watch this while I cook. [*Pushes a button on the remote and Booko appears on the TV screen.*]

What Booko Said about the Multiverse

Our present time is only one time among others. We call it alone present not because it differs in kind from all the rest, but because it is the one we inhabit.

—DAVID LEWIS, *Counterfactuals*, p. 86

BOOKO: Ahem. At the center of the multiverse is a dimension called the Time Room, believed to be the quasi-corporeal dwelling place of the almighty Prismo. The Time Room is the single dimension that exists outside of time. The Time Room produces time waves that are experienced by other dimensions. Some dimensions have permanent links that allow travel to and fro. Others become linked temporarily by naturally-forming Worm Holes. And others can become linked artificially by magical portals, torn open by items of great power. Once the last gem is inserted into the *Enchiridion* it will have the power to create a portal to any dimension in the multiverse. An activated portal creates a time dilation in which either end of the portal experiences a temporal synchronization allowing for the safe passage of particles [*Deep, elaborate breath*] through a non-local region of space-time."[6]

JAKE: I don't know what the Björk he's talkin' about.

PRISMO: This should help. [*Hands Jake some food.*]

JAKE: Bacon pancakes help everything! I love you, Prismo.

PRISMO: Oh yee!! [*Laughs and blushes.*] Well, it doesn't really matter exactly what Booko said. Basically, all that other stuff means is this: there are a lot of ideas about the Multiverse. Just to look at a few, we can start with the Many-Worlds Interpretation. It basically says that each event that *can* happen *does* happen on different worlds. Each event is a branch point that splits into countless different outcomes. The Lich taking Billy's body was a point that became different branches like different worlds. In one, branch Billy died; in another branch he didn't.

JAKE: So, when you put those bacon pancakes in front of me, in another world, I *didn't* eat them?

PRISMO: I know it's hard to believe. Usually we think that all possibilities disappear when one action happens. Like, you ate the pancakes, so the possibility of *not* eating them is gone. But this theory says that anything that *could* have happened *did* happen and that all possible histories and futures are real. Scientists even gave mathematical proofs that this is true.[7]

JAKE: Whoa, algebraic . . . and delicious at the same time.

ICE KING: [*Appearing suddenly on the TV screen.*] So if everything possible exists, that means that me and all my princesses are together and I'll never be lonely again! Everything happening in my imagination zone is really,

---

[6] Booko in "The Lich."
[7] Everett, "The Theory of the Universal Wavefunction."

really, real somewhere in the Multiverse . . . Me and
Neptr basking in the sunset as father and son, even if I
can't remember him . . . Me and my princesses doing
nothing but smooching and eating a whole bunch until
we get fat and die. I told you, Gunter!

GUNTER: Whac.

JAKE: Heeey! What the floe? How come Ice King can see us
through the set?

ICE KING: [*To himself, on screen.*] Stanky old wizard eyes. Is
this real?

JAKE: Dude, Cosmic Owl, is the Ice King right and somewhere he's with Princess Bubblegum, and all?

COSMIC OWL: Nah, he's just a sociopath.

ICE KING: Ad hominem, ad hominem!

PRISMO: [*Mutes the Ice King*] Even though some people
believe that all possibilities are real in the Multiverse,
that's just not the way it works. Here, let me remind you
on screen. [*Pushes a button on the remote to replace Ice
King on the TV screen with a previous image of himself in
the hot tub.*]

PRISMO: [*Speaking from the TV screen.*] You see, Jake, there
are rules to this stuff. If Ice King marries Princess
Bubblegum, think of all the stuff that will be different
after that, and all the stuff that would need to be different
to lead to that marriage. So. Memories will be destroyed,
babies will not be born. Potential worlds could be evapo-
rated by-your-wish![8] [*Jake looks a little distressed*]

PRISMO: [*not on the screen, but in the hot tub.*] You're not
going to be sick again are you?

COSMIC OWL: Whoo?

JAKE: [*Takes a moment to gather himself and his thoughts
and then looks relieved.*] Blubbpf . . . Naw Bro, I'm okay
now, I just needed to digest some stuff! Hey! These bub-

---

[8] "Jake the Dog."

bles are as fragile as my old perception of reality!

PRISMO: Those can't be hot tub bubbles. The jets aren't even on . . .

PRISMO AND COSMIC OWL: Ewww! Uugh!

JAKE: Hee, hee, hee.

PRISMO: [*Wishing he could actually forget some things tries to leave the "bubble incident" behind them, tragically, as a supreme being, he* cannot.] . . . Others have the notion that in lots of situations things could have turned out differently. They call these different outcomes "possible worlds," and say that those worlds are just like ours, but with different things happening. They say these actually exist, but what we call "actual" depends on what world we're in. So, if someone asked them how many worlds there are and what is going on in those worlds, they can't say because their answers would be from their imaginations rather than from those worlds.

JAKE: Okay, okay, I see. Different timelines but maybe not everything. But what's going on *here*, man, in the Time Room?

COSMIC OWL: Alright, I shouldn't be telling a singular this, but yeah, all the timelines are connected here and the past, present, and future of all the timelines are connected. Shoko's missing arm, Farmworld Finn's missing arm, both replaced by mechanical arms, both being abandoned by their parents, just like Marceline was, all raised by others.

JAKE: That's crazy biz, man. I still don't know what the Time Room is, Glob dog it.

COSMIC OWL: Outside of time and space, beyond three-dimensional understanding.

JAKE: Dude, you sound like Finn that time he put on Glasses of Nerdicon, . . . uh, I think. What *did* Finn say that time he put on the Glasses of Nerdicon?

PRISMO: Let me tune that in. [*Pushes a button on the*

remote.]

What Finn Said That Time He Put on the Glasses of Nerdicon

I do see a possibility of showing that the timeless reality would be, I do not say unmixedly good, but very good, better than anything which we can now experience or even imagine. I do see the possibility of showing that all that hides this goodness from us—insofar as it is hidden—is the illusion of time.

—JOHN McTAGGART, *The Relation of Time and Eternity*

But if time, as immediate consciousness perceives it, were, like space, a homogeneous medium, science would be able to deal with it, as it can with space . . . all the relations which cannot be translated into simultaneity, i.e. into space, are scientifically unknowable.

—HENRI BERGSON, *Time and Free Will*

FINN: Ladies and Gentlemen . . . and *Princess* . . . [*Winks at Princess Bubblegum, who waves back*] I'm here to talk about multi-dimensional bubbles! But I'm not *just* going to talk about blowing bubbles! I'm going to blow . . . your . . . minds!

PRINCESS BUBBLEGUM: Hmm?

FINN: [*Revealing bubble creator*] This is a bubble-blower of my own design. With this, you can blow bubbles in different dimensions. [*He sets the device to two dimensions and blows a bubble with no depth.*] This two-dimensional bubble casts a one-dimensional shadow. [*He sets the device to three dimensions and blows a normal, everyday bubble.*] A *three*-dimensional bubble casts a *two*-dimensional shadow. [*He sets the device to four dimensions and blows a three-dimensional shadow that appears to be a projection of a four-dimensional tesseract.*] A fourth-dimensional bubble casts a three-dimensional shadow . . . IT IS BEYOND COMPREHENSION! [*The audience is amazed.*] Beyond space!! Beyond time!!

PRINCESS BUBBLEGUM: Finn, . . . that would mean you've created . . .

FINN: Yes, . . . A BLACK HOLE!!![9] [*Prismo pushes the pause button on crazy, open-mouthed Finn laughing on screen.*]

JAKE: Awww! I think I'm getting wacked out poo brain.

PRISMO: Here, eat this egg—it's brain food.

JAKE: Ah, yeah!

PRISMO: Some philosophers have said that you can't understand time using space analogies or by thinking about it analytically at all, like all those A-theorists and B-theorists we just talked about. Instead, you have to just experience it. That means, time doesn't really exist in any way you can think of rationally. Just like Finn says in the rant.

JAKE: Right on, man. I *told* Finn not to use that science junk. Instead, he used it to say we can't understand things.

PRISMO: So here it is, the Time Room. Because of Einstein's Theory of Relativity, some scientists came up with the idea that time moves differently for people traveling at different speeds. They proved it by sending an atomic clock in a rocket around the Earth and then comparing it to a synchronized clock that had stayed on Earth. The clocks showed different times when the rocket came back. They also found that the speed of time was affected by gravity. The more gravity, the slower it goes. And you know what has the most gravity, don't you?

JAKE: An everything burrito?

PRISMO: A black hole.

JAKE: Huh. [*Speaking to Finn on the TV screen.*] I believe in you, buddy.

PRISMO: If you enter a black hole, time goes slower and slower until you get to the middle, where it stops completely.

JAKE: But you can't enter a black hole. I was almost the first one who died trying not to.

---

[9] Quoted from "The Real You."

PRISMO: Maybe. But maybe we're in a black hole right now.

JAKE: Huh?

PRISMO: According to a fancy-named idea called "black-hole cosmology," the universe is all the inside of a black hole, which is one of many black holes making the Multiverse. And do you know what's in the middle of our Multiverse?

JAKE: The Time Room!

COSMIC OWL: The only place beyond time.

PRISMO: The Theory of Relativity says that even though it seems to us that the shortest distance between two points is a straight line, space is actually curved. We only *think* it is straight because we see things in three dimensions. That is to say . . . [*Pushes the rewind button than the play button on the remote.*]

FINN: [*On the TV screen.*] IT IS BEYOND COMPREHENSION!

PRISMO: [*Pushes the pause button again.*] Did I mention time behaves differently in different places because of gravity?

JAKE: I don't know.

PRISMO: According to this theory, space isn't really 3D; it's 4D. By adding a fourth dimension that's the same as the other three, scientists showed mathematically how curved space is. One of them said that the fourth dimension is time.[10] Later, others said the fourth dimension is one of space like the other three, and time was a way to measure change in matter.[11] Either way, although things are four dimensional, we see them as three dimensional, because . . . [*Pushes the rewind button than the play button on the remote.*]

---

[10] This was Hermann Minkowski (1864–1909), Einstein's teacher.

[11] The article by Sorli, Klinar, and Fiscaletti, listed in the References.

FINN: [*On the TV screen.*] A fourth-dimensional bubble casts a three-dimensional shadow . . . IT IS BEYOND COM-PREHENSION!

PRISMO: I should also tell you that different places in the Multiverse are not as far apart as we might think they are. That's because space is not straight and long; it's curved and according to this theory, places in space that seem far away can be connected with worm holes, momentarily synchronizing time between those universes. So, it doesn't take that much time to travel a great distance. That's an illusion.

JAKE: My belly's fully. [*Yawning.*]

PRISMO: You see, my cube here at the center of the Multiverse acts in the same way as a worm hole. It's shaped like a Menger Sponge that connects the different dimensions through the different openings in the cube. It also repeats patterns over and over again. . . . [*Pushes the rewind button then the play button on the remote.*]

FINN: [*On the TV screen.*] Everything *small* is just a small version of something *big*!! I understand *everything*!!

PRISMO: [*Pushes the pause button again.*] That's how the Lich came into the Time Room from one dimension through that opening, and left to another dimension through that other opening.

JAKE: [*Asleep.*] *Zzzz.*

PRISMO: It's also how you get home again. Sleep tight, Jake.

COSMIC OWL: [As *Jake fades out of the Time Room.*] Woo.

[*Finn, back in Ooo, pulls Jake out of his pocket and rouses him.*]

FINN: You awake yet, little guy?

JAKE: Huh? Where am I?

FINN: You fell asleep in my pocket again.

JAKE: *Burrrrp.*

FINN: Oh man, bacon pancakes.

[*So, there you have it: a sleepy dog, his best friend, and the true nature of time. Wait, you mean you still don't understand how time works? That's okay; nobody does.*]

EDITOR'S NOTE: In an ironic twist of fate, not long after this conversation, Prismo died at the hands of the Lich. We will miss him . . .

[*Hey, guy, wait a minute, the time room is timeless. So it isn't like there is a "time" after my life in the Time Room. All you have to do is remember the past like it is the present, forget the present like it was the future, and reflect on the past like it will be the future. Easy. If you want to come back and hang out some time. Call me. I'll make pickles!* —P]

16
Ooo, Who's Dreaming?

CHRISTOPHER KETCHAM

Finn and the Flame Princess are an item, happily hanging out. Out of nowhere, the Ice King flies by hurling insults. Irate, Flame Princess gets hot and burns the Ice King's britches . . . humiliating him. The princess kicks the defeated wizard back to his castle, leaving a hot flame heart blazing in the sky. Finn blushes. . . . That night Finn dreams about getting flamed by the Flame Princess. It should hurt, but it doesn't. . . . In fact, it's awesome!

Finn tries to dream the hot dream again; he needs to know what it means. So he lies to get another fight going between Flame Princess and the Ice King. But everything ends in shambles—broken hearts, bruised bodies, and the Ice Kingdom is left in cinders. Finn, having learned a great deal about himself, is left alone, without the princess.

There's a lot more to the episode "Frost and Fire" than that, but here's what I think. . . . The convoluted plot of this story represents the intricate nature of our minds. Think about it, we spend a third of our time in sleep and a good part of that time dreaming weird stuff that can't happen when we're awake. Why weird stuff? Good question!

Scientists have discovered that dreaming somehow assists in our learning. "So, is weird also good? And, probably since we first began to think, we've wondered about the "cosmic" significance of our dreams and the future they foretell. So, is Finn's first dream really just a hot dream or is it a revelation of things to come? *Adventure Time* makes us ask the question, "How real can dreams become for us and, more importantly, how they can

impact our lives . . . if we let them!?" I need to explain what this all might mean, but first, let me get some shut-eye. It's so late . . . **Yawn**
Zzzzzzzzz

The Storyboard Place

Okay, this is weird, I'm on the set of Adventure Time. Well I think I am. . . . No, I'm sure I am! But it's where the storyboarding is done, just a simple room . . . no palaces or treehouses. It's a really white room with white whiteboards, white tables, white floor and white ceiling, white chairs and no windows. Am I dreaming?

Five people sit around the white table. All are dressed in white. Only their heads and faces have color. I listen to their chit-chat for a few minutes and pick up on their names. On the left, Suri has long straight charcoal hair and deep brown eyes. Benjamin seems taller and his blonde hair is spikey, not punk; but wild like, and his face is almost orange as if he had once been a redhead. To the right, Evelyn's cheeks are a bit sallow but her lips are ruby and her gray hair is pulled back-severely into a scrunchie. Saul's curly mop is a smallish but mushrooming afro and his cheeks are fat and the color of warm cocoa with darker black freckles. A charcoal colored electronic cigarette dangles from the lips of the angled ever so white face of Tatyana who sits at the end of the table staring over crisp brunette bangs from black rimmed glasses into a pile of erratically arranged white papers. The room is filled with white noise that I can't make sense out of . . .

QUIET ON THE SET. Shhhh. AND ACTION!

The Big Setup

TATYANA: Settle down, now. *She glowers.*
A white paper airplane floats across the table spearing her paper pile. I can't see where it came from; my camera angle is all wrong. I could be watching this like a movie, but I smell coffee. Lots of tall white paper cups with white lids. The producer in the back of the room seems to look down his horn-rimmed glasses at me.

TATYANA: Real Mature, Benjamin. . . . The question for this episode is, 'What is a dream?' *Groans from the group.*

TATYANA: All right, all right. Here's what we were thinking. Finn is awake and something happens to him that makes it into his dreams, maybe something a bit erotic. He wants to dream the dream again so he does something while he is awake to make the dream come back. . . . That's about it so far.

SURI: As always, well thought through by corporate. So, who else besides Finn's in this?

BENJAMIN: Princess Bubblegum . . .

SAUL: She's getting really old. What about a new character. We could call him Freudo!

SURI: In your dreams. *Moans fill the room followed by a rude gesture from Saul.*

TATYANA: Hey, maybe Saul has something. Remember Freud thought all dreams were wish fulfillments. What if Finn has a secret wish he wants fulfilled?

SURI: Why secret?

SAUL: Secret's more fun. Especially when Jake finds out he's been left out of the secret.

TATYANA: Is Jake in this?

AUL: What if Finn just explains the dream to Jake the next morning?

SURI: Boring. There has to be something in the dream that gets Jake worked up so that he messes with Finn. You know how he does that.

TATYANA: But what's this dream about?

SAUL: So, what if it's hard to know whether this is a dream or real? Isn't that what this whole story is about? If we know right away that Finn's dreaming then where's the weird?

BENJAMIN: WHAT IS REALITY?

SAUL: Dum dum dum dum . . . *Pounding Beethoven on an air keyboard.*

Hot Hot Hot

Benjamin is grinning.

BENJAMIN: I smell burning.

SURI: Tatyana's cigarette.

BENJAMIN: No, not that, figuratively . . . burning like in Flame Princess or Flame King.

SAUL: Hot dream! But who's Finn hot for?

BENJAMIN: Hmmm. How about Flame Princess and his hots for her? How else do you get involved with someone who's so hot you can't touch her? But *in a dream* Finn can get close without getting burnt!

SAUL: Sure it's possible. I get burned all the time by hot dates, and I'm not dreaming.

BENJAMIN: Saul, you don't know what hot is . . . So, okay, hot is hot and Flame Princess is Finn's hottie. Why not go back to Freud again? *'Oh, Flame Princess would you, could you be mine?' The canned laughter "wah, wah, wah," comes from somewhere and punctuates Benjamin's plea. It's getting very hot in the room. I loosen my shirt buttons. I hear knocking and realize it isn't a door but Saul pounding a drum riff on the table with his forefingers.*

Arte Speaks

Nobody is speaking, the only sound is Saul drumming. Then Tatyana looks up.

TATYANA: What about Artemidorus?[1]

SAUL: Oh, hell Tat, not another one of your obscure philosophers.

TATYANA: Hear me out. Old obscure Arte was where Michel Foucault got his inspiration for beginning to understand the sexual dream in *Care of the Self.*

SAUL: [*muttering*] And I suppose you're going to tell us how.

---

[1] Old-time Greek philosopher from Ephesus.

TATYANA: [*screws down her face and looks over her glasses at Saul like a schoolmarm*] I believe I will, Saul. But it isn't just about Artemidorus. After writing his first two volumes about the *History of Sexuality*, Foucault realized he had to go back to the ancients to better understand what sexuality meant to people then so that he could compare it to what sexuality has become today.[2] For the historical aspects he turned to Artemidorus.

BENJAMIN: [*in a hillbilly drawl*] Sex was different then?

SAUL: [*continuing the accent*] Sho 'nuff, it was brandy new and excitin' in them days.

SURI: You know, Foucault said today we pervert sexual pleasure, make it bad. Catch my drift? Why don't you just let Tat talk . . . ?" *A raspberry from Benjamin.*

TATYANA: Thank you, Suri. Artemidorus said that the dream tells us two things. First, the dream tells us what's real then it explains the consequences whether they're good or bad. What Artemidorus tried to do was develop a way to analyze dreams to see what practical consequences they would reveal for us when we're awake.

SURI: Fortune telling?

TATYANA: No he was more interested in where you were—your station in life. So it didn't matter the sex of your partner in the dream but if you were a slave-owner underneath a slave in a dream would mean ominous troubles for you; being over the slave, well that could be a good thing or just something neutral. But, and here is where it gets strange. . . . Because of the interpretations of the dreams, the things different people and relationships represent, if you're a man and have sex with your mother it is generally a good thing to Artemidorus!

SAUL: Say what?

TATYANA: I know it's weird. While Artemidorus was against incest he interpreted the mother of the dream into man's trade and naturally a man must be involved with his

---

[2] *The Care of the Self.*

trade, intimately. But on the other hand if you were physically sick and have this dream this does not bode well for
you because this is messing with Mother Earth, where
you are bound to go when you die. It gets complicated.

Sense from Nonsense

*Tatyana takes a puff from her electronic cigarette and stares
down at her papers. Benjamin stands and stretches then
looks at the group and raises his hands palm up.*

BENJAMIN: So, what does this all have to do with Finn and
the Flame Princess?

SURI: I think I'm getting it. See, there is a moral thing going
on at the same time there is a practical thing going on in
the dream. While Finn can be dreaming about having a
relationship with the Flame Princess, the circumstances
surrounding that relationship are more important than
whether the relationship is creepy. So, if Finn is honest
and forthright in his dream about her, well it's a good
dream which bodes well for Finn. If, there is some sub-
terfuge or something, or it's backwards, like if she is a
slave and he is under her . . .

SAUL: Quoth the Raven, 'nevermore'.

TATYANA: Exactly. The dream is how Finn thinks and this
translates into what he will do when he's awake. So, how
do we bring in the morality thing to this dream so that
Finn recognizes its significance?

BENJAMIN: What about Beemo? Beemo's like the ultimate
voice of reality.

SURI: Beemo's a box that does stuff on command. How is
Beemo the voice of moral reality?

Strange Interlude

*Wait, it's me. Sorry, but I have to stop this here. I'm waving at the pro-
ducer in the back of the room, but he isn't looking; he's texting on his
phone. I walk onto the set anyway. I'm trying to shout, "No, it's all
wrong, it's all wrong! It has to be the Cosmic Owl!" My mouth is open*

but nothing comes out. So I'm standing now and walking to a white-board to get their attention, but it's no use. My feet are like blocks of granite and I move as in slow motion and they keep talking and then there are windows in the room and the sun is going down. How long have we been here? The producer is glowering at me now. I slink back off the set.

It's a Hoot

Tatyana takes another puff from her electronic cigarette and exhales with a grunt.

TATYANA: The Cosmic Owl it is. But what does it say?

SURI: Beware . . .

SAUL: Naw. Too obvious. Remember that Freud said that dreams are a product of our subconscious wishes and traumas. Why not have the Owl be Finn's subconscious that bubbles up slowly through his dream and whispers something to him that he doesn't see in his dream?

BENJAMIN: Yeah, like you screwed up.

SAUL: Sure, something like that.

SURI: You know I read somewhere that scientists think there's more to dreams than what Freud and Artemidorus talked about. Some researchers think that dreams help us learn, especially the dreams we have around the time we go to sleep and wake up and this is connected to our deeper sleep dreams too. Dreaming somehow sorts things out that we learn during the day and helps us make stronger memories.[3]

On the other hand, when we get into deep sleep dreaming turns off things like our muscles and other parts of our brain. This is when weird happens because it is like we have two different conscious states, one while we are dreaming and one while we are awake because something in our brain turns off certain chemicals when we sleep and turns them back on when we wake up again. So I guess this is why our dreams when

---

[3] The article by Stickgold and others, listed in the References.

in deep sleep are certifiably strange. And, get this, in these deep sleep dreams our episodic memory function is turned off![4] Maybe that's where Artemidorus and Freud come in—with the really strange stuff that just pops out.

TATYANA: Okay, but how do we work learning and this other stuff into this story?

BENJAMIN: Well, this Flame Princess is the ultimate hottie. So, what if you learned a few things about how to get a hottie to want you and how to embrace such a fiery thing without getting burned. Wouldn't that add an additional dimension to the dream?

SAUL: Like, what would he learn?

BENJAMIN: Well, what do flame Princesses do to keep hot? Do they eat or are they just pyrotechnic?

SURI: I don't know. Maybe it's a dumb idea. But what if we made it, like Benjamin said, that Finn dreams about what it takes for the Flame Princess to always stay hot? What if he learns this from his dream but he never had this experience when he was awake?

TATYANA: "Sort of, he deduced it from what he observed?

SURI: Sure, people get all sorts of inspiration from their dreams and sometimes it's right and sometimes it's wrong and sometimes you have to dig deep to find out the association, like rubbing your face with dirt which really means you have dirty thoughts or you just dug a hole for yourself. Well, or . . . you get the idea.

BENJAMIN: It *has* to feel right in this case because Finn has to believe what the dream says, otherwise he'll think it was all just a kooky fantasy if it doesn't work out when he's awake.

SAUL: This has surely gone beyond me. So how does she stay hot?

---

[4] Hobson, *Dreaming*.

It's a Wrap

Tatyana looks up at the clock and Benjamin swipes his cell phone front and frowns.

TATYANA: It's getting late and so far all we have is a jumble. Good ideas, but still a mish-mash. Can we tie this up into something that the artists can sink their teeth into?

SURI: Well, we've got this so far. First we need to blur the lines of what's real and what's a dream. And we can do that simply by changing scenes. You know how suddenly the dream is here and then it's there? It's like the dream forgot where it was so there it is now and that's just fine because what was isn't there anymore!

BENJAMIN: So, what we could do is have Finn and the Flame Princess together in some common setting like a picnic or in the park and then the next moment they're in some kind of passionate embrace where Finn is covered by flames but this feels so good to him. And then he wakes up. So what was the dream? What if he is so involved in being awake and being in his dream that the two seem the same to him?

SAUL: I like that. Make the really strange stuff bubble up next to what seems to make sense. I am so involved in the dream I don't notice how bizarre it has become. Thus the dream is real in a real sense and then it's real in an unreal sense and who's to say whether our sleeping mind cares? Or does the waking mind care? Ow, my head hurts. I think that is why we've been given the gift to forget most of our dreams.

TATYANA: Yes, but Finn needs to remember this dream and take something from what seems real and the weird stuff like being smothered in fire without getting burned.

SAUL: But how do we keep out interference. So, what if the Earl of Lemongrab or Lumpy Space Princess just come walking on into his dream and send it off in a new direction? Dreams do that you know.

TATYANA: How does it serve this story?

SAUL: "Dunno, but that happens all the time and in our dreams we don't seem to be able to know what's coming next. Like someone is shoving you into random YouTube videos or something."

BENJAMIN: So, we turn on Beemo's EKG function and zap Jake when his rhythm goes random.

SAUL: Be serious. . . . By the way, does Beemo dream?

BENJAMIN: Okay, maybe we push it a little—Finn sets himself up to have this dream and only this dream. He, like, drinks warm milk and puts on soft music and says over and over again, 'There's no place like home . . . there's no place like home . . .'

SURI: Guys, I think we need to back out of that hole and move on. So, does this flaming interlude portend good or ill for Finn? Remember Artemidorus. What has Finn done to enflame the Princess? Or is this just his flaming passion for the Princess? Does even Finn know?

BENJAMIN: Oh, good point, Suri. He knows subconsciously he blew it with her, but his flaming passion is telling him one thing while the situation is saying something else entirely. Twisteroo!

SAUL: I'm getting dizzy. So what did Finn do?

TATYANA: He lied to her, maybe?

SURI: No, what if this hot dream was just that and at first it didn't mean anything specific but he wanted to have the dream again, so then he set up things during the day so that he could learn from his experiences so that he could have the same dream again and finish it. Finish it, because deep down he wants to understand the consequences—like Artemidorus said. Maybe even like Freud to see what he was really wishing for—*to break into his subconscious for answers!*

TATYANA: So, the first dream is a hot one, but it doesn't yet have the context that Artemidorus needed to finish the morality play.

SAUL: But there is a hint of the consequence in the first dream when the Cosmic Owl whispers, 'you screwed up' or something.

SURI: Yes. So Finn dreams this passion with the Flame Princess but it's incomplete. He wants two things. He wants desperately to have another hot time with the Princess but he also wants to know what the consequences of the dream are for him.

SAUL: And does he find out in the end?

TATYANA: I think his subconscious has known it all along.

SURI: But it needs to come out in the real as well as the dream.

SAUL: I got a problem. So, does anyone here have the same dream again and again? I mean, we all get anxiety dreams like for a test or something but for me they're all different—different people, different settings, different problems. Finn may think he's going to have this same dream again but I bet he gets Ice King snowballs thrown at him instead of passionate flame. That's what I think.

Sorry, Spoke Too Soon . . . Here's the Wrap

Tatyana glances up at the clock again and Suri taps her watch.

TATYANA: We are getting close. But what goes on in the world, in reality, while Finn is awake that makes this happen?

BENJAMIN: We know the Flame Princess is a hot head. No pun intended . . . Well! And what better foil to her than the Ice King. What if Finn in his dream stirs her passion by getting the two to argue, even fight?

SAUL: So, Finn gets turned on by the Princess and the King fighting?

SURI: Why not? Finn's hot for the Princess and this is just something that's part of his weird kinky dream. It's kind of a role reversal, where instead of the damsel in distress, the Finn is in distress and the Princess comes to his rescue . . . like Finn's under his slave . . .

SAUL: So many twists.

BENJAMIN: It's his dream. It can go wherever he wants it to go. It's without inhibition.

SURI: But it's this rampant spontaneity and his willingness to do things just to continue his own pleasure and it's his need to find the ending and earn his ultimate reward for the dream. . . . All that just gets him into trouble.

SAUL: So, are we saying that dreams are just an extension of reality and that somehow dreams and reality bleed into each other and somehow alter the reality of both the dream and what is real? Kind of like the fantasy affects the real which affects the fantasy and produces a new real?

SURI: Hmmm, I suppose . . . Yes, right, that's what it might be . . . But how do we know and will our audience know what's what?

TATYANA: Does it matter?

BENJAMIN: No, I don't think it does. See, the whole point of this is to consider the twists and turns of our lives—our sleeping lives and waking lives. They have to intersect, overlap and otherwise affect each other. They have consequences as ole Arte said and we need to be mindful of what we wish for and what our dreams are made of because they can affect what we know and what we learn and even what we forget. So Finn has deep passion but poor judgment and he ends up getting burned in the end.

TATYANA: There's a moral message in this?

SURI: And it goes back to your Artemidorus: there are consequences for all of our actions, even our dreams. We not only need to observe and keep track of our thoughts and thinking but beware where our passions are too hot and so hot they cloud our thinking.

SAUL: Sometimes we push too hard.

SURI: Yes, but we don't always know when that is.

BENJAMIN: Maybe a dumb question but does this need to be black and white? I mean, do we dream in color or black and white?

SAUL: Oh, and what about someone who has been blind since birth. What do they see in their dreams?

BENJAMIN: Nothing, nada. How could they?

SURI: But is that right? Think about the Doppler Effect when a car goes past you and the sound goes from higher to lower pitch. Blind people can sense distance from hearing sounds. Isn't that like seeing? So wouldn't they like see sounds when they dream?

SAUL: So I ask again, does Beemo dream?

TATYANA: Alright, alright this is all very interesting, but . . . Okay, so the sun is just coming up or is it going down? Hard to tell . . . Can we come back together with the artists tomorrow and lay out the whole thing? Saul, be the Ice King in your dreams. Suri, dream about the Flame Princess. Benjamin dream of Jake and find out more about the color thing and I, well, I will try to be Finn.

EVELYN: Anyone up for coffee?

I feel a nudge. My wife, holding a cup out to me. I smell coffee. I push down the white sheets from my chin. It's me, not yet me me, but just-awake me. My eyes are open. It's early, the sun is barely peeking through the shades of my bedroom.

"Did you sleep?" she asks.
"I guess," I say, "You?"
"Yeah, but I had these weird dreams," she says.
"Like?" I ask.
"Like I was in a cartoon and there was this boy with noodle arms who had, like, a white television for a head with his face inside and he had pointy ears and this fat dog was with him. And it was hot but there was lots of snow around," she says.

"Pointy, like rabbit ears?" I ask.

"Nah, like dog ears, but he wasn't a dog. Weird. How about you, did you dream?" she says.

"I don't think so. I guess I slept pretty hard," I say.

IV

What Are You?

17
When I Don't Remember You

NICOLAS MICHAUD

♫ *Making your way in the world today takes everything you've got.* ♫
      "Simon . . . NO!"
♫ *Taking a break from all your worries, sure would help a lot.* ♫
      "I have to, Marcy. I have to save you."
♫ *Wouldn't you like to get away?* ♫
      "Please Simon, don't. Don't do this. Don't leave me again. You
      promised!"
♫ *Sometimes you want to go.* ♫
      "I'm sorry Gu . . . Marcy. It's the only way."
♫ *Where everybody knows your name.* ♫
      "I love you, Simon."
♫   . . .   ♫
      "I love you too, . . . Gunter."

   . . . and that was the last time Simon put on the crown. It was then that
the Ice King was born, for whom Simon Petrikov is only a confused
and distant memory. It was then that little Marceline lost the closest
thing she had to a father for the last time, and she had to grow up.

Poor Simon. Poor Marceline. Poor, poor Marceline. What must
it be like to lose your dearest friend and protector? And then
lose him again? And then again . . . and then again? I wonder
if Marceline, as a little girl, asked herself, "Is this it? Is this
time the last time Simon puts on the crown?" Or did she just
assume, like children often do, that every time Simon lost himself in the Ice King, he would get better. Because he would *have*
to get better, right? All I can say for sure is it must have been

torture for that little girl to watch her only friend slip away into madness. . . . Was it a relief that last time, or did it break her already broken heart to cry out to Simon, and see nothing but cold fury in his icy eyes. What was it like for that little girl to realize, finally, that her only friend was gone?

Really, if we think about it, there's a worse nightmare for Marcy. Accepting that Simon was dead would have given her a kind of peace, a way to say goodbye, some closure. But he isn't quite dead, is he? The Ice King is still kind of Simon—worse, we have even seen Simon come back, if only for a little while. As long as Simon has those brief moments of consciousness, Marcy can never quite let go. I imagine it is like having a parent who slips into Alzheimer's. Caregivers sometimes dread the few brief moments of lucidity more than the moments when their parent doesn't know them—because in those aching moments of awareness, when you can look into their eyes, you have to tell them, again, that they are sick, dying, and won't remember you—at any moment they will be lost again. How would you hide the hurt and pain they cause while they are lost in the illness? We see Simon suffer this, realizing every time he comes back how poorly he's treated those he loves, only to disappear again, leaving Marcy with worse than nothing—leaving her with a broken friend. But maybe we can ease Marceline's pain. Maybe, even though Simon Petrikov *appears* to come back now and then, he is dead. Maybe Simon Petrikov really did die that day.

Nobody Wants to See This Old Skin

To help Marcy, the first thing we have to accept is that Simon and the Ice King aren't the same person. It seems pretty easy to confuse them. After all, isn't the Ice King just Simon with the crown on his head? Well, we can see that's not true. The Ice King is different from Simon in every way that matters. Let's think about it like this. . . . What stuff makes us who we are? And what is it that makes me different from you? I mean, what actually makes us different people?

Well, there are a few answers that we usually give to a question like that. To distinguish between you and me, we might say we have different bodies, we have different minds, and we have different souls. It seems that the Simon and the Ice King actually share some of those things. Even though their bodies are different in some significant ways, Ice King's body is actually Simon's, just with some magical transmutation. But when the curse is lifted, the Ice King's body is transformed back into Simon's. Simon's mind is probably also in there somewhere, right? Simon's mind, like his body, becomes *twisted* when he puts on the crown. And if they share the same body and mind, then it only makes sense that they have the same soul. Case closed. Simon and Ice King are the same person for the same reason you and I are different people. . . . Well, here's the bad news—though perhaps good news for Marceline—not really.

Check out each of the criteria we just listed. First, there's the whole body thing. You and I have different bodies, so we are different people. Simon and the Ice King have the same body, so they are the same person. Well, there is a *huge* problem here—because if it's your body that makes you, *you,* then you aren't the same person today as you were yesterday. The fact is, our bodies change *a lot.* Cells in my body die and new cells are made. In a decade, there's a good chance that none of the cells in my body will be the same. Worse, if what makes me, *me* is this physical stuff sitting right here at my computer, then when every atom that makes me up is gone and exchanged with some other atom as time passes, I cease to exist. That's what happens when I eat and breathe; I'm taking in the outside world and turning it into *this* body, and I expel parts of my body all the time. So we can't say that what makes me, *me* is my body.

Here's another way to look at it. Is Finn dead just because he lost his arm? If what makes Finn, *Finn* is his body, then how come we still think he's the same guy after he loses his arm? Remember Finn as a baby, crying, stuck to that leaf? Well, think of the young man he is now. All of his cells are different, all of the atoms that made him up as a baby have been exchanged with new atoms he's taken in from the world around him, *and* he's lost an arm! How can we say it's his body that makes him Finn? We can't! It isn't his DNA either! Otherwise, Finn would be the same person as his clone, right? If I have an identical twin, are we the same person? No, even if we have identical DNA! Our DNA is just a blueprint for making us, but it isn't *us* any more than the blueprint of a building is the building.

So we can't say Simon and the Ice King are the same person just because they share a body, even if the DNA is the same.

There must be something else that makes a person one person and not another. We had a couple of options left: the mind and the soul. When we talk about the mind, we want to be specific. We tend to say things like, what makes me, *me* is my mind. But what does that even mean? It can't be *your* mind if we don't even know what *you* are. Maybe we mean something like our memories, beliefs, or personality. It doesn't seem like a stretch to say that what makes Jake the Dog himself are his memories, beliefs, and personality.

I Know My Mind Is Changing

Well, we're gonna hit the same problem we do with Finn's body. What happens when Jake gets really hungry? Doesn't it seem like he totally changes, almost like he forgets everything that matters to him? After all, we've seen him get hungry enough to decide to eat Marceline, even though he's terrified of vampires! Also, we can't say that Jake's memories make him who he is, because what if he got amnesia? Would we say Jake was dead? Probably not, right? People with amnesia aren't dead; they've just lost their memories. Doesn't the same thing go for our beliefs? When Jake stops being afraid of Marceline, and changes his beliefs about vampires and become her friend, does that mean Jake has ceased to exist? No! Even if he changes his beliefs, he's still *Jake*. So what the heck makes Jake, *Jake,* if it isn't his body, his memories, or his beliefs?

Well, there's always the personality, right? If anything clearly is mine and no one else's, it's my personality! Well, there's the problem. Just like with body, memories, and beliefs, my personality changes. So if what makes you and me different is the fact that we have different personalities, how come we don't say the same thing about me of the past and me of the future? All of our personalities change a lot over our lifetimes. Think about the stuff that mattered to you when you were five. How different is a lot of that stuff now? And when we first met Marceline, she was a lot meaner than she is now; hanging out with Finn and Jake has reminded her what it means to have people who care about her. But even though her personality has changed, she stays the same person!

So we can safely say that it isn't your body or mind that makes you, *you* because even when we change those things, you are still you, right? So they can't be the center of your identity. It would be like saying that the Ice Kingdom is the Ice Kingdom because it has ice, then removing the ice and saying, it's still the Ice Kingdom! That makes no sense. If we defined the Ice Kingdom as "A Kingdom with Ice," then if we remove the ice, it isn't the Ice Kingdom any more. —*Or*, if we say, "No, it's still the Ice Kingdom even we change it so that it doesn't have ice," then we have to admit that the ice isn't that important *to the kingdom being "the Ice Kingdom"* because it's still the Ice Kingdom, even after the ice is gone.

Okay, so far it seems like I've proven the exact opposite of my point. I'm trying to prove that Simon and the Ice King *aren't* the same person. But all I've shown is that our bodies and minds change, and yet we remain the same person. So no matter how much Simon's body and mind changes, he's still Simon! But I've also shown something else—something kinda scary . . . it can't be our body or mind that makes us who we are, so it must be something else that makes us who we are, right? Something like the soul. . . .

Well, sadly, the soul seems to not help much at all. Because the soul, if it is what makes me who I am, must be different from everyone else's soul. —So the question is this: What is different about it? It can't be different because of memories or personality, because—as we've pointed out already—those things change over time without changing entire identities. So what's the deal? If my soul isn't different from everyone else's, it really isn't what makes me, *me* (and not someone else). On the other hand, anything that might be different about it, is likely different over time too—like the memories stored in my soul, my soul's personality, or my soul's beliefs.

I Can Feel Myself Slipping Away

So here's the problem. . . . We like Simon, and—if only for Marceline's sake—we really don't want Simon to be dead. So there needs to be some connection between Simon and the Ice King, something about them that's the same. The problem is that all of the stuff that could be the same between them is all stuff that—if we think about it—doesn't really make someone who he is.

There's a good chance you are asking yourself, "What's the big deal with change over time? So what if my personality changes over time or if my soul changes over time? It is still *mine*, so it is what makes me, *me!*" Well let's think about something else that changes over time, like the Candy Kingdom. What if we asked the question, "What makes the Candy Kingdom, the Candy Kingdom?" It can't just be the name. No matter how much I want to, I can't just decide to name a town the Candy Kingdom and poof! there it is! No, the Candy Kingdom is a specific place with specific people, right?

So the Candy Kingdom seems like it would have a physical existence, just like any other country does. But, if we think about it, the Candy Kingdom isn't really a physical thing. — Because although it has buildings and the palace and the people who live there, over time, all of those buildings will eventually be torn down and new ones built. Imagine the Candy Kingdom one thousand years later; it's likely a very different place. There's a good chance it will have all new buildings, and, all of the people who once lived there have likely died and been replaced by new people. This is the same problem as thinking that it's my body that makes me myself. My body will be very different thirty years from now with new cells and new matter, just like the Candy Kingdom will have new buildings and new people.

In fact, imagine that Lemongrab became the ruler of the Candy Kingdom again, just like when Princess Bubblegum was too young to rule. Imagine that he takes power, but no shots are fired, no one dies, no bombs are dropped. It's not hard to also imagine, then, that Lemongrab decides to remake the Candy Kingdom in his own image. He would likely rename it after himself—maybe "Lemongrab Kingdom"—and he would change the very way the kingdom works. He would change the rules and the laws to suit himself. So, the Candy Kingdom would be gone. But notice, here, that in this case all of the people are still there and all of the buildings are still there too. It's like Lemongrab killed the Candy Kingdom without doing anything physical, almost like he killed its *soul*.

Oh. I . . . I See. It's all Making Sense Now

What we realize is that our way of thinking about the soul, the very heart of what makes us who we are, might be very wrong. Maybe the "soul" of the Candy Kingdom is really just the way the ruler, the laws, and the people work together. So even if you change rulers or the people grow old and die, the Kingdom still exists because it is the way everything coexists. Some philosophers, like Gilbert Ryle, think that the whole idea of a soul is really just a way of saying "the way our brains work to produce us." Just like the way the people work together to produce the Candy Kingdom.

The point is just this: we're trying to figure out what makes us who we are, but there doesn't seem to be one physical thing that does that. Even the soul is really best understood as something that doesn't have a physical (even magical physical) existence. Really, it's better understood as the way physical stuff works with other physical stuff to make something. A quest isn't the hero. It also isn't the treasure or the monsters. A quest is all of the stuff added together: the hero, plus the quest, plus the monsters, plus the working together in a specific way that makes "quest." If the hero and the monsters travel down to the dungeon and have tea, it isn't a quest, even though it has a hero, treasure, monsters, and a journey. A quest only happens when all those parts work together in a very *specific* way. And so it might be the same way with us. *I* only exist when the cells of my brain interact in a certain way. Yes, some cells can grow and others can be lost, but they must keep working together in the same way . . . or I cease to exist, just like if Lemongrab takes over the Candy Kingdom. All the *stuff* of the brain could still be there, but if it doesn't function the right way, I'm gone.

And I Need to Save You, but Who's Going to Save Me?

So. There isn't something magical that stays the same that makes me, *me*, like a soul. And it can't be my body or mind; all of the reasons we give for saying you and I are different people turn out to be differences I also have from my past self. That's a real problem. And that's why Simon Petrikov is dead.

It's true that Simon and the Ice King are very interconnected. You might say that Simon is what causes the Ice King to exist. But being the cause isn't enough. You aren't your parents even though they caused you. Even if Simon and the Ice

King share the same body and mind (though, truly, it seems that they don't) that *still* isn't enough to say they are the same person. The soul doesn't help. Think about how different Simon and the Ice King are. Simon is extremely intelligent, brave, self-sacrificing, and thoughtful. The Ice King is generally shallow, cowardly, selfish, and thoughtless. So if they do share the same soul, it seems that the soul doesn't really count for much. If it is supposed to be the magical thing that makes us who we are, but it doesn't account for our intellect, virtues, or personality, how does it really matter? . . . So we're stuck.

Now, let's not forget that Simon comes back on a rare occasion. It might be even that he can be brought back for good. But notice that to do this, we have to lose something else—namely, the Ice King. If I'm right, bringing Simon back requires killing the Ice King. So we're trapped between two very bad options. If it is the mind and body that makes us who we are, then Simon and the Ice King are different people, as their bodies and minds are quite different. But we've said that the mind and body don't really make us who we are, as we remain ourselves despite all that stuff changing all the time. Maybe it's the soul, but that doesn't seem to help us much, either: the soul, if it does make Simon himself, is either lost when he becomes Ice King (making them two different people), or it is the same . . . but really pretty meaningless. Because, like I said, if the Ice King and Simon have the same soul, well . . . *Cabbage!* What is it good for, if it doesn't prevent Simon from becoming a cowardly, selfish, lunatic?

So if we want Simon back, we basically have to kill the Ice King, because having one means getting rid of the other, which is a tragic option. After all, the Ice King is pretty endearing in his own way. And while Simon is obviously the better guy, is it right to get rid of the Ice King just to bring Simon back? What would poor Gunter do?! The most obvious evidence for the tragic nature of bringing Simon back at the expense of eliminating the Ice King is the fact that Simon himself is very unaware of what he does when he's the Ice King. And the Ice King doesn't remember being Simon. In every way that we think about what makes us who we are, they are two totally different people. And I can't imagine that the Ice King would agree to the argument that he should cease to exist so that everyone can have Simon back.

What Am Us?

The realization, then, is very dark. It's *vampire* dark, actually. To bring back Simon permanently is (assuming there aren't any magical options) to delete the Ice King. Simon isn't trapped inside of the Ice King; he's gone. And sometimes, we can bring him back. It's a bit like turning a computer on and off. If I turn off my computer and load in a new operating system and turn it back on, it will basically be a completely different machine with different programs and functions. I can turn it off again and reboot the old operating system, but I can't really have both running at the same time in the same machine. —Not unless I want to have some sort of weird simultaneous split-personality thing going on. Imagine what that would be like for Simon and the Ice King! If we had both of them existing in the same body at the same time, . . . they'd be miserable!

The problem gets even worse. In showing that the Ice King and Simon aren't the same person, we seem to also have proven that we aren't the same person as our past and future selves. So far, we've found nothing that makes us who we are over time. There seems to be no one specific thing that we can find that holds us together. In the same way that Simon and the Ice King are not the same person despite sharing a body and brain, we would be different from our past selves. The fact that they're so connected makes it even worse. Simon can kind of vaguely remember being the Ice King, and the Ice King seems to have some very vague connection to Simon, even recognizing that he once wore glasses. But despite that connection, they aren't the same person, any more than two people who share similar memories are the same person.

In splitting apart the Ice King and Simon Petrikov, we seem to also have split apart ourselves. No wonder Marceline is so messed up. If she separates the Ice King from Simon, that means her friend is completely dead, but if they are the same person, then her friend doesn't remember her, doesn't seem to really care about her, and is often pretty mean to her. It might be just easier for her to believe that Simon is actually dead. And all the evidence about personal identity seems to support this; when the Ice King exists, Simon is really dead.

♫ Please Forgive Me for Whatever I Do . . . ♫

Well, there is one upshot to all of this. If it's true that all of us are different people when our bodies and minds change, then it's also pretty much true that the old version of us is constantly being deleted and a new one is constantly coming into existence. In other words, the person who started reading this chapter is dead. Whoever that person was, with particular cells, DNA, beliefs, memories, and so on, is gone. That person was replaced with a person with very similar cells, DNA, beliefs, and memories—so similar that we might as well just keep calling that person by the same name as the old person. It's kind of like we don't rename the Candy Kingdom every time a new building is built and an old one is torn down. But it also isn't the same Candy Kingdom, and if we stepped away from it for a thousand years and came back, we likely would think it was a different place.

Maybe in this way we can give Marceline a kind of peace. Death is a pretty scary concept, and it sucks to think of losing your best friend. But if there isn't really anything all that magical to death and to who we are, then we die a thousand deaths every day. As we grow and change, we leave behind the *self* that was once us.

So, when I get scared of death, I remind myself that I already have died, and it doesn't bother me that much. Weird thought, I know. But, seriously, the person I once was is gone, but he doesn't know he's gone. There is a new present (or future) self who has taken his place, and when that present person goes, he won't be around to be sad about it. He won't even know.

So maybe Marcy can have some peace.

Just one more thought, though. Remember what Death tells Simon when Simon is dying: "Get real, man. You're gonna be the Ice King till the sun blows up." Notice he said, "*You're.*" This seems to imply that Simon *is* the Ice King. And we do know that Simon has a very vague awareness of what he does as the Ice King. In other words, he's in the limbo that scares us all the most. That's the world in which Simon Petrikov still exists. My past self doesn't get to come back, but my present self can still regret the decisions of that past self, and mourn the losses experienced by that past self. So although the past self doesn't have to continue to suffer the guilt and loss, that guilt and loss can continue to be transferred forward to a new entity—one who didn't even exist at the time. This sounds like the Hell to which Simon is condemned . . . having to know that he might come back at any time, perhaps at the very end of time, and have to bear the guilt, shame, and losses of his other life.

♫ . . . When I Don't Remember You. ♫

—The Ice King and Marceline
. . . together.

18
When My Gameboy Became Self-Aware

DAVID DEGGINGER

Finn and Jake are walking through a long, grassy field together after saving yet another princess from the clutches of the Ice King. Finn turns to Jake as they stride toward the treehouse, "Hey, Jake . . ."
"Yeah, buddy."
"I was just thinking, what does it mean to be alive?"
"Have you been eating nachos before bed again? It always makes you all existential and junk," Jake replies, making a face.
"No, for real, Jake," Finn pounds his fist into his palm for emphasis, frowning. "The idea has been stuck in my dome piece for days."
Jake, now looking like he's eaten a bad burrito, ventures, "Well, I don't know. I guess being alive is about having a heart and lungs and blood and guts and junk."
"Yeah, . . . I guess." Finn's young brow furrows deeper as he gets to his real worry . . . "But what about Beemo, then? Is he alive, too? He doesn't have a heart and guts and all that bizz, but he seems alive to me. He hangs out with us and skateboards and laughs at my jokes . . ." Finn's question hangs in the air between the two friends.
*"**Cabbage**."*
The two heroes walk on in silence, hoping to slay something soon.

In a land filled with talking animals, talking inanimate objects, and candy people, it seems almost ludicrous for us to question the consciousness of Beemo. So, why is there a dogma in popular culture that only organic beings can be fully conscious?

It's strange that we're easily willing to accept that a radioactively enhanced dog can be fully conscious, but with Beemo we're skeptical. Yet we are. It seems odd to argue that a

Gameboy could be a person, but Beemo appears to be just that. Everyone in the Land of Ooo seems to be completely capable of accepting Beemo's wishes to be treated like a person, but even Finn and Jake chuckle at her often futile imitations when she play-acts at being a boy or a hard-boiled detective.[1]

You may think that Beemo is simply a complex machine and nothing more, but I'm going to prove that Beemo *is human in all the aspects that truly matter.* She demonstrates all the factors that make us human *persons* like 1. intelligence and 2. consciousness. So, if we determine that she's alive and conscious, and if we can at least entertain these ideas, what do we make of the fact that Beemo believes she is a person? She pretends to eat, drink, sleep, brush her teeth and pee in the toilet but does Beemo's belief in her own personhood make her a person?

Do Robots Dream of Electric Dogs?

Beemo's not the only robot on the show that has some capabilities of interacting. There is Neptr (Never Ending Pie Throwing Robot), a machine that Finn haphazardly constructs in order to do an elaborate prank on Jake (to be fair, he did start it; throwing a bag of butter on someone is a pretty good gag). If we compare Beemo to Neptr, there is a distinctive difference between their mindsets that makes Beemo, at least, more human-like. There's an episode where Neptr says to Beemo "we should hang out more, we are both robots," Beemo replies "No Neptr, I am not like you." Whoa . . . *Burn!*

But why does Beemo feel the need to make that distinction between herself and her metallic comrade? Well here's part of it. . . . Neptr lives to serve his creator while Beemo can be defiant and creative. Beemo doesn't want to be seen as a robot because she truly believes that's not who she is. She thinks she's something more than Neptr; she's more than a robot.

Remember those robot dogs that did flips and barked? They have a set programming with instructions on what they are capable of doing. Beemo is not your average robot. She is not a flashdrive of fixed information; in fact, she's the opposite. She

---

[1] Throughout the show, Beemo's gender differs depending on who's speaking because, as a robot, Beemo has no biological sex. For the most part, I will refer to Beemo as "she."

learns how to act and be a person through observation much like a human child does. She is constantly gaining new knowledge. She is kinda like if your six-year-old cousin became fused with a Gameboy. You know, the cousin that everyone wonders if she's going to end up being normal.

Being Itself: Is Beemo Even Alive?

I know what you're thinking: "How can a machine be alive? That don't make a lick of sense." But there are many living things in the Land of Ooo that don't exist in our own world, so suspend your disbelief a little bit further. Sure, there are plants and animals in Ooo but some can talk! There are also some plants that do not move or talk; however, we know that they are 'living.' So, what does it mean to be alive? Some would say life is based in cells—little organic cogs that allow the living animal or plant to function. But, if we look at a character like Beemo, we may want to consider the possibility that there must be other things that factor into what constitutes life. She just seems to be so alive.

Robert Pepperell has argued that life is not necessarily defined by biology. Life is about a motivated meaning which means that living things need to be aware of their environment in order to survive and sustain their life and it is their ability to carry out these needs that makes them alive. Taking Finn as an example, it's clear that he knows that in order to survive he needs to eat food, drink water, and defend himself from things that may harm him. In order to eat and drink, Finn needs to know where to get these necessities otherwise he will die and that wouldn't be very math. Even plants do this. They grow in areas where they can get sunlight and water and the ones that survive are ones that are hard to be eaten by predators.

I know what you are you are thinking. "Okay, smart guy, you have proven to me that things I know to be alive are alive but I am not swayed on this talking Gameboy you keep bringing up!" But, seriously, Beemo has motivated meaning too! She displays an understanding of her environment and how to manipulate it in order to survive. Unlike other machines which simply power down if not provided a fuel source, Beemo changes her own batteries because she understands that they are what keep her functioning. We've seen her do it! She picks up a pair of batteries and places them in just the right spot. Then, she takes out her batteries and falls directly onto the new ones as she powers down.

Beemo is also aware of the difference between helpful and harmful beings; in one instance, she's abducted by a giant bird which attempts to feed her to its young. Beemo understands that this is not a desirable scenario for her to be in so she escapes. This may not seem like a big deal, but I don't see your laptop inching away from the mug of coffee you set maliciously next to it. If we can accept that Beemo has motivated meaning then we should accept that Beemo is, at the very least, alive and not an inanimate object, even though she has a very different kind of biology. But that doesn't necessarily mean she is conscious in the same way that humans are.

Consciousness and All That Bizz

Consciousness is a tricky thing to measure in a definitive way because it's impossible to ever truly know what is going on in the mind of another being. We can guess through observation, but grasping exactly what constitutes consciousness has been the subject of debate. It's hard to get away from the idea that consciousness is entirely a human trait. Tracking back to René Descartes's famous argument, "I think therefore I am," we can see where the human-centered idea of consciousness arises. Descartes concluded that he is conscious because he is aware of his own existence and aware of his own thought.

But do you have to be human to be aware of your existence *as human*? Robert Pepperell argues that there are seven attributes of consciousness which can be observed: thought, emotion, memory, awareness, intelligence, self-knowledge, and a sense of being. He also argues that there are "varying layers and densities of consciousness," meaning that some beings can express a few but not all of these attributes. Beemo expresses all of these characteristics in a much more meaningful way than your average Gameboy or even very young human children!

Music to My Sound Receptors

Computers have memory but that does not mean that they cherish these memories and have an emotional and self-identifying connection to them. The fact that my computer has three thousand or so songs stored inside it doesn't mean it will protest if I decide to delete them all. It may ask "Are you sure you want to get rid of these files?" but that is more to serve me than any personal connection it feels to Bob Dylan's "Like a Rolling Stone." Beemo, on the other hand, has a favorite song that she shows Finn and Jake. Unlike my computer, which only serves me, Beemo associates music with her own happiness.

Beemo clearly connects her experiences with her sense of who she is. She recognizes Finn and Jake as her friends—not her masters. One day, Finn and Jake have a silent contest and this throws Beemo off. She asks, "Where is the real Finn and Jake?" she calls them evil "doppelgangers." In this same moment, she displays what appear to be genuine emotions of fear. She's afraid that her friends have been taken away by something strange and foreign to her (which is not all that unlikely in the land of Ooo) so she hides in the wall. The fear she seems to display could be just sophisticated imitation, but, again, do we have any more reason to believe that a six-year-old human child is "really" afraid when she hides from the monster under her bed? We *assume* her feelings are genuine. But we do that because of the actions we *see* her take. Why should it be different for Beemo?

So, we've established that Beemo displays emotion and remembers her buddies, but is that enough to make her conscious? We're going to have to prove that she understands complex ideas like friendship (awareness), memory loss (self-knowledge), and intelligence. She is also going to have to prove that her ideas are her own and that she exerts some form of thought independent from the opinions of Finn and Jake.

I'm Incapable of Emotion, but You're Making Me Chafed!

In the scene we just discussed, Beemo does not blindly follow the commands of Finn and Jake by waiting at their beck and call. She apparently thinks for herself. If we compare her to Neptr, we see a fundamental difference. Neptr cannot help but obey Finn even when he's treated terribly by Finn. When Finn and Jake are rummaging through their basement for some supplies to build a heat-proof battle suit, they find Neptr hidden under some old boxes and he exclaims "You found me!" It turns out that they had been playing a hide and seek game with Neptr several months earlier and had simply forgotten to ever look for him. Most people conscious of themselves and their own feelings would never put up with that treatment. I imagine that even if Beemo forgave the guys for such an insult, they would get an earful.

Neptr does not hold a grudge against his creator and decides to help them build the heat suit while singing a song where he repeatedly says "working for the master." He is like that friend that tries just a little too hard. It's clear that Neptr does not have free thought like Beemo does. Beemo frequently is defiant of Finn and Jake's wishes, we see this when Beemo refuses to play a card game with Jake because he is a sore loser. Imagine your Xbox not wanting to play Call of Duty with you because you always throw the controller when you die (which, seriously, is not good for the controller—just sayin').

Be More: Beemo and His Memories

An example of Beemo's desire to retain her memories—which have become a part of her identity—comes when Beemo accidentally deletes her core system drivers. She tells Finn and Jake they need to take her to where she was created in order to get fixed, otherwise she would lose her memories and their time spent together would "vanish like tears in the oven." This uncharacteristically morbid statement is significant because it shows Beemo's complex understanding of language; she can use metaphor to articulate the gravity of a situation. When the factory robots attempt to do a "total personality wipe" she resists because she values her sense of self.

Later in the episode, it's revealed that Beemo is one of a kind. Her creator, Mo, explains to Finn and Jake that Beemo was made to be his son's friend, understand fun, and how to play. Beemo was designed to be able to comprehend personal interaction but that does not necessarily mean she is a person. Her speech is not always clear and she's often unaware of the difference between her imagination and reality.

Despite the overactive imagination, it's clear that Beemo does display an array of attributes that we associate with consciousness. She displays the ability to have emotion, understand herself through memory, she has thoughts, and is aware of who she is, but is this enough to call her a person? She does other things that seem human-like but is this instinct or imitation? And does that even matter? Beemo is quite similar to a child in many ways. Everything impresses her and she gets completely lost in her own imagination—like those little girls who wear their princess gowns from Halloween to picture day because they really *are* princesses.

Haters Gonna Hate

Some philosophers believe that even if machines could respond and interact with humans in a seemingly human way they cannot be considered human. Descartes explains that there are two human factors that no beast or machine can replicate:

1. **A machine could not replicate how men use words and signs to declare their thoughts to others.**

and

2. **A machine would not be enabled with enough reason to act in a way that could replicate all the complexities of life.**

According to Descartes's view, Beemo is not alive at all, she's simply a complex mechanism that does not understand the language she replies with. It's merely a function of her machinery that it makes her *seem* alive.

A similar argument is made by John Searle against Allan Turing's "Turing Test." In the Turing Test a human asks a series of questions to two entities he can't see; he can only judge them by their answers to the questions. One of the entities is a human person and the other is a machine like Beemo. If the interrogator cannot tell the difference between these two, the machine can be considered intelligent, according to Turing.

The reason for this is simple. It is our conversations with other humans that make us think they are conscious and thinking, not their bodies. Isn't that how we tell the difference between a living, conscious person and a corpse, or someone in a coma? Breathing and a heartbeat isn't enough for us to assume you are conscious (as opposed to say, alive but brain dead). We assume other humans are thinking things *because of the way they respond to us.*

So if Beemo responds to us in a way similar to the way humans do, should we treat her as a thinking thing? After all, I can't hear your thoughts, but I assume you are a thinking thing if you argue with me about Beemo's intelligence. Imagine that you were talking with Beemo, but she was behind a door, and you didn't know she was a machine. In fact, during your conversation you assumed that she was a human. Much to your surprise, when the door opens, you realize she's a robot! If you suddenly decide, "Whoops! I thought I was talking to something intelligent, but it was just pretending," then isn't the *only* reason you change your mind because of her body, *not* her mind? Aren't you just being a *species*-ist?

John Searle's Chinese room argument is supposed to prove Turing wrong. The argument goes something like this. Imagine that Gunter (you know, the penguin...) is locked in a dungeon in the Candy Kingdom with no windows but only two tiny slots. Also imagine that Gunter has no knowledge of the English language but has with him a book of instructions written in "penguin." On the outside of the room, there is a slot for questions that come in and a slot for answers that he puts out. As cards in English come in, Gunther flips through his instruction book and formulates responses based on what the book tells him to write. He then puts his responses through the other slot.

The people outside the dungeon may think that whatever's in the dungeon understands and responds in English but this is actually not the case. Gunter is merely interpreting signs that he does not understand. In this analogy, Beemo is Gunter in the dungeon. The argument is that she's not really thinking, but merely takes in symbols and has a preprogramed response to those symbols. But they mean nothing to her! So even if it looks like Beemo understands what we're saying to her, it's really just an elaborate system of set responses.

As I argued earlier, however, Beemo often displays very complex interactions with others that do not follow a simple set of pre-programmed responses as our Penguin Room argument outlines. John Searle's Chinese room argument assumes that the conscious being is passive, but often it's Beemo who instigates conversation. Searle's argument also does not account for

Beemo's conversations with herself in the mirror or the situations she creates through her imagination.

It's clear from these examples that Beemo's thinking is more complex than simply an input of perceived information and an outputting of programmed responses. We've already agreed that Beemo illustrates intelligent conversation, so we can say that she passes the Turing Test and disregard the Chinese Room argument that Searle presents because it reduces interaction to a simple input and output of information even though it is way more complex than that.

Pepperell summarizes Turing like this, "What constitutes intelligence is our subjective experience of what we think intelligence is, regardless of precisely how it is being generated." In other words, because we can't reach into other people's minds, our understanding of them as thinking, as conscious, is based on our own experience of their behavior. Heck, in Beemo's case, we can reach into her mind by jacking in to her virtual reality capabilities, which is in some ways like directly accessing her mind. But even Finn and Jake can't actually experience her intelligence by jacking in, they can experience the same way they do with everyone else... *through observation and experience.*

Imagination Isn't Just for Turbo Nerds Who Can't Handle How Kick-Butt Reality Is

Intelligence does not constitute personhood, however. How much of a person Beemo is still needs to be worked out. Beemo often imagines that inanimate or unintelligent animals can talk and have personalities. We can view this imagination as being similar to that of a child's. She creates these imagined scenarios to entertain himself while her friends are away on adventures. Think castaway without the constant threat of starvation. Beemo imagines an entire noire-style detective story with household animals and inanimate objects to explain how she misplaced Finn's sock. Her imagination is pretty elaborate.

There are a few instances where we see Beemo talking to herself in the mirror while Finn and Jake are not around. She calls her reflection "Football," and she asks herself "Beemo, are you a robot?" to which she replies "Oh, no Football. I am a real living boy." She then proceeds to imitate brushing her teeth, washing herself, and peeing in the toilet in order to show what it is like to be alive. We can view this as an expression of Pepperell's requirements of awareness and self-knowledge because not only does she acknowledges herself as "I" and distinguish herself from a simple reflection in the mirror but she's expressing what it means to be alive as well. From her observations, she has realized that to be alive is to do things that organic beings need to do like bathe and release bodily fluids.

This conduct could be seen as a bit delusional because it doesn't seem as though Beemo is willing to accept her robotic appearance. However, in another scenario, Football tells Beemo she is a little girl now and cites the fact that she can smell flowers and hear squirrels screaming, but Beemo does not believe that is enough. What Football describes are simply expressions of a sense of being; she is aware of the sources of her sensory mechanisms, but Beemo says that is not being a person. She then explains that Football needs manners "otherwise you will be all alone. . . . I will not always be here to protect you, Football." This is a recognition of another human invention; society. She has learned that in order to have company, be safe, and have memories worth saving she needs to interact with others. What Beemo is realizing, here, is the key component to what makes someone a person—recognition from society *as* a person.

Really, being a person is all about what the community has decided is a "person." Things that aren't "person" can be property. Which is why we can "own" for example, gorillas, orcas, and other intelligent animals. Heck, that's why here in the States slaveholders could own *humans*. Society decided that the "black race" was property, and society acted accordingly. There have been many groups of humans through history that were not considered persons, and because of that they were enslaved, tortured, and often killed. Beemo is beginning to see this when she realizes that she will be alone without the recognition of others. Being a person means being recognized *by people*.

Robot Tears

After reviewing the scenes with Beemo and Football it becomes clear that Beemo is in the stages of learning what it means to be a person, much like a child would. We can see another examples of how Beemo imitates things he perceives as being related to personhood when Beemo has taped a cup to her mid-section and placed a chicken egg in it. He sings about the fact that he is pregnant and that a mysterious electrical force told him to protect the child that was inside. Immediately after he finishes singing, a butterfly knocks the egg from his hands and he begins to cry.

This scene is important because, after the egg cracks and Beemo begins to cry, James Baxter (a horse that jumps around on a beach ball) quickly cheers him up. This shows that he did not truly believe that the egg would spawn a human child—which further disproves the theory that he is disconnected from reality—but, rather, it was a pretend game he was playing. The fact that he can easily forget about the made-up situation he created means that it was just a fun way to pass the time for him and not his reality. We could even imagine this whole scenario being played out by replacing Beemo with a child. Like a little kid on Halloween who believes he *really* is a pirate and is finally told that he's not, Beemo cries but is eventually consoled and brought out of the pretend scenario he had created for himself.

More Human than a Human

When Finn meets Beemo's creator, Mo, he asks "Wait, are you human too?" The man in question has a mechanical heart and mechanical lungs on the outside of his chest; he uses another robot to move around and looks extremely disheveled. In response, Mo says "My skin is human." When he first says this, you're thinking that's a really weird way to say "Kinda." What is he really trying to say, though?

Mo is saying that it really does not matter how much of a person he is biologically; as long as he has a working mind, he doesn't seem to care what you call him. The point is that it doesn't seem to matter whether or not Beemo is biologically a person. We cannot define it through biological factors because even in our current world there are people like Mo. There are people on life support and people who have prosthetic limbs—are they still people if being a person means having only "human" parts?

Perhaps death is the distinction; people all eventually die, while Beemo has the potential to live forever. Even if she gets powered down for an extended period of time she would still be the same once she recharged. However, if her system drivers are removed permanently, she would essentially die because the person she was would be erased entirely. But this is really a question of aging. Beemo, like everyone else, will eventually wear out. It's not her fault we just happen to age a lot faster.

Maybe the better question comes down to, "Why don't we want to treat Beemo like a person?" Is it because our ability to treat her like a possession is more valuable to us? Treating her like a toy allows us to play mathematical video games and watch movies but treating her as a person means showing genuine concern for her feelings and wants. Believing she's a person would make that whole using-her-to-do-what-we-want-when-we-want experience a bit awkward.

So maybe we don't know, for sure, what makes someone a person. But we can say this, the one criterion we know *shouldn't* be used is, "Because I find it really convenient that *it* isn't a person!" In other words, we shouldn't get to define slaves as property because we don't want to do our own work, and we shouldn't get to deny Beemo her much desired status as a person, just because we don't want to have to pay attention to her inconvenient feelings. That wouldn't be very *humane* of us, would it?

19

Imagined Worlds and Real Lessons

DANIEL VELLA

With a sad little frown the rounded, frumpled, blond and graying bearded man closes the notebook in front of him heavily. He looks over his rounded little glasses, cracks his knuckles, and the lines around his eyes deepen, just slightly.

"Well, I guess that's a wrap."

The eclectic group of men and women sitting at the table look, blinking, at each other and laugh. The sound is empty.

"Hey, we got that last fart joke in right? It was a good run . . . Wasn't it?"

The flanneled man couldn't remember his reply, waving behind him, his knit cap on his head, notebook under his arm, as he walked out of the building. "It was a good run. Wasn't it?"

There, in that tattered notebook, are the final sketches and lines. The words engraved there will be the final words aired by Finn and Jake. Closing that notebook was like closing a coffin.

"What happens to the boys now, now that he's grown up?"

"Will his adult life have room for any more adventure time?"

"Or are they all just gone . . . poof?"

As Pendleton Ward muses about the final episode of his beloved creation, he wonders what impact the world he created had. He can't help but wonder, almost as if squinting hopefully across a great distance at his own lost youth, if anything of that adventure will live on. Did our game of Adventure Time *change anything? Or was it just "play?" And now, we just go back to very mundane lands . . .*

Something strange sets *Adventure Time* apart from most other examples of the sword-and-sorcery genre to which it appears to belong. Yes, all the elements are present and accounted for: We have the hero and his sidekick, princesses in distress, quests, fearsome monsters and perilous dungeons, magic swords and tomes. We can confidently place a big checkmark next to every single item on the Checklist of Generic Clichés—but something's still not quite right.

It's not just that the colors are a little brighter than we would expect, or the characters a little (or a lot) wackier. It's not that all the generic elements of the fantasy quest are a little too perfectly arranged, so much so that the characters themselves seem to be aware that they're performing the motions of an age-old generic formula, almost like a ritual. And it's not even the fact that Finn, our hero, doesn't behave quite like we would expect him to, usually embarking on his adventures not with trepidation and fear, nor even with courage and bravery in the face of danger, but with laughter and joy. These are all important details, but they are only symptoms of something bigger.

What is it, then? The clue is in the opening. Every episode of *Adventure Time* begins with an invitation to the viewer. "Come on and grab your friends," the theme song beckons, "We go to very distant lands." There's a reason why this familiar call strikes a chord. It resonates with the nostalgic memory of childhood escapades: It's the call to playtime, and the distant lands we're being summoned to are the infinite realms of the imagination and make-believe.

Here's what makes *Adventure Time* different. . . . Its stories are not just stories of adventure—even more importantly, they are stories of play. Play is everywhere in the series, whether it's Finn and Jake engaging in a board game, picking up one of BMO's controllers, a game of make-believe that gets out of hand, or battling with Prizmo's. *Adventure Time* reminds us that play has a huge role in human existence. It shows us just how important it is to play—and how play can create new worlds that can reshape reality.

Miniature People, Real Problems

The "adult world" of work, routine, seriousness, and responsibility tends to sideline play. Still, if every adult remains, somewhere deep in their heart, the child they once were (and how sad it would be if they don't!), then they will remember the fantastical worlds of the imagination into which they used to escape. With the opening up of a book, or the powering-up of a games console, or even the simple statement, "Let's pretend!" we can recall the play-filled worlds of our childhood. These worlds might even have looked a lot like the Land of Ooo, which comes across as a supercharged combination of every realm of childhood adventure. Finn and Jake's expansive tree house, and the traditional "boy and his dog" image that they live up to, bring to mind the freedom of carefree countryside escapades that apartment-bound city kids could only dream of. And there are other worlds of the imagination, too: the primary-colored worlds of sixteen-bit-era videogames and the treacherous, monster-filled dungeons of pen-and-paper role-playing games are all ingredients that go into the make-up of Ooo.

But this is all child's play, right? When we grow up, we put away childish things. We live in the "real world" (whatever that is) and set aside the many worlds of play. Johan Huizinga (1872–1945) argued that, when people talk about play, they most often talk about it as something that is "not serious." When we say we're "only playing around," or that someone is "just playing," this is exactly what we mean, that it's not serious. If Jake teases Finn too much and hurts Finn's feelings, wouldn't he say, "Relax! I was just playing around, dude!" What Jake is saying there is that it shouldn't be taken personally . . . it was just "playful!"

Huizinga thought that it is this "separateness" from the ordinary world that defines the meaning of play. Play is not "serious," not "real"—it's something separate from the everyday world, and it's exactly because it is separate that it is play. But this doesn't mean that play is just a pointless bit of fun. On the contrary! Huizinga insisted that play was of the utmost importance. Play, he said, lies at the basis of all human culture: art, religion, ritual, and law are all result of our ability to play!

What gives play this amazing power? Huizinga wrote that "all play presents something." In other words: careful! Play is never as innocent as it seems, and it's never just playing around about nothing: all play is about something. When we play, something is being played, and the act of playing creates something that wasn't there before. Many people experience this with *Adventure Time*. At first they may take it really lightly. It's just a playful cartoon, right? But when you really spend some time with it, Pendleton Ward's playful creation makes something really different and powerful.

Hans-Georg Gadamer said something similar about play. Play is always a "presentation." When we play, we are presenting something—to our fellow players, to anyone watching us, but, most importantly, to ourselves. When Finn struggles with growing up or Jake struggles with being a parent, part of what we're seeing is the play of cartoonists and writers, but it's also presenting something that reflects us, that reminds us about the difficult of growing up and the difficulty of raising children.

And what is it that we are presenting? When we "play" something, Gadamer believed, what we are presenting is its "truth." This seems very strange—in fact, it seems like the exact opposite of what we would normally think. Don't we usually think that play is what is not true? Finn and Jake are fake, right? What can they tell us about ourselves and the real world?

When we play, we have to follow the rules of the game. These rules shape our behavior, leading us to move and act according to the patterns of the game. Play is a "patterned movement," something like a dance. When we play something—for example, when we play a role in a game of make-believe—we express it in fixed, rule-bound patterns. Because of this, we transform it into a clear structure that allows its true, essential nature to be revealed.

Finn, the protagonist of these tales of adventure, clearly desires to be a legendary hero. But what does it mean to be a hero? Finn has to work it out for himself, but, luckily, he has a very clear idea: being a hero means embarking on dangerous quests, raiding dungeons, facing monsters and devious traps, obtaining loot and rare magical items, helping innocents and rescuing princesses. This hero's code of conduct that Finn follows determines every aspect of his behavior while he's in hero mode, and he sticks to it religiously. In fact, when Flame Princess refuses to stick to the rules of how a hero should bust out of a dungeon in "Vault of Bones"—flaming her way through traps, obstacles and enemies, rather than patiently trying to find the "right" solution, Finn gets really upset!

Finn is playing a hero in much the same way that anyone might create a hero in a tabletop role-playing game. It's by "playing as" a hero that Finn can genuinely act as a hero, and make himself into one. "Playing" hero reveals to Finn *and to us* truths about what it means to be a hero. As he plays hero he learns more and more about what it means to be a hero. And the fact that he is playing allows for him to make changes and adjustments to his game, as long as he doesn't break the rules!

The same is true whenever the situation calls for a different approach. As all youths do, Finn tries out the roles he has learned and "plays" them according to their fixed rules, following the established patterns of behavior set down by these directions and limitations. When Finn is faced with mysterious events, as in "Mystery Train" or "The Creeps," he drops the role of the questing hero and adopts another, equally familiar, role: that of the detective in a murder-mystery, hunting out clues, interrogating suspects and forming hypotheses. Again, rules determine the situation down to every detail: in "Mystery Train," Finn rejects the first, most obvious suspect, just because, in murder-mysteries, the first suspect never turns out to be the murderer. That's not how the game works.

How Can Something Be What It's Not?

So far, Huizinga and Gadamer have helped us understand that all play is about something, and that something is presented whenever we play. But the philosopher who will be the best help to us in looking at what play means in *Adventure Time* is Eugen Fink (1905–1975). Fink said that play has a very special role in human life. Everything we do, as humans, has a purpose. We study in order to pass our exams. We work because we need to earn a living. We eat and drink to sustain ourselves. We sleep in order to rest for the next day.

Play, however, is different. Play has no purpose—or, rather, it has no purpose outside itself. It is its own purpose. We do not play because we want to get something out of it, but simply because we want to play—the activity of play is its own purpose. This special quality of play makes it stand apart from all other areas of human life, and, because of this, it has the power to help us reflect on our lives and see things differently.

How does this happen? Let's look at a basic example of play in action: what happens when Beemo plays detective? Looking at the scene with our spoilsport common-sense glasses, what we see is a machine walking around as if it is a human talking to chickens who have no idea what the heck is going on! This is undeniably true, but the child in us is already screaming in defiance: "It's not just a chicken, she's Beemo's suspect!" And the good news is: our inner child is completely right

Fink tells us that, when we play, the plaything has "another, mysterious reality." The chicken stops being only an animal that doesn't understand—in Beemo's imagination she becomes Lorraine, a real dangerous suspect with motives and even malice!

No wonder that Fink calls play "magic": it has the capacity to focus the powers of the imagination into the creation of new beings and things that seem to come alive before our eyes as we play. Immanuel Kant (1724–1804), for one, considered the imagination, or "image-making" to be one of the vital ways we make sense of the world, since it allows us to create mental representations of things we perceive in the world. And, influenced by Kant, Samuel Taylor Coleridge (1772–1824) spoke of the productions of the imagination as a "secondary act of creation," a reflection in our minds of the creation of the universe in the mind of God. Is it really that much to think of Ward's creation of *Adventure Time* and all of its facets and intricacies as something like the creation of our universe itself?

It is by drawing on this creative capacity of the imagination that, according to Fink, playthings earn their own particular, troublesome kind of reality. What starts off as play can soon become all too real. When Finn and Jake sit down to play a board game in "Card Wars," the game comes to life before their eyes, their card moves playing out as an animated, magical battle on the table at which they sit. And, in "Guardians of Sunshine," the dangers and enemies in the title's action-adventure videogame become genuinely life-threatening when Finn and Jake enter the world of the game.

But we'll save the most powerful example for last. In "Rainy Day Daydream," Finn and Jake, stuck in their tree house because of a knife storm, fall back on their imagination to come up with a new adventure. Everything seems perfectly fine until the products of Jake's imagination become a little too convincing. Despite Finn's bold proclamations that he can "master reality," and tell the difference between what is real and what is "only play," he soon realizes that Jake's imaginings cannot be so easily dismissed. When Jake imagines that the floor is covered with lava, it genuinely burns Finn, "pretend" though it may be. When we face playthings, we know perfectly well that they are only products of the imagination, that they are not "real," but they can take on a life of their own.

This leaves us with a very strange understanding of play! When we hold a plaything in our hands, we're holding something that is two things at once. Fink was not the first to notice this. The anthropologist Gregory Bateson (1904–1980) wrote that, when we observe animals playing, we see something that's difficult to explain. Two dogs might appear to be fighting, and we might see one dog biting the other dog, until we realize that they were actually play-fighting. This means that the bite we saw was actually only a play-bite—not really a bite at all.

That is the paradox of play. What we are seeing is both a bite and not a bite at the same time. In the same way, when we're children and play with a doll, we believe it to be a real, living child. But at the same time we're also fully aware that it is only a piece of plastic. The fact that it stands apart from ordinary life, by being "not real," means that it is "safe." If something bad happens when we're playing, like if we neglect the doll, and it gets hurt, then we can always say that it's only play and it doesn't really matter. But the fact that we also, on some deep level, genuinely believe the doll to be a real child (despite knowing it's really not) gives play its unique power to hold up a mirror to our life, which is we still feel guilty if we let something bad happen to our toys!

In "All the Little People," Finn is given a magic bag containing miniature, but apparently living, play-versions of the show's cast of characters. At the start of the episode, Finn is lost in thought. Having experienced the woes of unrequited love and the difficulties of maintaining a romantic relationship in his dealings with Princess Bubblegum and the Flame Princess, Finn is perplexed about matters of the heart. As he sits on a cliff with Jake, he is troubled by big questions: what is love? How do you know who's the one?

These are important questions that many teenagers—and adults—will have to tackle. When he starts playing with the lives of the little people, he realizes he can use them to try to find answers to his questions. They represent all the characters in Finn's life, including himself, but, because they're "not real," Finn feels that he can manipulate them as he wishes, playing out all the relationship permutations he can imagine in his attempt to find an answer to the questions that have been troubling him. After all, mini-Finn is not Finn, so it doesn't matter if his heart gets broken.

Still, as we've already said, play has its own, strange reality, and we can't just dismiss it as being "not real" and consequence-free. When Finn makes mini–Lady Rainicorn break up with mini-Jake and fall for mini–Mr. Cupcake, Jake is understandably upset despite Finn's assurances that it's all just a bit of harmless play. Even though the play-version of Lady Rainicorn is not the real Lady Rainicorn, it *represents* her, and in playing out the break-up of her long-term relationship with Jake, Finn is presenting his friend with some pretty troubling imagery. No wonder Jake decides he needs to go away and spend some time with the real Lady Rainicorn. Play showed Jake some very possible consequences before they actually happened.

The Worlds of Play

Play has the power to give a peculiar kind of life to play-things—to make them something they're not. But the magic of play doesn't stop there. Fink tells us that play goes one step further, and it's with this step that its greatest power comes to light. The plaything doesn't just bring this imaginary being into existence, it brings with it a whole other imaginary world.

When the child moves the doll across a table, the table can become a sunny park, or a busy street. Whenever we play, we create a play-world of the imagination, different and separate from the "real" world in which all our other actions take place, but that represents it and comments on it. We can learn things about ourselves, whether we're poor losers, what our fears are, and what we believe a hero should *really* be like. After all, wasn't it Finn's own imaginings of what Billy the Hero *should* be like that lead to his disappointment when he met the real Billy, *and* led Finn to inspire Billy to heroic deeds again?

This means that the play-world holds up a mirror to the real world. That's why, as Fink knew, play is one of the most powerful tools we have for making sense of the world. Play can make us see things in the "real" world in a new way, and can even make us aware of things we never knew about the world—and, crucially, about ourselves. Our play-worlds, like the Land of Ooo, reflect the "real" world. In Ooo, we can trace the mark of aspects of our daily life. But it's not a simple imitation—often, our play-worlds show us how things could be different.

When we play, we don't just play with our toys, we also become a part of the act of play. The player is a member of the play-world. When Beemo plays with the chicken, the chicken changes into Lorraine, and the world around them becomes a truly dangerous and mysterious place, but it's also Beemo who transforms herself. Beemo pretends that she's human and is learning to understand the complexities of human relationships, romances, and deceits in the same way human children take an imaginary role and become themselves a part of the play-world.

We see this when Finn takes on the role of the hero when he plays out his adventures, and how this shapes his understanding of what it means to be a hero. But, there is a particular *Adventure Time* episode which really showcases the power of the play-world, and the ease with which the player can fall down the rabbit-hole of the imagination.

"Puhoy" begins with Finn and Jake building a pillow fort, and it's harder to think of a more emblematic image of the safe, concealed, sheltered space of childhood imagination than a pillow-fort. As in "All the Little People," it's Finn's relationship issues that spur this escape into make-believe, with our protagonist having realized, through obsessing over a seemingly unimportant event, that maintaining a relationship takes a lot of work, and causes a heavy emotional toll.

This time, the escape into the other-world of play becomes even more total and radical. When Finn is alone in the pillow fort, he finds a doorway that leads, Narnia-style, into a whole new imagined world—a Pillow World, complete with pillow-people and a blanket dragon. The humble pillow-fort has become the gateway to a complete play-world that stretches as far as the eye can see. Finn's immersion in this secondary world is complete—with the door back to Ooo vanishing behind him, he has no way of returning to the "real" world. For the rest of the episode, Finn lives out a complete alternate life in the Pillow World, growing up into a man, marrying Rosalinen, the mayor's daughter, having two pillow-children and, gradually, growing old and arriving at his deathbed surrounded by his loving family. He even renounces the "real" world in his old age, deciding that his place is with this Pillow World family.

The Pillow World is a dizzying example of how immersive play can prove to be when taken to its fullest extreme. Finn lives out a complete, secondary alternate life, one that, for the duration of play, entirely eclipses his "real" life and becomes primary. You might say, "But Pillow World was real!" And to that I reply, "Yes!" But not just because it might actually be an alternate dimension, because, even if Finn "only" imagined it up, it was real enough, he learned from it, and even if he doesn't remember it, his experiences with Pillow World changed him.

All Played Out

"Puhoy" paints a vivid image of everything we've said about the meaning and importance of play. When it ends, we're left with many troubling questions, and no easy answers. How real are Rosalinen and Finn's pillow-family? What happens to them when Finn leaves the Pillow World and returns to the "real" world? How does Finn's playing-out this play-narrative of committed love reflect his real-world emotional difficulties in his relationship with Flame Princess? How is Finn changed when he returns to the "real" world at the end of the episode, having lived out a full play-world life? Does he bear the mark of his play experiences?

One thing is certain. After watching *Adventure Time*, it's very hard to keep thinking of play as something that's "not serious" and that has no purpose or consequence. Finn and Jake's escapades show us what Huizinga, Gadamer, Bateson, and Fink spoke about. In them, we see the unique power of play in action. We see how play is always about something, and that whatever play touches is touched by a strange kind of magic. Whenever we play something, we see it in a new light, and learn things about it we never knew before. And this is because the productions of our imagination in the act of playing, the wonderful people and endless worlds of play, are not real, but they are also not not real. They have their own, special play-existence, and they can change our understanding of the "real" world. Finn and Jake's playful adventures teach us many things that we should take with *real* seriousness, like what it means to be a good parent, a true hero, and a lonely child, and those are lessons we take with us when the TV turns off, we leave Ooo, and return home.

20
A Buff Baby Who Can Puncha Yo' Buns

M. BLANKIER

Finn, riding to the rescue astride a massive Jake, finds Princess Bubblegum in grave danger. The Ice King has trapped PB in a glacial cage. Ice King zaps ice bolts at Finn and Jake while he laughs maniacally! "You can't save her this time, Finn! My Wizard's cage is too strong! Its bars are unbendable, like month-old, unwashed underwear! She will become my frozen princess-icle and love me forever!" Finn swings down next to the cage, frantic. Princess Bubblegum reaches out to Finn futilely; she's turning blue. She won't be able to withstand the cold much longer!

Finn swings his sword at the bars, but nothing happens. He looks over his shoulder to see Jake dodging and snaking around the Ice King, trying to catch the mad wizard off guard. Ice King just continues to zap away, gleefully.

"Idea!" Finn yells out. "Mathematical! . . . Jake, keep it up, but swing over here!"

"What?! But the Ice King might zap you, Bro!"

"No he won't. I'm too heroic for that! But he might hit the bars of the cage!

"Whoa, Bro, good plan!" Jake continues to dodge and duck, but makes his way to the front of the ice cage as Finn ducks out of the way. BAM! Ice King, who really should have been eavesdropping on the boys' plan, zaps the bars of the cage, and Princess Bubblegum falls out, free! Finn gently catches her in his arms.

"Oh, blast!" laments the defeated wizard.

PB places her arms around Finn's neck, and the two seem about to kiss . . . finally. Suddenly, Finn drops PB, turns to the forlorn Ice King and embraces him passionately. As the Ice King and Finn kiss

deeply, Jake only shakes his head and mutters to himself, "Well, I guess the old man is kind of cute . . ."
Whaaaat????

That doesn't sound right, does it? Well, what if you replaced "Finn" with "Fionna" and "Jake" with "Cake"? Does that make it all better? When our hero embraces the evil wizard, it seems a lot less problematic when they fit the gender roles we are comfortable with. . . . Finn's a man, well a boy, right? And he should act like one! But what does that mean?

As (probably) the only human left on Earth after the Great Mushroom War, Finn's got a lot of responsibility on his shoulders. Whether he's saving princesses, protecting the Candy People from a zombie onslaught, or, in one case, preserving the delicate sensibilities of a sensitive mountain, Finn's a hero, a protector, and Princess Bubblegum's knight in shining armor.

Finn walks in the path of the well-tread Hero Myth. He joins a long line of masculine warrior-types who've come before him, beginning with the many adventures and romances of questing knights-for-hire from medieval poetry, and Japanese tales of samurai and ninjas. There are lots of versions of this myth: the cowboys and pioneers of the Western and the gumshoes of detective stories are some examples. But the action heroes of the 1980s and 1990s, and even the heroes of role-playing games like *Dungeons and Dragons* and *Legend of Zelda*, are also part of the Hero Myth. This tradition of heroic men is a rich and diverse one, and Finn is a worthy addition to it. As a lively, impulsive kid with an irrepressible spirit—he's got so much energy that he can actually power an underground world-flipping machine—Finn seems to be a classic example of bouncy, bubbly boyhood.

But one of the many things *Adventure Time* does really well is the slow reveal of complex details behind its deceptively simple appearance. As the show goes on and Finn experiences life as a growing teenager, we see him struggle to cope with the burdens placed on his shoulders. The Season Five episodes "Davey" and "Puhoy" are especially good examples of Finn trying to find ways to escape the weight of expectations that go along with being a hero. In "Davey," Finn creates an alter ego, "Davey Johnson," a normal guy with a normal job, so that "no one can bother him about being Finn." In "Puhoy," Finn escapes to a dream world of pillow people where he can start over as a family man. And it's not just these episodes that reveal how hard it is to be a guy. Finn may be an archetypal hero, but over the course of the series, he's forced to learn again and again that being a hero—or even just being a man—is a lot more complicated than roughhousing with Vikings and being nice to ladies.

So what does it mean to be a man?

Princesses and Kings

If I had beautiful shiny hair, no one would look at my muscles!

—Muscle Princess

Since we're asking what it means to be a man, it makes sense to ask, what does it mean to be a woman? Am I manly if I like to fight and go on adventures? Or womanly if I'm all about the lumps? Both as individuals and as societies, we find ourselves constantly butting up against the gender expectations of our cultures. The growth of feminism over the nineteenth and twentieth centuries has led modern Western culture to face (if not ignore) many of the inequalities that exist between men and women in society. As studies in feminism have evolved and changed, it seems natural for questions about women's roles to become questions about the roles of women *and* men in society. These questions have a lot to do with questions of power: what power means, who has it, and who doesn't have it.

Adventure Time spends a lot of time asking these questions. Sometimes, it plays easily into the traditional expectations we the audience bring to the show. Other times, *Adventure Time* shows us answers we don't expect. In the Land of Ooo, for example, political power is held almost entirely by women. Princess Bubblegum is not only the leader of the Candy Kingdom, but she is its creator and primary representative as well as a generally Very Important Person in Ooo. There is no Candy Prince or King. Marceline is the Vampire Queen, and though she's had boyfriends, she's the chief holder of vampire political power.

There are minor kings scattered across Ooo—the Ice King, King Worm, the Fight King—but their domains are small, and they are really more of a nuisance than major power players. Outside of Ooo, though, the underworld and outer realms are governed, or at least controlled, by men: Hunson Abadeer in the Nightosphere, Lumpy Space King in Lumpy Space, and the Flame King in the Fire Kingdom (until he's overthrown by Flame Princess). It seems fair to say that political power in *Adventure Time* isn't obviously biased towards men or women.

On the other hand, all of Ooo's various fighters, warriors, and guardians are definitely male. Men like to roughhouse and compare armor. They like to fight just for the sake of fighting, and they're quick to make fun of Finn when he shows any weakness. "Blood Under the Skin" is a Season Two episode in which Finn tries desperately to recover from being continually embarrassed in front of a very manly knight, Sir Slicer. But Sir Slicer ends up looking pretty ridiculous himself by following a kid around all day to prove his own manliness, while Jake saves the day wearing lady armor: a hero doesn't always need to *look* the part of a manly man. Finn learns another similar lesson about heroism in "Ocean of Fear": heroes can have fears and flaws, and still be brave.

Another big part of traditional gender roles is *behaving* the way we as women or men are *expected* to behave. On the outside, Princess Bubblegum seems like a traditionally feminine character: for one thing, she's pink, a color we think of as feminine. From time to time, she needs a hero to rescue her. These seem like traditionally 'feminine' traits, sure. But she's also totally unsentimental. Being sentimental seems like *kind* of a feminine thing, right? Princess Bubblegum also has no interest in romance, and has devoted her life to governance and science. So, . . . definitely not 'traditionally' feminine.

Jake and Lady Rainicorn also behave in interesting ways when dealing with their puppies. Jake is terrified that the pups will suddenly die or get into serious trouble, while Lady sits back and happily lets the puppies make mistakes on their own. Where we would expect Jake, normally a cool, collected sort of guy, to be a hands-off father, he instead acts like a total helicopter parent.

Fine, so, men and women can both rule, they can both be embarrassed . . . so what? Well, if men and women can do the same things, and behave in the same ways, then what's the difference between being a man versus being a woman?

Biology and Ideology

Did you take a bath in rainbows and cupcakes?

—JAKE

At this point, you may be thinking that the answer's pretty obvious: there's a basic biological difference between men and women. The feminist philosopher Judith Butler agrees that this answer does seem obvious . . . too obvious. So let's do Princess Bubblegum proud and have a bit of Science Time!

In her book *Gender Trouble*, Butler talks about an experiment from 1987 in which a group of MIT scientists tried to discover a "master gene" that determines an individual's sex. In this experiment, researchers took DNA samples from people who had been medically assigned a particular sex—individuals who were considered men because they had penises, and others who were considered women because they had vaginas—but had the chromosomes of the *other* sex—men with penises and XX chromosomes, and women with vaginas and XY chromosomes. Butler finds a lot of problems with the experiment. First, the subjects are called "male" or "female" based on their external genitalia, but not their *internal* function (none of the subjects could produce sperm or egg cells). More importantly, the researchers were trying to prove that men have a specific gene sequence that was "missing" or "passive" in women.

Butler says that while sex can be biologically determined most of the time, we bring a lot of cultural ideas to sex and gender: for example, that women are "passive," or "missing" something that men have. She says that *cultural conventions* that are associated with external genitalia are the only thing that led the team of researchers to decide that a person with an unclear biological sex is a man or a woman. But is this good enough? What if a "man," with an XY chromosome, loses his penis in a violent explosion during a battle? Or what if a "woman," with an XX chromosome, must have an operation to remove her reproductive organs? Sure, an unclear sex is unusual, but Butler points out that it is the unusual that calls our attention to the things we normally take for granted. Namely, what we're taking for granted, here, is that *man* and *woman* are somehow *opposites*; a person *must be one or the other, man or woman, at least so we think!*

We can see this in play in *Adventure Time*. We can probably take for granted that Finn and Jake (among others) are boys and Marceline and Princess Bubblegum (among others) are girls. We don't really need to see the evidence (children watch the show, after all). But what about the King and Queen of Lumpy Space? They share one body! How can we call that body male or female? We have no way of expressing what they are, because they're both male and female at the same time. What about Flame King? He's a flame! In a suit! And we usually don't think of fire as male or female (well, I don't, anyway). The point here is not to say that we need proof, or that we're being misled by the show's creators, or that it's impossible for a flame to be male (or wear a suit). But in the *Adventure Time* universe, where anything is possible, why are there only two possible sexes? This brings back the earlier idea that the difference between men and women is obvious. But it only *seems* obvious because people have for centuries assumed that penis = man, vagina = woman.

To complicate things some more, sex and gender are two separate ideas. Sex is biological, but gender is created by cultural expectations and meaning. Butler says that even if you take for granted that there are only two possible sexes, you can't assume gender from sex at all. For example, a person can seem "manly" to us in every possible way—that person can be muscular, tough, unsentimental, and so on—except that they have a woman's genitalia. We should also remember that the two genders that we take for granted today have changed a lot over centuries, over decades or even years, and from culture to culture. We can easily say that our modern ideas of "masculinity" and "femininity" are constantly being changed. A few decades ago, a lovesick guy like Finn would have been considered feminine, and an independent, sword-wielding gal like Fionna would have seemed unnatural.

Gender theorist Todd W. Reeser says that one of the best ways to think about masculinity and femininity is to consider them "ideologies," or systems of ideas and beliefs that affect our behavior. Ideologies are deep-rooted in our culture. We find their expression in language, politics, and mass media. Often, we buy into these ideologies and without even realizing it: these ideologies seem totally natural to us. The question then becomes: how much do we buy into *these* ideologies on a daily basis? Just how much do the cultural ideas associated with being a man or a woman make up our own identities? And if being a man or woman is a cultural idea and not something "natural," does that mean our identities are also created by culture, or are they "natural" too?

Adventure Time addresses this question in an interesting way in the Season Four episode "Goliad." Princess Bubblegum creates Goliad, an immortal cat-like clone of herself from one of her baby teeth so that, in some form, she can continue to rule the Candy People even after death. Other than her mondomama brains and pink color, Goliad isn't necessarily similar to Princess Bubblegum. Instead, Goliad is something of a blank slate: she tells Finn and Jake that she's excited to learn what they have to teach her about life. But she misinterprets Jake's lesson about cooperation and quickly becomes a ruthless tyrant, using her psychic powers to take over Princess Bubblegum's castle. To fight her, Princess Bubblegum creates Stormo, a clone of Finn (with a feline body and an eagle's head). With Finn's "heroic DNA," Stormo is born a good guy. Without hesitation, he sacrifices himself to keep Goliad in check for eternity. Finn's behaviors—his sense of self-sacrifice and his desire to do good—are part of his DNA. Finn and Stormo don't choose to be heroic: they just *are* heroes.

In Goliad and Stormo, we see two different ways that character and identity can develop: Goliad *becomes* selfish and tyrannical, while Stormo is *naturally* selfless. Is it possible that these qualities are split along gender lines—males are born to be good, while females are more impressionable and less innately heroic? It's possible, but when we look at Finn himself, it's obvious that the expectations of manly behavior weigh much more heavily on him than they do on his clone.

Acting Manly

A bumbling baby beau bereft of bravado

—JAY T. DOGGZONE

Butler explains that, rather than being born a man or a woman, language and culture create reality. Finn isn't a "hero" in any sort of automatic way, but everyone calls him that. Being called a "hero" over and over is what makes Finn a hero; *language determines who Finn is.* And because the word "hero" has so many pre-existing ideas already attached to it—in Ooo, as in our world, the expectation is that a hero is manly, strong, and fights evil—Finn acts out those expectations in his daily life. The Land of Ooo may be full of the unexpected, but Finn himself, as written by writers at the beginning of the twenty-first century, both meets and responds to contemporary Western culture's own ideas of masculinity and heroism.

Finn's own hero is Billy, a giant man who slew an evil ocean, defeated the Lich, fought a bear, and has his own theme song. Finn's idolization of Billy combines with the cultural and linguistic associations of the word "hero" to determine Finn's behavior. Even when Billy encourages Finn to help out his community without violence, Finn shows that violence is "awesome," and restores Billy's heart. Butler would say that Finn is "performing" masculinity. In other words, he's acting the way he believes a heroic, masculine person acts. In doing this, Finn makes the ideas that he (and we) attach to heroism and masculinity seem totally natural.

Many other characters in *Adventure Time* perform in the same way. Mannish Man, the minotaur and guardian of the *Enchiridion*, is so manly (it's right there in his name—twice!) that when he flexes his enormous muscles, each muscle flexes its own little muscles. Joshua, Finn and Jake's dad, calls Finn a whiny baby and makes a dungeon just for Finn, so that Finn can "toughen up." Mannish Man and Joshua are both satirical examples of manliness: they're over the top, and in Joshua's case, flat-out wrong about manliness. But these characters are partly meant to call our attention to our preconceived ideas about masculinity and how silly or even harmful those ideas can sometimes be.

Finn still buys into our traditional ideologies about masculinity, and as the series progresses, we see that he is buckling more and more under its weight. When he tries to teach other characters about the "proper"—that is, the expected—way to do things like be nice ("Donny"), romance ladies ("Slow Love"), and explore dungeons ("Vault of Bones"), those other characters end up showing him that his way isn't the only way. Even before Finn starts creating different, non-heroic lives for himself in "Davey" and "Puhoy," he reveals how exhausted he is by expectations, and how frustrated he is by the lack of control he has over his own life.

In "Who Would Win," Finn tells Jake that spending time with other people sometimes feels like a chore, while in "All the Little People," Finn abandons his own life and spends months watching the lives of tiny toy Ooo people, controlling their relationships and acting godlike. Sometimes, Finn responds to the strains of being heroic by embracing traditional masculinity so tightly that he doesn't even care about the consequences: in the Season Six episode "Dungeon Train," Finn hops on an endless train with compartments full of bad guys and tells Jake that he never wants to leave, because "stuff makes sense here." While he tries to bolster himself and draw strength through these exaggerated performances of masculinity, we may yet see him only more frustrated by them.

Finn alternates between rejecting the role of the manly hero or embracing it in an over-the-top, destructive way, revealing a young man who's deeply conflicted about who he is and what it means to be both a man and a hero. We can call this tension, between the way Finn sometimes wants to behave when he rejects expectation, "the subjective," and the way he sometimes feels he should behave, "the objective," a *crisis of masculinity*. Finn finds himself torn between what society says a man is, and the *person* he is. It's hard to see a complete resolution to this tension. Finn, and by extension we, will always have our own experiences that make us different from how society dictates we should be.

Finn's Awakening

The sword is after my flesh!

—FINN

But there's some hope for Finn as he tries to find himself, without having to just be what society wants him to be. First, of course, there is Finn's faithful sidekick, Jake. Jake's often unfocussed and sandwich-obsessed, and not always without his own issues, but he helps Finn understand that the way things *seem* is not always how they *are*.

Finn never wants to leave the Dungeon Train: he can battle and win loot forever, without the pressure of having to actually save anyone. Finn compares being on the train to polishing off a batch of Jake's delicious biscuits. But Jake explains that Finn only liked his biscuits so much because they were full of butter, and you can't really live on buttery biscuits forever; you need real food, real sustenance, and variety to be healthy. The train is "just butter."

The Season Six episodes "Grass Blade" and "The Vault" do something a little different, and show Finn a couple of ways he can free himself, at least in part, from the weight of social expectation, and that he can be masculine in his own way. In "The Vault," Finn's haunted by a ghost whose existence he's stored in his memory vault, where he puts the stuff he "can't handle." But he soon learns that the ghost is his own past life: Shoko, a female mercenary, an orphan girl who is tough, independent, and, like Finn, conflicted about herself and the person she's become.

After Finn helps Shoko resolve her ghostly problems by returning the amulet she stole from Princess Bubblegum decades (centuries?) before, he says, "My vault feels lighter." He may not yet realize that Shoko's struggles have a parallel to his own search for identity, but it may be a step towards resolving his identity conflict. And the metaphor in "Grass Blade" seems pretty obvious, especially when you think about the fact that Finn is thirteen—right around puberty! Okay, I'll spell it out for you . . . Finn buys a new sword . . . the grass blade has "a mind of its own" and fuses to his body, standing at attention in response to Finn's thoughts (oh, my!). At first, Finn's nervous, but as he learns how to use the sword to its best advantage, having the grass sword as a part of him for all eternity is pretty cool—once he's accepted it, he can control it.

Finn is learning that being a "man" is something he has to determine for himself. But he has to be careful because there are always others who are going to try to decide what that means for him. Princess Bubblegum often represents the pressure society puts on Finn and us to blindly do and be whatever society wants. But, often, what society wants isn't what is always best. Think of how many women and men have been harmed by the way we define "manly!" Heck, men aren't supposed to cry (or else be called babies!) But not confronting our emotions, even those we think we shouldn't have, can lead to all kinds of problems. And maybe even worse, we think crying is a weakness, but we *expect it* from women—like they are supposed to be weak! (Don't tell that to Muscle Princess.)

If Finn really wants to be happy, he has to face who he really is, without worrying who will call him "girly," "a baby," or even "lumpy." By embracing and resolving his troubled inner life with the appearance and performance of masculinity, Finn can be a hero in a greater, truer way: *his own.*[1]

----

[1] I owe a huge debt of gratitude to Mike Blankier, Aaron Feldman, Darius Fox, Dennis Gonzales, Miles Link, Asher Novek, Ben Spergel, Dan Tooley, and of course, Nicolas Michaud! Thanks for Feedback and Editing Time! You're all extremely mathematical.

21
Beemo Unplugged

CHRISTOPHER KETCHAM

*F*inn and Jake are happily playing with Beemo. Pixelated characters fight and run across her screen as the boys laugh and elbow each other.

"I've got you now . . . 16-BIT CRUSHING SPIN COMBO TIME!" yells Finn, jumping up as he moves in for the win.

"No way, you don't! ARG . . . CABBAGE!" shouts Jake, the perpetually bad loser, yanking Beemo's cord just a little too hard as we see her wince. "That was an illegal move!"

"Was not!"

"Was too!"

The boys are about to beat some buns when Beemo deftly deflates the situation. In her awkward and somewhat robotic English, she asks, "Who wants scrambled eggs?"

"Yeah!" The boys exclaim in unison, high-fiving each other.

"That's a great idea, Beemo!"

Our heroes sit down for egg sandwiches, once again laughing as Beemo cooks. They hear delicate footsteps enter the tree house and turn around, surprised at the arrival of Princess Bubblegum in her full science research gear.

"Good, I'm glad you're all here. Will you two do me a favor and turn off the BMO? I'd like to take her apart and figure out how she works; that way, we can make lots more of her.

"A machine that can pretend to think is a very impressive technological feat! And I'd like to know how she does such a good job of appearing to be an intelligent machine. After all, there must be a scientific explanation for how she works, and it's up to us to figure it out! Of course, she won't survive the process. But that's what

*machines are for . . . To serve us, right? Okay," she continues
while pulling out a menacing looking hacksaw, "Who wants to do
the honors?"*

We know Beemo is a boxy thing that speaks in a Korean accent
and cooks eggs. We know she (or he?) is a video and game
player, and has a cracked screen-face. . . . But come on now, isn't
there something about Beemo that makes her as intelligent as
the other human-like residents of Ooo, not just a "pretend"
intelligence? Isn't her intelligence like the princesses and the
Ice King or Finn the human or even egg-cooking Jake? Or, is
Beemo just a modified Gameboy?

We know that Beemo has the physical attributes of some
kind of machine-box: drawers, screen, and plugs and buttons,
but also arms and legs, or something like arms and legs. We
understand from "Be More" that when you look inside her she's
got a medal, a heart, and a diploma like the Wizard of Oz gave
the Cowardly Lion, the Tin Man, and the Scarecrow. But does
that diploma mean that Beemo is as smart as a human? Some
of you will ask, "Why does it matter?" Well it matters to Beemo.
. . . After all, if she's intelligent, doesn't she deserve to be
treated with some of the respect and dignity we automatically
give humans and, yes, the other people who live in Ooo? Or is
she just fodder for an over-zealous scientist's hacksaw?

The Singularity

Okay, let's say, since there may only be one human left in Ooo,
that it doesn't matter what Beemo is; what matters is whether
Beemo is as intelligent a being as, say, Finn. Whether she's
physically human is not nearly as important as whether or not
she's actually intelligent, or is it?

But first we have to define "intelligent." Techno-geeks are
clamoring for the advent of the "Singularity," the moment
when machine intelligence exceeds our own. So, when IBM's
Deep Blue beat Chess Grand Master Garry Kasparov in
1997 or when IBM's Watson won on Jeopardy in 2011 was
either of these the moment? Well, Deep Blue could only play
chess, not cook eggs, and Watson was just a disembodied
answer. Beemo is mobile and can also speak. But is that
enough?

Breaking the Intelligence Code

How do we figure out whether Beemo is genuinely intelligent and not just "smart" technology? (Smart technology like a sophisticated videorecorder that just responds to inputs and outputs that make it seem like it's responding to our questions). Alan Turing thought he could answer that question. Turing, a World War II code breaker, is considered by many to be the father of modern computing. Turing developed algorithms and memory storage concepts we still use today.

In 1950 Turing devised what has been called the "Turing Test" to find out whether an "artificial intelligence" was actually thinking, intelligent.[1] So how would you give this test to Beemo? Say you hide Beemo in another room. You ask her questions and see what the answers are. If they sound like something an intelligent human-like being would make, give credit to Beemo as having a human-like intelligence. But, if she answers like a machine might, without emotion or empathy, well you're talking to a "smart" machine, aren't you? You and I know some people who are stiff and mechanical, but wouldn't you know the difference? That's the idea of Turing's test.

In other words, if the machine can fool you into thinking it's a human, then shouldn't you think the intelligence it displays is "real" rather than just "pretend" intelligence? Turing thought this was a good test because it really is the test we use on each other. The reason why I think the humans I am speaking with are living, thinking people is because they respond to what I say in ways that make sense. When we speak, you show understanding of my questions, concerns for my worries, and empathy for my emotions. In other words, if we only *heard* Beemo, or read what she said over text messaging, wouldn't we assume she was a human—a human who could *really* think? Well then, says Turing, why not just assume she's intelligent? Give her the benefit of the doubt in the same way I do with you! After all, I can't hear the thoughts in your head; I just assume that they are there because of our conversation!

But the only way Turing left us to determine whether something has human-like intelligence is questioning. In other words, through conversation. You couldn't put the machine through its

---

[1] "Computing Machinery and Intelligence."

paces in an actual setting, say for example, make it re-enact a love scene in a play. Turing was not willing to handicap the machine because of its physical limitations. Remember, in Turning's time computers were room-size machines that could not move and had no audible voice. But Beemo can move, can talk, and can interact one-on-one with humans in the human world, well at least the Ooo world. Is conversation the test of human-like intelligence for Beemo, or do we need to know more?

What kind of relationship could you have with Beemo? Let's make it slightly different. . . . What if Beemo, instead of being a boxy thing, looked human? What would you think then? Is intelligence just lots of smarts or is it also emotion and empathy? . . . Or is it *looks* too? Because Beemo seems to display intelligence *and* emotion. So is the only reason why we think she isn't "really" intelligent is because *she isn't human?* How would you know the difference between the really high-quality human-appearing android and a human if both were crying in front of you? Would a Turing Test alone make the case? This was the problem facing the protagonist of Philip K. Dick's novel, *Do Androids Dream of Electric Sheep?* He had to kill human-looking androids that had gone wrong, while avoiding killing any real humans, no matter how lacking in emotion some of these might be.

I ask you, "Can you have empathy for Beemo?" And is Beemo an intelligent being, intelligent enough that she could have empathy for you?

Turing It On

So, let's conduct a modified Turing Test and see what we can find out from questioning alone. We are not going to put Finn (the human) in one room and Beemo in another and disguise their voices when we ask them the same question to determine which one might be a machine. I think we can agree that Beemo is some kind of machine, though with the progress we have made with human prosthetic devices and artificial organs, that distinction may be difficult to make in the future. So what we want to look at is whether we can determine whether Beemo has human-like intelligence from questioning alone.

We're going to go through episode after episode after episode to find places where Beemo has a solo act or interacts with other characters in Adventure Time. . . . Well, I will do this for you. I will then ask Beemo a question about a scene in the episode or about something in general and you will see Beemo's response. In the end, we should both have a better idea about whether Beemo has human-like intelligence—at least I hope we will.

Are you ready? For some of you this round of questioning may sound like the Inquisition. However, Beemo was a willing participant.

The Test

CHRIS: Beemo, do you have any relatives?

BEEMO: Football!

CHRIS: Is Football, whom we met in "Five Short Grables," a relative or a friend?

BEEMO: Football is my friend. Football is like me.

CHRIS: Is Football a boy or girl?

BEEMO: Football is like me.

CHRIS: Are you a boy or a girl?

BEEMO: Sometimes I am a boy. Sometimes I am a girl.

CHRIS: In "Five Short Grables" you were a little boy. And in "James Baxter the Horse" in the scene "BMO's Pregnant Song," you were a girl, weren't you? So what are you really?

BEEMO: Now I am a boy. But I can be a girl if you want.

CHRIS: Okay, we'll move on. When Jake burst your Bubble in "BMO Lost" what did you feel?

BEEMO: I cried and cried.

CHRIS: But what did you feel?

BEEMO: Like crying.

CHRIS: Okay, in the same episode Bubble asked you to marry it, so how did you feel?

BEEMO: Oh I did I did I did!

CHRIS: Did what?

BEEMO: Want to marry Bubble.

CHRIS: Was that how you felt?

BEEMO: Yes.

CHRIS: Okay, then your burst Bubble came back as air and said to you, "Nooo, see that's what's so great. Now we can be together forever, BMO, every minute of every day. No more privacy, no more quiet, no more alone. Every room you ever go in, I'll already be there . . . waiting . . . forever and ever, until the end of time." How did you feel then?

BEEMO: I said Yaaaay and made a big smile and waved my arms up and down.

CHRIS: You cried again in "BMO's Pregnant Song" when the butterfly knocked your egg to the ground and broke it. How did you feel then?

BEEMO: I was singing and dancing and then I was crying over the broken egg. The butterfly was very pretty.

CHRIS: Fine. Okay, now in "Holly Jolly Secrets Part I," you, Jake, and Finn hid from the Ice King because you didn't want to see him. Then your 'Finn's bath time' alarm went off. Can't you control the alarm function?

BEEMO: But it was Finn's bath time! Jake and Finn pressed my buttons and it was okay again.

CHRIS: Alright. When you are a game console, what is it like?

BEEMO: Like being a game console. What is it like for you?

CHRIS: I've never been a game console, so that's why I asked. Can you tell me more?

BEEMO: Well, it's like a game, being a game, like being a game console.

CHRIS: Sure. Okay, in "BMO Noir" you said that Lorraine was, 'red hot like pizza supper' and you blushed. So, do you have a relationship with Lorraine?

BEEMO: So, it depends on what the meaning of the word 'is' is.

CHRIS: What?

BEEMO: It's what Bill Clinton said. I stand by what Bill Clinton said.

CHRIS: I get it. But Lorraine mentioned in the same episode that the missing sock was in 'our secret grown-up kissing spot'. What did Lorraine mean by that?

BEEMO: What would it mean other than it is a secret grown-up kissing spot? For grownups. For kissing. It was where the sock was. That's all it was.

CHRIS: Just a few more questions. Okay?

BEEMO: Yaaaay.

CHRIS: In "We Fixed a Truck" when Jake asked you if you knew how to fix a truck you said no.

BEEMO: Nope.

CHRIS: No?

BEEMO: I said nope.

CHRIS: Oh. Well anyway suddenly you seem to know a lot about fuel-air mixtures and aerodynamics and stuff. Where did that come from?

BEEMO: It just did. Where do your questions come from?

CHRIS: Fair enough. Just one more line of inquiry. I am going to the "Be More" episode. In it you had a glitch. What was that?

BEEMO: Like a stutter but it isn't a stutter. I needed new system drivers! I had to go home where I was born to be fixed.

CHRIS: Like to a doctor?

BEEMO: No, to the MO factory. I know the way there.

CHRIS: I see. Do you have a father and mother, then?

BEEMO: Mo built me.

CHRIS: Mo in the Mo Co is a human, right?

BEEMO: Yes. I was built to take care of Mo's son but Mo never had a son.

CHRIS: How does that make you feel?

BEEMO: Without a Mo Boy to take care of.

CHRIS: I think we're done, Beemo. Thank you for taking the time to take the Turing Test. You are free to go.

BEEMO: Yaaaay.

Now let's think about the answers Beemo gives. . . . Because she sure seems to avoid the questions about her emotions, right? Think about it like this, if someone asked you how you felt when something bad happened, you might say, "I felt like crying" just like Beemo might. But if someone asked you why you felt like crying you'd say, "Because I was sad." So does that mean you feel emotion and Beemo doesn't? Maybe. But what if I asked you, "What does it mean to feel 'sad'?" You'd probably say, "Well feeling 'sad' means feeling like crying." And we'd just go around in a circle! It's really hard to put emotions in terms beyond the words we've been taught. When we cried as children people told us, "Oh, you must be sad!" so we learned to attach that word, 'sad', to whatever we were feeling while crying, though no one *knew* for sure that we were sad. That's why it's really confusing, still, when a happy person is crying!

Maybe Beemo, like any child, is trying to figure out what it means to feel emotions and how to express them, except *we*, her makers, told her that she doesn't feel them! Notice when she says it to the *very* annoying Donny, "I am incapable of emotion, but you are making me chafed!" If we asked Beemo, "Why are you chafed?" Wouldn't she say, "Because Donny is annoying!"? But if we asked her, if she "feels" chafed, she'd say, "I am incapable of emotion." That's like the difference between "feeling sad" and "being sad." Or maybe even like the difference between "being sad" and "crying because "my egg broke." Is there a difference?

Your Turing Test

Now it's your turn. What do you think? Can you have empathy for Beemo? Could you be Beemo's friend? How would Beemo respond to your friendship entreaties? And, does Beemo have human-like intelligence? Can you answer all these questions from Beemo's interrogation, er, inquiry alone? Let's dig a little deeper.

We know that the Mo Co designed Beemo to be a companion. How good a job did they do in that? Would Beemo make a good companion to a child? So, if you were the child's mother would you put restrictions (besides limiting tube watching!) on companion Beemo and Beemo's interaction with your child? If you say none, why none? Come now, ask yourself, Is Beemo mature enough to be an adult-like companion to a small child? But how does that relate to intelligence, you ask? Certainly children learn; couldn't machines be programmed to learn? If a machine can learn, perhaps with an infinite capacity to learn new things, is that not like what humans can do? But, of course, the ultimate question for you, Mom, is whether Beemo is mature enough today to be a child's companion without restrictions. The same applies to other children and even to some adults, does it not? So does being immature mean lack of intelligence, human-like intelligence?

And there's the whole issue of Beemo's gender confusion—well is that really an issue any more? But how solid is Beemo's conception of love and romance? Can a machine love, be truly empathetic towards another being? Can we ever build an algorithm for that, or will there always be a limitation of the physical in the machine? I realize that the easy answer is "no." But remember there is already an excellent example of a machine (an arrangement of matter that does work) that can think and feel . . . You! You are proof, even though we can't actually "hear" your thoughts, that matter in the world can be arranged so that it can feel love, anger, confusion, hunger for burritos. . . . Right?

You might say, "But I also have a soul!" Okay, but how do you know Beemo doesn't have a soul? Couldn't Glob (or God if you prefer) give any machine (whether built like us or not) a soul if it wants? Aren't you the best proof that Glob does, at least on occasion, decide to give intelligence to machines? You are proof that inert matter . . . protons, neutrons, electrons, can be arranged to make something that can think and feel all kinds of stuff!

Are we just biased because Beemo isn't human? Could you love Beemo and could Beemo love you back? Is love no more than what you think or say, or does love also require the physical? And if so, what does that mean for Beemo and love? If the physical is not an issue, would you, could you, ever love the box? If not, then, in your eyes, could Beemo ever hope to have human-like intelligence?

Children animate stuffed animals as they play. Is Beemo just another sophisticated stuffed animal—a toy? Certainly you, the mother, would have empathy for your child playing, but would you also have empathy for the toy? So, even though the toy is smart because it can do lots of stuff, something has to trigger empathy and emotional attachment, a moment of realization that this other is another with intelligence and emotional capacity like me even though it doesn't look like me.

You Be the Judge

So, at the end, what do you think? I know you would like to ask a thousand more questions. I know I would, but we ran out of time. So, what will it be?

Beemo is intelligent!

Beemo is faking it; open her up, let's see what makes him tick! Mom, where's my hacksaw?

What's a Beemo?

V

For Righteous
Eyes Only

22
Finn's No Hero!

SCOTT FOREST AIKIN

Princess Bubblegum holds up in the dim light a magical globe. Finn's eyes grow large in its luminance.

". . . It's a book meant only for heroes whose hearts are righteous . . ."

With those words still ringing in Finn's ears, Finn and Jake begin their quest to Mount Cragdor. As they adventure, numerous perils confront them, and Finn seems up to the task . . . mostly. Finn shows great strength and ingenuity, when suddenly, a massive lumbering ogre eats Jake, but Finn kicks the ogre in the stomach and saves his friend. And he shows great compassion when confronted with a dark magician who he kicks in the crotch to save an ant. . . . But Finn does leave a few old ladies to die when he runs away . . .

In the end, though, the boy hero beams as the manly minotaur hands him the Enchiridion. *Within it are the secrets meant only for true heroes.*

"You're the goodest of heart and most righteous hero I've seen here. Tenderness, ingenuity, bravery, nard-kicking ability . . ."

And isn't it really there that our story begins?

Finn faces the trials to test if he's really a righteous hero, and after a shaky start (mostly the deserting old women being killed by evil gnomes part), he passes the tests and receives the *Enchiridion* for being the most righteous hero Mannish Man ever met. . . . Awwww, Yeah!

But there are two things I've got to know. The first is: what makes Finn righteous? Why is it that he deserves the *Enchiridion* and, say, you or I don't? Given the trials, it seems being righteous means facing danger, slaying evil things and refusing to slay good guys. It also seems like Finn is supposed to know when enough punishment is enough, refuse to follow unjust orders, and have the right motivation for his heroic deeds. But should we buy these criteria for heroic righteousness? I'm not convinced these tests are really enough to say Finn's righteous. Doesn't it seem like righteous people (even the heroically righteous) shouldn't be so quick to use violence? Finn uses a lot of violence, pretty quickly. In fact, as his attempt to follow Billy the Hero's pacifism proves, he kind of sucks at being non-violent. Not to mention, doesn't it also seem like Finn uses pretty weak proof to decide who's evil, who isn't, and whether or not to slay them!? That's totally not righteous, dude.

My second question is what the *Enchiridion* really should be. It is a book meant only for righteous heroes, but what information should we expect in such a book? We see that there are instructions for kissing a princess, and in a later episode, there is lore regarding Cyclopes and their healing tears. We get some brief glimpses into some other chapters, but really we don't know much. True, the book has other uses—it can be thrown at worms and is used to knock food out of a dopey bear's mouth. It also has powerful magical properties, as it is a portal to travel between the multiverses. But I want to know what is *in* the darned book!

What *should be* in a handbook for righteous heroes? An *Enchiridion* is literally "a handbook," and so it should play a major role in the hero's life! It needs more than being a source of obscure facts about medicinal tears or methods for smooching royalty. Here are things I think a true *Enchiridion* needs:

1. **It should have explanations of how to improve your virtues**

2. **It should help prepare you for the inevitable decline in ability that comes with age—all heroes must face this, even Billy**

and

3. **It should have an account of how to face defeat and how to acknowledge mistakes—as heroes, being heroes, are used to winning and being right (but since they are fallible, they will not always win).**

The Stoic philosopher Epictetus (55–135 C.E.) wrote an ancient *Enchiridion,* a handbook to the "good life" a *life of righteousness.* Epictetus calls us to a life of righteousness, and he identifies ways we can be pulled astray, ways our lives can be upset by accident and by age and death. Even heroes. In other words, a truly righteous *Enchiridion* doesn't just explain how to win, it explains how to lose. A truly righteous hero needs to be ready to improve and be ready for losses. Is this true of Finn? Or was he rewarded for being "righteous" just a bit too soon?

Epictetus thought that being a hero requires focusing on our duties, having the right motivation, and even recognizing that doing the right thing is sometimes a drag. Okay, this sounds like a hummer. All this focus on loss and losing isn't very heroic-sounding, but the reality is that life is grittier and less glamorous than heroes Finn and Jake make it out to be. And it's really too bad for Finn—the Land of Ooo can be a pretty dark place, and anyone who wants to be a good person there needs all the help they can get.

Finn's Three Trials

There are three tests of Finn's righteousness in his quest for the *Enchiridion*: the illusionist gnomes, the confrontational giant, and the encounters inside the temple at the top of Mount Cragdor. What we see is that in all three cases, Finn displays *some* admirable qualities. But, *not all* of Finn's actions are admirable. . . . I think Finn may not be righteous!

The gnomes and their illusions are first. After entering the forest at the foot of Mount Cragdor, Finn and Jake hear cries for help in the forest. They rush to find three gnomes in a pit of lava. They pull the gnomes out—very heroic, brave, and so on. Moreover, Finn even admits that saving the gnomes may interfere with the quest for the *Enchiridion*. This is pretty good-hearted—Finn is willing to do something for others, even if it means his quest is interrupted.

Then trouble arises. The gnomes, as it turns out, are evil. Once released from the lava, they start destroying old ladies. Finn is horrified! He objects, but the gnomes reply that the more he objects, the more old ladies they will destroy. Finn is even more horrified, and the gnomes really twist the knife and tell him that if he acts sad about the old ladies, they will kill more! Finn retreats. (Jake then grabs the gnomes and tosses them back in the lava, where they belong!)

Finn's reactions are all appropriate—objecting to the harm done and feeling remorse for having, even inadvertently, contributed to it. This all expresses good moral character, and Jake clarifies the situation further by noting two important things: those were likely not old ladies (what would they be doing out in the woods like that?) and these are all tests of Finn's "heroic attributes."

Jake, of course, is right in the end. Finn shouldn't pay attention to gnomes and their illusions—they're just gnomes and illusions. But Finn is rightly troubled by his performance. He needs to be righteous, but he's not doing so well. He admit he is instead, "wrongteous, stupidteous."

Notice that Finn doesn't have the clarity to see that in these encounters, he's being tested. He's only reacting, responding only on impulse. It takes Jake's reflection to refocus Finn, to remind him that it's all gnomes and illusions.

Finn doesn't have long to worry about his shaky start, since he must face the second test: the bulgy-eyed giant. The giant crashes through the trees, pops Jake in his mouth, and hollers that "You cannot pass!" Pretty random.

Here, Finn is being doubly tested. First, he is on a quest, and so he must actually pass the giant—that's how he needs to get to Mount Cragdor. So he faces a physical confrontation with someone *a lot* bigger than him who has already defeated Jake. Finn's in serious danger. In a way, it's exactly the kind of challenge we'd expect Finn to have to face in a quest to test his heroism. What would a heroic quest be without a battle with a giant?

Second, Finn suddenly must face this challenge without Jake. And, as Jake has been eaten, it becomes clear he may not have Jake with him for any future battles, either. You see, after Jake pops out of the giant's nostril and ear hole to show he's okay, the giant reports that Jake "fell into my stomach," and so likely is a goner. The challenge, now, isn't just to fight the giant, but to face the loss of a friend. Things just got real.

Finn, in a rage over the prospects of losing his friend, steals an appropriately giant dollar from the giant's wallet and hang-glides away with it. The giant is furious, "Hey! My big money! Give it back!" Finn proposes a deal: the dollar for Jake. But the giant claims he's killed Jake. Finn glides back and furiously kicks the giant in the belly, which causes him to barf up Jake. Reunited, the two glide to a perch up on Mount Cragdor.

And with that, it seems the test is done. But it isn't. The giant is crushed—Finn has stolen his dollar. He blubbers and cries, and he suddenly looks more like a giant baby than a giant ogre. Finn pauses to fold the dollar into a paper airplane and he tosses it back to the giant. Jake, witnessing this, remarks: "You know what that was? That was righteous."

For sure, Jake is right. Finn showed himself to be brave, inventive, and even merciful. The giant hardly has any right to say he deserves his dollar back—it was his eating Jake that led to his losing it. But, amazingly, Finn holds no grudge. He takes pity on the blubbering bulgy-eyed giant. Finn shows some mercy with the giant, even if he really doesn't deserve it.

But the whole situation and Finn's mercy are perplexing. Finn never asks the giant his motive for preventing them from passing. Was the giant merely there as a guard, or is he another illusion? Is he simply a giant spoiling for a fight? Compare this gesture of goodwill from Finn to Jake's tossing the gnomes back into the lava. Keeping people from passing doesn't require that you eat them—the giant meant to do *real harm* to Jake. The gnomes were only destroying *illusory* old ladies. Yet the giant gets his dollar bill back and the gnomes get thrown in the lava. That's weird—the guy trying to really hurt real people isn't punished at all, and the guys only pretending to hurt illusory people get thrown in lava. How is that fair or even?

The Candy Kingdom and the Land of Ooo generally make for a morally strange place, and it seems that real righteousness should require that we understand why a giant must eat travelers or why gnomes would perform illusions. To be hurdles for hero-tests is an insane explanation. Imagine that as a job, *your* job. You hang around in the forest waiting for some knight or random hero to come along. Then your job is to test him or her. What might you do in the meantime? Talk to the other testers? Read? Surely, the denizens of the forest at the base of Mount Cragdor have reasons for what they do. They stand as tests for heroic virtue, and that means they put themselves in harm's way. To test a hero's virtue is to put yourself on the wrong end of a sword. What makes that job worth it?

Couldn't righteousness here be, instead of running around fighting willy-nilly, seeing the insanity of the quest and the tests? Wouldn't a thoughtful hero wonder what kind of heroic tester would risk the lives of a bunch of people just to test a hero's valor? And what kind of hero would want to pass, or even take, such a test?

These questions bring us to the third test. Finn meets a creepy mage inside the temple, and the mage takes him into his "brain world" for the final test. First, Finn must slay a beast. It's pretty hideous, with a heart-looking shape for a body and a big, glowing skeleton arm. Finn asks the mage if it is evil, and the mage assures him that it's "completely evil."

Finn replies, "Shoot, yeah, I'll slay anything that's evil! That's my deal!" He and the monster fight, and the monster explodes in a shower of blood. Finn, covered in the gore, is pumped. He feels the bloodlust.

The mage then challenges Finn to slay an "unaligned ant." But Finn can't bring himself to do it, and he breaks the brain world illusion. He promptly kicks the mage in the nards.

We should applaud Finn withholding violence against the ant. This is an important thing, and it is something we had not seen in Finn—he'd seemed pretty much happy to fight anyone, but he draws the line with the ant. But now notice a few things. First, all Finn's slaying, though rightly directed at things with the alignment 'evil,' depends entirely on *being told* who is evil and who is not. Finn is just tossed into a "brain world" and is told that something's evil. And then he just kills it. That's all it takes, and he doesn't test out his sources! He kills the heart-beast simply on the say-so of the creepy mage. Being inclined to slay evil things is righteous to a degree, but being inclined to slay anything you're told is "evil" is not righteous. It's dangerous. It's wrongteous, stupidteous. What if the dark mage had said the ant was evil?

A perfect picture of Finn's failure of careful distinction between evil and non-evil happens right after the third trial. The Key-per arrives dressed as a devil (with a little red jumpsuit with a horned hoodie and pitchfork). Finn promptly sets to walloping him. It is revealed that the devil costume is Key-per's pajamas (but why the pitchfork?). Key-per was simply hurrying over to congratulate Finn for completing the tests. For his trouble, as we see, he receives a beating. Why? To Finn, only *seeming* like a bad guy is enough to start kicking butts! That's not virtue. That's just looking for excuses for violence . . . it might just be viciousness!

The Manly Minotaur along with the Key-per sit down with Finn for a picnic of spaghetti and juice. The Manly Minotaur gives a little speech with the presentation of the *Enchiridion*:

> Yes, Finn, you are the goodest of heart and most righteous hero I've seen here. Tenderness, ingenuity, bravery and nard-kicking ability. And when you took that ogre's dollar . . . [*laughs*] Man! The Key-per nearly fainted!

But what about the cowardice, lack of fairness, gullibility, and hasty violence Finn has shown?

So, Is Finn Righteous? No

Okay, look, we all love Finn. I don't mean to trash our righteous young hero. But that's the point, isn't it, he's a *young* hero. The trouble is, Finn is good of heart, but he has no wisdom. He is impulse, no thought. He can't distinguish the good from the bad on his own—it must be done for him. And when the wrong people do it for him, he is easily fooled.

True righteousness requires the wisdom to know that we must be careful distinguishing good from evil. Especially when slaying stuff is on the line. I don't mean that Finn is himself evil, but his virtues . . . bravery, ingenuity, good cheer . . . are incomplete without good judgment.

Virtues are virtues only when exercised with good judgment. Without good judgment, virtues become bad things. Bravery is no virtue if we are brave for the wrong reason. A Nazi can be brave, a terrorist can be brave, heck even the Lich can be brave. . . . Bravery is no great thing if it is not deployed for the morally right purpose.

The reality is that Finn is still a kid. And though he has remarkable resilience, skill, and enthusiasm, he has a lot of growing up to do. The problem is that there aren't many better examples of righteous heroism for Finn around.

The *Enchiridion* should go to the *most* righteous hero. If Finn earned the *Enchridion* then that means *there isn't anyone more righteous than him in Ooo*! This says something horrible about the Candy Kingdom and the Land of Ooo generally. Finn is not particularly righteous, but he is the *most* righteous. That makes Finn the best, but we have to admit he is missing at least one really important righteous quality . . . wisdom. That means that every other hero in Ooo is less righteous than an impetuous and often unnecessarily violent boy! I'd said earlier that the whole place is morally strange, and awarding Finn the title of "most righteous" proves that. The Land of Ooo is a broken, fragmented place. Perhaps we shouldn't be so surprised that Finn is the best it can do.

Who Could Write a Decent *Enchiridion*? Not Billy

So far, I've argued that Finn isn't particularly righteous. That's bad news. But the good news is that he gets a book that might help—the *Enchiridion*, a handbook for heroes. The trouble is that the book, at least what Finn reads of it, is not a resource for improving his character. Instead, it's more like a book of useful information—how to kiss a princess and other things heroes might need to know. This comes as no surprise, as the Candy Kingdom and Ooo do not seem to have, really, anyone capable of writing a book more helpful. That is, if you're going to have a good book for righteousness, you'd need someone who knows what righteousness is to write it. Who in Ooo could write *that* book?

Maybe Billy? After all he's the supreme hero and subject of Finn and Jake's adoration. But I don't think it's likely. What we see of Billy does not inspire much confidence. He strikes me mostly as a lunkhead. When we first meet Billy, he's completely given up on fighting evil. That sounds interesting, but his reasons for retirement are very, very strange:

> All my life, I've beaten on evil creatures . . . [*sighs*]. But new evil keeps popping up. Kicking their butts was a worthless effort!

And when Finn explains that he saved a MiniQueen from an evil creature just a few minutes ago, Billy replies:

> You know where she is right now? She's probably being eaten by a different monster.

Billy's point is that the hero's life is wearisome, draining. But the challenges continue. That is, of course, not a reason *to give up saving people*! Just because a job is repetitious doesn't mean it's worthless. Finn asks what else he should be doing to help if not kicking butts, and Billy answers:

Nonviolently! By being active in your community.

But Billy doesn't seem to believe what he's saying. Is he being active in his community? No! He sits locked in his cave, rotting away with his treasures and the skeleton of his dead magic dog. He gives Finn and Jake no direction as to what activity they should take in their community, which, of course, leads to disaster. Billy might have been a great hero, but he sure doesn't have any idea how to help Finn and Jake.

Even Ooo's greatest hero is a bit morally disappointing. After all, if he really believes its *right* to be active in his community, shouldn't he get off of his big blue-gray butt and *do* something???

Even Kicking Ass Gets Boring

Shouldn't the *Enchiridion* have a good answer to Billy's challenge? There is evil in the world, and even if new evil is to arise later, we must face and oppose it. The reality of any life, heroic or not, is that we face the daily grind of work, housekeeping, obligatory social gatherings, classes, and so on. There's a special Latin word for the grind of small details and tasks that eat up our days: "*quotidia*." Our *quotidian* lives are filled with repeated micro jobs that, when seen from the perspective of having to do them again, again, and again, are burdensome . . . or even absurd. You make your bed, again, and again, and again. Only to mess it up that night, again, and again, and again. Same for cutting the grass, getting a haircut, trimming your nails, going to school or work, paying bills. It's the same grind, same thing, a rat race. Absurd, and hardly worth it. Sigh. That's what Billy was complaining about . . . the *quotidia* of being a hero.

For the hero, fighting evil becomes quotidian, just like doing homework or doing taxes. That is horrible news for someone who wants that life for its excitement and glory. The life of the hero is supposed to be exciting at its core, to be a break from the kind of lives we normally lead. It's strange to hear from Billy that it's not. But then, again, maybe it's not so strange.

But Billy's forgotten something. He has a duty to others. Imagine a teacher saying something along Billy's lines:

> All my life, I've been teaching kids. And every time I teach a kid, the kid needs to learn something else. Even worse, half the time they forget what I taught them and I have to teach it again!

We might reply that to be a teacher is, for sure, to face this kind of grind, but good teachers are resilient. They find ways to effectively motivate not only their students but themselves. Duty is the motivation in these circumstances—*even though the job is repetitive, it must be done, and it is my job to do it.* Taking ownership of a role, seeing how it fits with the rest of the whole, doing it for the sake of the others it benefits (even if temporarily and contingently)—that is true heroic motive. Living otherwise, expecting otherwise, isn't realistic. That's stupid. Problems are never permanently solved, nothing stays fixed forever, selfishness and violence recur. But that is no reason not to solve problems, fix things, or stand against evil. That is the reason why the hero's life, like the teacher's (or the parent's, student's, office worker's, doctor's, or dishwasher's) life is full of the continuous and repetitive work of doing one's duty in light of one's role. The object is to do it well, but Billy just checks out. Some hero. Some role-model.

A handbook for heroes would prepare a hero for that challenge, the challenge Billy faces and fails. A real handbook for heroes would prepare the hero for other challenges: future failures, misunderstandings, errors, and the hero's own limitations. Heroes aren't gods, they aren't immortal. They have limitations. And the reality is that they will always bump up against those limits. Even Billy, the greatest hero, wore down and checked out. The *Enchiridion*, if it's a real handbook for heroes, needs to have some of that wisdom. Righteousness is hard to keep up.

How to Stay Righteous

In Epictetus's *Enchiridion*, he outlines the way a person can, in heroic fashion, become invulnerable to the world, to be invincible to the opinions of others, to do one's duty, and to be content with one's life. For better or worse, Finn's *Enchiridion* demands comparison with its ancient namesake.

Epictetus's *Enchiridion* was literally a handbook for Stoic living (*en-cher* being ancient Greek for *in-hand*). The Stoics were philosophers living in ancient Greece and Rome, and the core tenets of their philosophy were that only virtue is valuable, and that we have to master our emotions in order to be virtuous. A Stoic is *indifferent* to all things except virtue. And so, the Stoics think it doesn't matter whether they are rich, healthy, well-liked, fancily dressed, yada yada. The only thing that matters to a Stoic is whether she is a good person— whether she keeps her word, stands up for what's right, treats others with respect, and does her job. The satisfactions of fame, riches, and pleasure are the satisfactions any thief or liar could appreciate, but the satisfactions of the job well-done, of doing the right thing, of having been morally attentive are satisfactions only the righteous can enjoy.

This Stoic perspective of self-control and duty is both stark and appealing. It is stark for sure, since the Stoic must view pain, poverty, and ill-repute as no big deal. This is a difficult position for most people. But the Stoic perspective has its appeal, too. Consider someone you've admired. If you've admired *the person*, it doesn't matter whether they are rich or poor, healthy or sickly, famous or not. If you admire the person, you admire how they handle adversity or how, when success comes their way, they don't let it go to their heads. If you admire someone because of their clothes or wealth or fame, you don't admire *them*, you admire the clothes, wealth, and fame.

The Stoic strategy is to be the kind of person someone could admire no matter how you're dressed, no matter your wealth or social station. It is the dignity we keep in doing our jobs and keeping our word, no matter how small the deed or repetitive the task, that we find that we are admirable. Embracing that perspective yields a good life. It may not yield wealth or fame, but it yields a job well-done, a life of dignity. That's what really matters.

A handbook for heroes needs a lesson like that. Billy could have used that lesson. Billy wants to defeat evil once and for all. But that's impossible, so Billy checked out. What about Finn? He reacts, on instinct and impulse, to the things around

him, and that is sometimes good, but not always. He needs
direction, guidance. But Jake will not always be there for him,
nor will Princess Bubblegum, or any of the other characters.
Finn needs to develop his own perspective, his own life; to be
more than someone who just reacts to the things around him.
He needs good judgment. Finn could use the Stoic *Enchiridion*
to remind him to focus on virtue rather than on loot, butt-kicking, and the fleeting fame that often comes with being a hero.

Flawed Heroes

Finn is a good guy. But he is incomplete, and I think that drawing him that way makes him interesting, but not admirable. It's
a better story, for sure, with a flawed hero. But you nevertheless have a flawed hero. But Finn's flaws, are not *tragic* flaws,
well not yet anyway. They could become really bad in the wrong
circumstances. Think about how easily Finn is led by others—
this can yield terrible results if he started taking orders from
the wrong people. Finn is exceedingly enthusiastic to slay evil,
which is why he starts pummeling Key-per. Good thing for
everyone that it was just a punch in the gut and the Key-per
could take the blow—if it was a blow delivered with a sword,
Finn's enthusiasm might have resulted in the murder of one of
the good guys! Finn could use a little Stoic virtue. . . . Maybe
that's the lesson that should be in Finn's *Enchiridion*—a hero
is just another murder with a sword unless he tempers that
violence with vurtue and good judgment!

23
How to Be a Hero

GREG LITTMANN

Everything you need to know about being a hero is in this book.

—FINN

Finn closes to grapple with the blue marauder chief and clasps the metal feathers of the warrior's helmet. He grits his six teeth, and his rubber-hose limbs shake from the strain as he pits his strength against his roughhousing foe. Suddenly, the sound of crying can be heard in the distance! Finn's sneer of exertion melts into a frown of sympathy. He tosses the chief aside and springs into action, announcing, "This is serious! I gotta go find out where that crying is coming from!" The time for games is over. It sounds like somebody out there needs a hero!

What is it to be a hero? The question is as modern as *Adventure Time* and at least as ancient as the earliest literature. With the exception of tales about the gods, tales about heroes have probably been the most popular form of story in history, while today, the likes of James Bond, Captain Kirk, and Batman are among the most widely known and loved fictional characters.

Different cultures have had different ideas about what it takes to be a hero, but all regard heroes as examples of life lived well. The hero may have flaws, even flaws that eventually lead to a tragic end, but the hero still serves as a standard for human excellence: someone inspiring to look up to. To ask "What is a hero?" is to ask what is important in human life, the most pressing question faced by every human being. To ask, "What is a hero?" is to ask "What sort of person should *I* be?"

In *Adventure Time*, Finn owns a guidebook to being a hero, the legendary tome known as the *Enchiridion*. As he explains to an ambitious bear, "Everything you need to know about being a hero is in this book." We never get to know much about the book's contents before it is finally destroyed by Finn to open a portal, and must make do with tantalizing glimpses—strange geometrical figures, information on Cyclopes, advice on how to kiss a princess.

If we want to learn the secrets of heroism the book contains, we may need to work them out for ourselves. One good place to start would be to take a look at people who have been considered heroes, to work out which features we think really matter. Let's see how Finn stacks up against some of the archetypical heroes from mythology. It turns out that in many ways, Finn's spirit is as ancient as civilization. On the other hand, the boy in the bear hat has worked out a few things about heroism that the ancients didn't twig to until the birth of philosophy. Philosophical!

A Hero Is a Warrior

I'm a tough tootin' baby, I can punch-a your buns! Punch-a your buns, I can punch all your buns!

—Baby Finn

In the Land of Ooo, to be a great hero, you have to be a great warrior. A song relates the achievements of Billy, Finn's hero: "Who's the greatest warrior ever? A hero of renown! Who slayed an evil ocean? Who cast the Lich King down! . . . Also, he fought a bear! Billy!" In the same spirit, when Finn saves an old lady from a swamp giant, she tells him, "Like a true hero, you were born to punch evil creatures." To say that Finn was born to fight is an understatement. His ass-kicking ability is far greater than any real person could hope to match. He takes on opponents ten times his size and faces armies and hordes single-handed.

Finn is not just good at fighting. He *loves* it. He laughs as he battles his way past evil dungeon monsters. "I'm in my element!" he shouts with joy, leaping through the air. When he comes across a "dungeon train" with an infinite supply of monsters, he enjoys the constant combat so much that he never wants to get off. Jake shows him his future in a magic crystal: "Look. That's you, dude. You're old, you're alone, and you're still fighting on this dumb train." Finn is delighted, crying, "Whoah! I'm going to have the best life!" Tree Trunks once asks Finn what he would do if he could do anything. Finn replies, "I'd catch a shooting star and travel to outer-space and fight space monsters."

The belief that the best and most heroic life is the life of a great warrior is an ancient one. Perhaps the most common trait of the heroes of myth and folklore is that they kick much ass. The oldest hero tale that we have is the Mesopotamian *Epic of Gilgamesh*, dating as far back as the fourth millennium B.C.E., almost twice as far from the birth of Jesus as we are. King Gilgamesh was such an excellent fighter that he had "unexampled supremacy over the people, victory in battle from which no fugitive returns." When Gilgamesh introduces himself to the goddess Siduri, his self-description reads like Billy's song: "I am Gilgamesh who seized and killed the Bull of Heaven, I killed the watchman of the cedar forest, I overthrew Humbaba who lived in the forest, and I killed the lions in the passes of the mountains." Of course, Billy only fought one bear. That's nothing to Gilgamesh, who boasts: "I killed bear, hyena, lion, panther, tiger, stag, red-stag, and beasts of the wilderness."

Perhaps the most famous heroes of myth are those of ancient Greece: bronze age warriors of the second millennium B.C.E. The Greek hero Achilles is such an incredible combatant that victory in the Greek war against the city of Troy depends on whether he will fight or just sulk in his tent. Likewise, in Ireland around the first century, the Irish hero Cú Chulainn takes on the army of Connaught all by himself and holds them off, saving the army of Ulster, whose soldiers have been incapacitated by magic.

To truly prove a hero's prowess, though, defeating mere armies is not enough. To make Finn cry "boss fight!" in delight requires a *monster*: something awesome like a brain with tentacles, or a semi-invisible panther creature gifted with "approximate knowledge of many things." Likewise, Gilgamesh slew the fire-breathing giant, Humbaba, the Greek hero Perseus decapitated the snake-haired Gorgon, Medusa, and the Scandinavian hero Sigurd butchered the dragon Fafnir and bathed in his blood! Even Finn's belief that eternal fighting is paradise is an old one. Norsemen who proved their worth by dying in battle were admitted to Valhalla, hall of the God Odin, where they get to spend every day in battle, endlessly respawning from death like monsters in a computer game.

Glory at Any Price

Being the third best at something is math and deserves respect.

—FINN

Heroes, as traditionally conceived, must achieve fame and glory, publically distinguishing themselves from lesser individuals. For Finn, fame and glory matter, at least some of the time. For example, he insists on fighting the champion "The Farm" just for the glory. He tells Jake, "If we beat him, we'll be crazy legends. . . . Winning this battle could take our reputation to a whole new level!"

Nor is competition and glory from combat the only competition and glory that he cares about. He's only too happy to accept Jake's suggestion: "D'you know what's really cool? Tough guy contests!" Such contests include not just wrestling, but competitive furniture destruction and pinching each other hard enough to bring tears. Similarly, Finn lets Jake wear him as a suit, betting Jake that no matter what he does while wearing Finn, Finn can take the pain. Finn refuses to back down in the face of everything Jake dishes out, even letting Jake get to the verge of dipping him in a volcano. Likewise, Finn and Jake both refuse to lose a bet by being the first one to speak, even as they are violently attacked by angry "bikini babes."

Gilgamesh could understand. He sets out to kill the giant Humbaba, not because Humbaba is hurting anyone, but just for the glory of it. By killing the terrifying Humbaba, he will show everyone what as astounding bad-ass he is, for ages to come and throughout the world. Just as Jake and Finn seek out the champion "The Farm" to prove their worth, Greek heroes in battle seek out famous heroes on the other side, challenging them to duels to establish who's the greater warrior. Both Achilles and Cú Chulainn are offered a choice of fates between either winning glory as a warrior but dying young, or living a long life without glory. For both the Greek and the Irish hero, glory is the obvious choice.

Like Finn, early heroes saw no need to limit competition to the battlefield. The Greek epic the *Iliad* describes in detail the athletic contests of the warriors in the Greek army. Like a bronze age sportscast, the epic fills us in on stories such as how Diomedes outdrove Antilochus in the chariot race, and how Ajax and Odysseus wrestled each other to a standstill. Cú Chulainn was a champion at the sport of "hurling," something like hockey, only even more violent. As a child, he won a match single-handed against a hundred and fifty older boys (who then, understandably, tried to kill him). The Scandinavian hero Beowulf, subject of an Anglo-Saxon epic composed over a thousand years ago, enters a swimming race with his friend Breca, and they keep it up for seven days and nights. A poor loser, Beowulf complains that he would have won, but he had to stop to kill a sea monster.

People who seek glory take insults seriously. At least some of the time, Finn sees being insulted as grounds for violence. When the fashionable Sir Slicer points out that his armor is so much more "ch'k ch'k" than Finn's, Finn tells him to "come here and say that to my fist." Cú Chulainn was no less touchy. When a poet named Redg threatens to write a poem making fun of Cú Chulainn if Cú Chulainn doesn't give him his famous spear Gae Bolg, Cú Chulainn gives the spear to him . . . through the neck. Even this is a minor case of pride compared to that of Achilles. Achilles's honor is insulted when he's denied his fair share of war spoils by the high king Agamemnon, so he goes back to his tent and refuses to fight the Trojans anymore, denying the Greek army his superhuman abilities, and as a result the Greeks come damn close to losing the war. For Finn, at least, defending his honor is less important than saving people. Finn is offended when the Marauder chief calls him a chicken for refusing to roughhouse, but he can't ignore a nearby cry for help, and lets the insult slide.

As skillful as Finn is with his weapons and fists, he's as likely to outwit his opponents with a clever trick as he is to beat them in a fair fight. For example, he defeats Xergiac's army of giant-eared earclopses by attacking them with sound, clapping loudly and shouting "Wawawa" through a megaphone. Similarly, to defeat a giant-eyed cyclops, Finn fools him into leaning down to hear his whisper, then sucker-punches him in the eye. The tricks get dirtier yet. Jake reminds Finn:

"What'd I teach you, dude?" and Finn answers, "Not to scorn the kicking of people in the crotch." Just in case they've forgotten this important lesson, a dream messenger reminds them to fight dirty against The Farm, finally allowing them to defeat him by catapulting mud into his eyes, baring his ass, and biting it.

Likewise, the goal of the mythological hero is generally to find a way to win by any means, rather than to offer a fair fight. Rather than enter combat with the monstrous Humbaba, Gilgamesh allows the giant to surrender, and *then* thrusts his sword through his neck. As for the Greek hero Odysseus, he's the very model of Finn's cunning, a point not missed by the Origami warrior Paper Pete, who compliments Finn: "You have the cunning of Odysseus!" Finn's ingenious victories over cyclops and earclops alike are based on Odysseus's victory over the cyclops Polyphemos, from whom the Greek hero escaped by getting him drunk and stabbing him in his eye.

It was likewise Odysseus who finally ended the ten-year Trojan War by coming up with the idea of hiding the Greek army inside a hollow wooden horse, predicting that the Trojans would take it inside their city walls. When Cú Chulainn finds himself evenly matched in combat against the warrior woman Aife, he finally defeats her by pretending that he has just seen her beloved chariot plunge off a cliff, thus causing her to turn around to look. If that dirty trick sounds familiar, it might be because the Ice King uses it to defeat the magic hit man Scorcher, telling him "someone got hit in the boin-loins! Hit in the boin-loins! Boin-loins!"

Look After Your Own

No matter how messed up and lumpy I get, this guy never turns his back on me.

—Jake

One of Finn's defining traits is his loyalty to, and love of, his friends. He and Jake are inseparable. In fact, after saving Jake from drowning in a rocket ship accident, Finn promises to "never leave your side ever again for the rest of our lives" so that Jake will always be safe. Risking his life to save Jake is routine for Finn, who journeys as far as the depths of Lumpy Space, the Chaos Dimension and, most frightening of all to him, the ocean. As Finn notes, "Homies help homies, always." He stands by this maxim even when it requires self-sacrifice. When Tree Trunks is attacked by evil signposts, he places his own body between the blows and his elephant friend. Likewise, when Lemongrab fires a sonic sword-blast at Princess Bubblegum, Finn throws himself in the way as a human shield. When Finn and his friends are surrounded by goo monsters in the Desert of Wonder, Finn is ready to give up his life for his pals: "One of us has to eat the big one so that the others can survive. And I'm going to be that one. . . . This is what it means to be a hero."

Here again, Finn follows an ancient tradition. Heroes care about their friends. Just as Finn adventures with Jake, Gilgamesh adventures with his beloved and inseparable pal Enkidu. As the goddess Ninsun predicts, "You will love him . . . and he will never forsake you." When Enkidu dies from sickness, Gilgamesh is overcome with despair. Likewise, when Achilles leaves for the Trojan war, he brings along his best friend, Patroklos. The two share a tent on the field before Troy, just as Finn and Jake share a tree house. When the Trojan hero Hector kills Patroklos by skewering him on his spear, Achilles is so upset that he dedicates himself to avenging Patroklos by killing Hector, even though he knows that he is fated to die shortly after Hector does. When Odysseus's son Telemachus goes searching for his father, who failed to return from the Trojan war, he turns to his father's old friends and comrades, knowing that they would do anything they can to help Odysseus.

Of course, you don't have to be Finn's friend to get his help. Finn keeps his whole community safe, protecting the Candy Kingdom from all comers, from zombie donuts, to genetically engineered psychic sphinxes, to a giant angry Gunter made of Gunters. Likewise, mythological heroes tend to be defenders of their communities against outside threats. Gilgamesh is king of the city of Uruk, and saves the city when it's attacked by a gigantic monstrous bull. The great Greek heroes are likewise kings or princes, who, when not off on adventure, keep the peace at home. When youths from the city of Athens are being sacrificed to the minotaur, it is up to Prince Theseus to track the monster down in its labyrinth and slay it. Cú Chulainn defends the province of Ulster against the armies that attack it, and Beowulf, King of Gotaland, defends his people when their farms are being incinerated by a disgruntled dragon.

What makes Finn (and many other more modern heroes) stand out most from the majority of mythological heroes is their willingness to help and protect those with whom they have no relationship. For Finn, even an anonymous cry for help must be answered at once. He explains to the Marauders: "I vowed to help anyone in need, no matter how small their problem." To his mind, this is what heroism is all about. Approached by a tattered homeless man begging for food, he judges, "A hero always helps someone in need." Finn can't stand the thought of harming the innocent. He refuses to kill an ant because the ant is not evil, but "unaligned," even though killing the ant is a requirement for receiving the *Enchiridion*. When Bubblegum orders Finn to keep an innocent Ice King in the candy dungeons, Finn imprisons himself rather than let the injustice stand, though the Ice King is his archenemy.

For most mythological heroes, their moral duties extend no further than their relationships. They must be loyal to their friends and family and must protect their community, but outsiders are largely fair game. When Gilgamesh is described as victorious in battle, the implication is not simply that he defended Uruk, but that he aggressively promoted its interests. Conquerors in the ancient world were respected for their strength and success. Greek heroes like Achilles and Odysseus would lead their armies to attack and sack cities for their treasure, seeing such raids as glorious adventures to boast about. They viewed foreign cities much like Finn views dungeons filled with evil creatures: as a source of challenge, excitement, and booty. Whereas Finn cannot kill an innocent ant, Achilles honors his dead friend Patroklos with a human sacrifice of twelve Trojan children. When Cú Chulainn's son Connla dies, the hero laments that together they would have conquered as far as the gates of Rome and beyond. Even the early King Arthur, who would come to represent a new kind of hero, devotes himself to such conquest, leading his armies as far as Rome before having to turn back.

We'll Always Need Heroes

Listen up, you cold-hearted marauders! Somebody's out there crying for help and I'm not gonna ignore that!

—FINN

In many ways, we today are still in the grip of the early heroic system of values. We still enjoy violent conflicts—at least, as long as we're on the winning side and our own casualties do not grow too high. Victory in war brings glory and popularity to leaders just as it did in the days of Gilgamesh. We are still obsessed with glory from other forms of competition too. For many of us, the pursuit of "success" through work becomes an end in itself. To gain money and status is to "win", even if we must all but sacrifice our lives to achieve it.

This is an attitude parodied when Finn and Jake find some businessmen from our world frozen in ice, and unleash them onto Ooo. The businessmen don't care what they do, as long as they do it well. All they want is jobs at which they can excel, even if they spread unhappiness, rampaging in a giant Finn robot and sucking up the "fuzzy friends." We mostly see our moral duties in terms of our relationships. We recognize duty to family and friends, as well as some duty to protect our community if, for example, our country were to be attacked by a foreign power. Unlike Finn, we generally see ourselves as having little duty to help strangers, regarding the fate of most people on the planet as being nothing to do with us.

Western moral philosophy began in Ancient Greece around the fifth century B.C.E. as a response to traditional values that were still largely "heroic." Achilles, if he ever lived, had been dead for seven hundred years by this point, but most Greeks still viewed living life well as a matter of being powerful, outcompeting others, and promoting the interests of your friends, family and community. Socrates (469–399 B.C.E.) urged his fellow Athenians to concern themselves with the state of their soul rather than devoting themselves to money and status. His pupil Plato (429–347 B.C.E.) went so far as to invent an entirely new social system in which citizens would work for the common good instead of for their friends and family.

Plato's view was still parochial. The citizens of his theoretical city are not particularly concerned about the wellbeing of outsiders, and non-Greeks were to be conquered and enslaved. However, the Greek philosophers were nevertheless laying the foundations of a morality built on a dedication to the common good instead of on competition, a morality that recognizes that the value of other human beings doesn't lie in our relationship to them.

The German philosopher Friedrich Nietzsche (1844–1900) claimed that with the arrival of these Greek philosophers, Western moral thought took a wrong turn, forgoing the healthy competition of heroic values for social restrictions that hold back the gifted. Personally, I prefer the values of a hero like Finn to those of a hero like Achilles, who would probably beat me up and take my wallet.

The sort of heroism I admire is best demonstrated by the giant lemon Lemonjohn. When the starving lemon people march on the candy people with intent to eat them, Lemonjohn gives his life to save both sides by turning himself into pieces of lemon candy. He reasons: "If I act, the candy people will suffer. If I don't, the lemon people will suffer. The greater good demands but one course only: that I dissolve the bonds uniting me and become component to all." Lemonjohn values the candy people as much as his native lemon people, and treats everyone's life as being as valuable as his own.

The old hero Billy urges Finn to give up the way of the warrior: "All my life, I've beaten on evil creatures, but new evil keeps popping up. Kicking their butts was a hopeless effort." But Billy is wrong. Humanity will always need warriors, just as we did in the days of Gilgamesh and Achilles. Without soldiers and police, we would be as helpless as the people of the Candy Kingdom without Finn and Jake. Yet when we have such forces at our disposal—as citizens of democracies do—we need to take care that we are using them for the good, not just for the good of those we care about.

Just as important, we need to recognize that being a hero need not always involve the use of force and violence. Billy recommends: "Help people by being active in your community." Someone feeding the hungry or building homes for the homeless is also a kind of hero. Finn's the right kind of hero for his circumstances. What Ooo needs is someone who can save them from the dragons, earclopses, and other monsters that plague their sugary lands. But what makes Finn a hero isn't that he is greatest kicker of butt in Ooo; what makes Finn a hero is that he does whatever needs to be done for the common good. That's the secret of the *Enchiridion*.

24
Our Real-Life Enchiridions

MICHAEL J. MUNIZ

After a lifetime of searching, you've finally found it. Your hands quake as you reach toward a dusty old relic. You hesitate and wipe the blood off of your hands onto your pants. An artifact such as this should not be soiled with the gore of monsters. Your foes lie dead around you. Decapitated heads, limbs raggedly torn from bodies, blood and bile fill the dimly lit room with a sickly sweet stench. It was fun getting here.

"Come on, pick it up, Dude! It's yours!"

You bite your lip so hard that you draw more blood; you can taste the dirt and dust of the room around you. The sacred item seems to pulse with power as your old hands close on their prize. The leathery cover seems to have a fluid quality; it is as if the runes that cover it are alive. Your eyes have difficulty focusing on them.

"Open it!"

The room becomes brighter as you carefully open to the first ancient page. You decide to share the ancient wisdom with your friend, reading the first line out loud. . . .

"Firstly, show righteous dudeinous by showing mercy to your enemies. Even gross monsters and stuff should be allowed to live, especially when fighting for awesome prizes like this one."

"Cabbage."

What if I told you that there was a manual of *"Righteousness"*? You remember, "The Enchiridion!" In it, the most important object in Ooo is revealed to us: *The Enchiridion* (aka: *The Book of Heroes*, or *The Handbook*, or *The Manual*).

This book, supposedly is the book of all books, a hero's manual for being, well, a *real* hero! According to Princess Bubblegum "it is a book meant only for heroes whose hearts are righteous" ("The Enchiridion!"). So what exactly is the *Enchiridion*? What does Finn's righteousness have to do with getting the *Enchiridion*? And are there any real-life *Enchiridions* that we can get our hands on? I think the answer to that last question is "Yes!" There are manuals for heroes, even in our world, if we are righteous enough to find them. . . .

Righteousness or Wrongteousness

According to Mannish Man the Manly Minotaur, Finn deserves the *Enchiridion* because Finn is "the goodest of heart and most righteous hero I've seen here! Tenderness, ingenuity, bravery, nard-kicking ability" ("The Enchiridion!"). According to the morals of the Land of Ooo, these qualities are known as virtues. These virtues, and others, exist in our reality as well.

In fact, there are those who spend their whole lives studying "virtue ethics." Virtue ethics is the idea that morality is really about developing into a good person, instead of a list of things that are right and wrong. In other words, virtues like courage, gentleness, and friendliness are excellent personality traits that can motivate us to constantly behave in a way that benefits ourselves and others.

Finn's heroism is modeled after this ethical theory. But, more importantly, his heroic actions are products of a heroic personality. When Finn and Jake are on the quest to get the *Enchiridion*, they hear cries for help and find some gnomes trapped in a lava pit. Finn and Jake rescue the gnomes, but then the gnomes immediately begin to kill old women. Ultimately, Finn runs away. Jake puts the gnomes back into the lava pit and tells Finn it was just an illusion, just "a test to show his heroic attributes."

What the flip?! Where the heck do these "heroic attributes" (in other words "virtues") come from? At least Finn gets his hands on the book, but are there any *Enchiridions* that anyone can read? Because, I don't know about you, but I don't really feel like battling giants and fending off murderous gnomes *before* I know what virtue is!

Nicomachean (And You Thought *Enchiridion* Was Weird!)

Aristotle was a Greek philosopher who was also the tutor of Alexander the Great (the sorta kinda real life version of Billy the Hero—well, if Billy took over the world . . .). Aristotle wrote this really long book about politics and how people should live. The second half of the book is known as *Nicomachean Ethics* (or just plain *Ethics*) because it talks about how people should live in a society. The best part about this book is how mathematical it is.

Aristotle wrote about this thing called the "Golden Mean." Basically, the Golden Mean is the key to finding virtues! What you do is figure out the most reasonable path between extremes. A virtue, according to Aristotle, is kind of different from the way Finn would think of a virtue. While Finn thinks being a righteous hero is about being balls-to-the-wall brave, Aristotle thought it was about knowing when to fight and when to run away. "Bravery" really means not fighting when you don't have to, but fighting when you know you should and can!

Really, the Golden Mean is about balance. If you don't balance yourself, you'll end up in one of the two vices: either excess (too much) or deficiency (too little). Just like when it comes to your physical health, if you eat too much, especially candy, or eat too little (or nothing at all) you can totally damage your body, or as Jake often says "your bread and butter." So, you should keep a balance of your virtues.

The best example that I can use deals with the virtue of courage. Aristotle spends a ridiculous amount of time talking about courage, which is saying a lot. If Finn has the virtue of courage then he should be able to keep a balance between the two vices: cowardice (being a wuss) is the vice of "deficiency"— too little courage. Foolishness (being stupid-teous) is the vice of "excess"—too much courage.

Just about every virtue has a middle way. Friendliness (like Jake) is in the middle of being annoying (deficient) and flattery (excess). Truthfulness (like Marceline through her songs) is between sarcasm (deficient) and bragging (excess). Gentleness (like Princess Bubblegum) is between being depressing and low-spirited (deficient) and being easily provoked to anger (excess). Once a hero has found the balance of the virtues, only then can they proceed to heroic action!

Enchiridion (Not to be confused with *The Enchiridion!*)

Another cool figure in the history of philosophy was the Roman philosopher Epictetus. He was so cool that he never actually wrote anything down. His disciples and followers wrote down all of his teachings. These writings eventually inspired the Roman emperor Marcus Aurelius. He was like the real life Princess Bubblegum (or the Ice King; it depends on how you look at it). In Marcus Aurelius's own writings, he talked about how Epictetus's teachings were influential in his decision-making as a ruler. Anyways, the primary text that we have today from Epictetus is called *Enchiridion* (or *The Handbook*). It's actually a shorter version of a much longer work called *The Discourses*. It's so short and simple that even Finn could read it in less than a day.

Throughout his life, Epictetus promoted a philosophy called "Stoicism." Stoicism mostly dealt with physics, logic, and other areas. Epictetus's form of Stoicism mostly deals with morality. He tries to show people how to live better and happier lives. This book would be great for the Ice King because it's basically a short account on how to be more successful. Every time the Ice King captures a princess he always seems to be depressed. Well, Epictetus's *Enchiridion* could teach the Ice King how to be happy, whether or not he kidnaps a princess. The main teachings found within this *Enchiridion* that are suitable for the Ice King are simple ideas such as:

- **His ability to be happy depends on himself.**

- **Events are either good or bad based on how he reacts to them.**

- **He can't try to predict or control what happens, but rather he should just deal with it calmly.**

There's a whole lot more. In fact Epictetus's *Enchiridion* is written pretty much like that: simple sentences and paragraphs.

The best part about Epictetus's *Enchiridion* is how it's quite similar to *The Enchiridion*. There's even a section on how to deal with women. In Finn's *Enchiridion*, Chapter 5 teaches heroes how to kiss princesses. In Epictetus's *Enchiridion*

Section 33 says: "As to pleasure with women, abstain as far as you can before marriage: but if you do indulge in it, do it in the way which is conformable to custom. Do not however be disagreeable to those who indulge in these pleasures, or reprove them; and do not often boast that you do not indulge in them yourself" (p. 15). Overall, Epictetus's *Enchiridion* is the most realistic version of Finn's Enchiridion. It's also worth considering that these two texts are the same, as they can tear through time and space.

How to Kick Buttocks

Okay, kissing princesses might be fun, but let's get down to real heroing . . . fighting stuff! Christine de Pizan (1364–1430) was asked by the royal family to write a book on warfare. This rather large book is called the *Book of Deeds of Arms and of Chivalry* and mostly focuses on battle tactics. So, in a swapping sense, it's like if Prince Gumball asked Fionna to write a book about how to fight off the Ice Queen.

What makes this book really about heroes (as opposed to a long manual on how to kick butts) is its discussion of a hero's *behavior*. Section 28 discusses the way leaders should act *when they lose*. She writes that

> it is a good thing to consider in advance the unexpected adventure, which means thinking about how a trap might be laid, so that the enemies who have been pursuing them should suddenly encounter them in some unexpected place or several places. (p. 77)

This means that when Finn and Jake are about to go on an adventure, they should be prepared for anything, even losing. But, they don't have to lose if they prepared properly, like setting traps. So, if the hero is forced into battle, this real-life *Enchiridion* could be a valuable read.

In Praise of Finn and Jake's Folly

Remember when Princess Bubblegum told Finn and Jake to capture the Ice King without giving any reason ("What Have You Done?"). But, by the end of the episode, we're told that Princess Bubblegum wanted to torture the Ice King and use his

howls to cure the ice plague. Well, once upon a time, in the
medieval period, when the Church pretty much dominated just
about everything, they imprisoned people without any reason,
or because they smelled really bad. They even tortured the
innocent because they believed that would bring an end to the
Bubonic Plague.

But by the end of this period there were a few who were
willing to bring light into this dark world. Desiderius Erasmus
(1466–1536) was one of them. Besides his funny name, which
literally means "desire, desire," he totally wanted to change
how righteousness was viewed both inside and outside the
church. So, he wrote from the point of view of Folly
(Foolishness). It was a neat trick to get the attention of everyone around, especially of those in charge. *In Praise of Folly*
became his most popular work, even though he had written
much more. One of Erasmus's other writings was *Enchiridion
Militis Christiani* (The Handbook for the Christian Knight).
Unfortunately, this book did not make it onto the medieval
times best-sellers list.

So why is *In Praise of Folly* important? Simply because the
very ideas expressed in the *Enchiridion Militis Christiani*
were retold in a new way and with new flare in *In Praise of
Folly*. It's like when Finn and Jake get retold from the Ice
King's point of view as Fionna and Cake. And, the best part of
it all is that *In Praise of Folly* makes fun of smart people by
claiming that they're too smart for their own good. It mostly
criticizes people in high places, like The Ice King, Bubblegum
Princess, Lumpy Space Princess. Yet, it suggests that if you
want to be "heroic" you can still treat them with respect. *In
Praise of Folly* is a tricky book, but it can still be used as a
guide from a sarcastic, or Marceline-songbook point of view. It
makes Finn and Jake's "foolish" behavior seem like noble,
genius, and righteous.

I Kant Get the *FPotMoM*

So, the most recent and most studied real-life enchiridion in
this chapter is Immanuel Kant's *Fundamental Principles of the
Metaphysics of Morals*. Yep, it's a really long title for a really
short book. Depending on which publication you get, it can be
as short as 64 pages. However, don't be fooled, this book can

take forever to read which might make Finn chuck it outside his tree house.

The most important thing you can learn from this book is Kant's concept of duty. If heroism is about fulfilling the duties of a hero, then Kant's *Metaphysics of Morals* is the book that'll teach you how to do it. In this book Kant—a German philosopher—introduces the word "deontology". It kinda means doing duty for duty's sake. Most deontologists (duty-doers) focus on doing the right thing all the time rather than just focusing on the rewards or consequences.

But, the most mathematical part about Kant's book, much like Aristotle's *Ethics*, is that Kant gives us a guide point on how to act. He calls this the "categorical imperative" and it means, "Act only on that maxim whereby thou canst at the same time will that it should become a universal law." To put it in Ooo terms, Finn should only do those things that he wouldn't mind other citizens of Ooo doing in the exact same circumstance.

For example, back in Season One's "The Enchiridion!", since Finn stole the dollar from the giant baby monster that swallowed Jake, Kant's categorical imperative suggests that if Finn were a giant baby monster that swallowed a hero's best friends then he would be okay with his own dollar to be stolen by a hero too. Just by following the rules of respect and dignity, Kant's categorical imperative can provide meaningful rewards that you were never expecting in the first place.

Conclusionation

Being righteous is hard. There's so much a hero has to do to maintain his righteousness. Luckily for Finn he has a powerful handbook that can help him through his adventures in the Land of Ooo. Meanwhile, we too are also lucky because we have several different handbooks that can help us along the way if we want to be righteous. Although our monsters may not be exactly like the ones in *Adventure Time* (Giant Tax Monster, Evil Road Rage Racers, Germy Dust Balls from Outer Space) neither are our heroes (UPS Delivery Men, Hialeah Adjunct Professors, Nurses). And, our real-life enchiridions can help us develop our righteousness that Finn, Jake, and Princess Bubblegum can approve.

If you believe that *The Enchiridion* is also for us as much as it is for Finn, then it's also okay to believe that our several *Enchiridions* can be okay for Finn and Jake. So, since it will be fun if you consider that their text really is also our text, they give us a good idea of what their manual says.

25
I Want to Be Your Hero, Maybe!

RAKEL BLÖNDAL SVEINSDÓTTIR

Sucking at something is the first step to being sorta good at something.

—JAKE THE DOG

Looking down at the puny figure before him, the giant's brow furrows. "That'll be $19.95, or two giant dollars, if you prefer."

The massive monster thrust his hands into pockets the size of swimming pools. Sheepishly, he offers the boy standing on the ground before him one giant dollar.

"It's alls I gotz."

"Mr. Giagantorhills, isn't it? I don't think that I've been clear," replies the boy, pointedly polishing his grass blade sword. "You asked for my help. I dispatched the What-wolves that were harassing you. And, now, you owe me two giant dollars . . ."

The little dog next to the boy looks uncomfortable. "Dude, maybe we should let this one slide. . . . One giant dollar is a lot of money for this bloke. And it was a pretty easy gig. We are awesome, right? We used to do stuff like this all the time, for free. We're heroes. . . ."

Finn doesn't bother to look at the little dog. "Look man, if you are going to be all down on my stuff and math, you can just head home. This monster is going to pay what he owes, or I'll have to make an example of him," sparing a meaningful glance up at the cowering giant.

"But that's alls I g . . ."

Finn's blade comes to rigid attention as our hero's patience ends. Jake jumps aside, a hair's breadth away from becoming a good deal less stretchy, as the boy swings the sword back and leaps forward.

The giant doesn't have time to even brace himself. "It's Payment Time!"

"Awww . . . yeah?"

You can save hundreds of lives and not be a hero, if your only reason for saving the screaming victims is to get paid. But, on the flip side, you can possess the virtues of justice, wisdom and courage, and never find the time and place to actually *act* like a hero! And, so, it ends up counting for nothing. When do you actually *become* a hero? Is it when you save the day, or is it something in your *heart*? To that question, Finn would answer: "Did you hear that? Someone is in trouble! Let's go, Jake!"

The True Hero

Makes Sense: You Do Bad Stuff, I Punish You!

—Finn

The basic concept of the true hero is someone, like Finn, who's motivated by shared sense of the public good. He takes responsibility for the lives and circumstances of those around him. It seems like a hero is someone whose actions and efforts improve the lives of others—someone who defends against hostile forces regardless of personal risk or gain. Finn certainly seems to have those qualities.

Remember way back when Finn saved the Candy Kingdom from the zombies, all the while he kept the threat a secret to make sure the candy people didn't explode in fear? To cover up the mess with her failed decorpsinator serum, Princess Bubblegum "throws a slumber party" and she and Finn play loud music to keep the candy people from hearing the zombies growling outside of the castle. Because, annoyingly enough, when candy people get scared, they explode!

When the zombies invade the castle, Finn quickly blindfolds the candy people, hands them wooden sticks and gets them thinking it's time for the piñatas and orders them to start smashing away. *"I'm hanging the piñatas . . . They are all around you! Smash the piñatas!"* Through fantastic ingenuity he gets much needed help stopping the zombies without the candy people seeing the danger and exploding. Finn saves the day yet again—*"trust pound"*!

A virtuous hero is not a hero by accident! A virtuous hero must intentionally, and selflessly, uphold moral virtues like kindness, ingenuity, justice, compassion, love, and peace—knowing the full risks and consequences of his actions. In other words, a knee-jerk reaction, like running into a building to save a friend in danger isn't the best description of a heroic action. When Finn saves the candy people, he does so knowing the danger, and he chooses to stand by them, even in the face of likely failure. In the world outside of Ooo, we have seen this kind of heroism in civil rights movements, democracy movements, peace movements, and individual acts of kindness. Heroes are not perfect humans, without blemish or errors. They may not have achieved their goal while alive, but they made a heroic effort to do so.

An ancient saying goes: "Tell me who you admire and I'll tell you who you are." Heroes define what values mean and they show us those values in action. Though it sometimes is a lesson we learn a bit backwards. . . . Like when Finn meets Billy the Hero, Finn learns an important lesson: Sometimes our heroes don't have the virtues we'd hoped for. And, so, we have to determine our own path and purpose to become a true hero. Finn learns this painfully, though, *after* experiencing a disappointing encounter with his own lifelong hero, Billy.

The Limitations of Rules

I'm Going to Blow Your Minds.

—Finn

For many people, the fundamental question of ethics is "What should I do?" or "How should I act?" Ethics is supposed to provide us with moral principles or universal rules that tell us what to do. This sometimes means following rules like the Ten Commandments. But there are lots of ethical rules that don't have anything to do with religion. John Stuart Mill helped to develop a system of ethics called Utilitarianism. Really there's only one rule: "Everyone is obligated to do whatever will achieve the greatest good for the greatest number." Then again, there's also the system developed by Immanuel Kant (1724–1804) who wanted all of us to follow the rule, "Everyone is obligated to respect the dignity and moral rights of all persons." He believed that we should follow the rules even if it led to bad consequences. As Kant said, "Let justice be done, though the world perish."

Moral rules are not the only way to think of ethics, though! The problem is that one rule, or even a set of rules, can't take every situation into account. It's hard to figure out what the Ten Commandments, Utilitarianism, and Kantianism have to say about human cloning or killing zombies to save candy people! That's why some people think that ethics, and being a *true* hero is more than slavishly following moral rules that would have us constantly checking our every action against a table of do's and don'ts. We should not focus so much on the question of, "What should I do?" but instead "Who should I *be*?" Finn comes across this kind of challenge when he must decide whether to follow his great hero Billy's advice to give up on violence as a way to fight evil.

Virtue ethics deals with exactly that question: "Who should I be?" Virtue ethicists try to figure out not just how a hero acts, but who a hero *is*. The key to being a hero, or just a plain ol' good person, is looking at your character. In virtue ethics, there are certain ideals, like excellence and dedication to the common good, toward which we should strive. It's those virtues—kindness, bravery, diligence, compassion, and so on—that allow the full development of our humanity. These ideals are discovered through thoughtful reflection on what we as humans have the potential to become.

The philosopher Martha Nussbaum says that in order to truly unleash human potential, we must bear in mind the idea of the citizen as a free and dignified person and that everyone is of equal dignity and worth, no matter where they are situated in society. Therefore becoming virtuous is a matter of the common good. Being a virtuous hero is a matter of good heroic practice and respect for the worth of others.

Practical Reason

But Strength isn't your strength. Adorable cuteness is!

—Finn

What virtues are key to becoming a hero? Virtues are the attitudes, dispositions, and character traits that enable us to act in ways that develop every creature's best potential, not just our own. Virtues enable us to pursue the ideals we have adopted. Courage, compassion, honesty, generosity, fidelity, self-control and prudence are classic examples of virtues. Those virtues help us achieve the ideals that we believe are worthy. Being brave, for example, helps Finn create a world free of evil monsters. His bravery guides him and helps him achieve a common good for everyone. And how do we develop those traits of character? As Aristotle explained, a person can improve his character by practicing self-discipline, and virtues are developed through learning and practice. By *practicing* the virtues, they become habits—they become our *character*.

Classic character building in literature often symbolizes the child as somebody who brings on a new beginning, like Finn. He seeks to help the good regain control in the chaotic, post-apocalyptic aftermath of the Great Mushroom War, bringing new hope to the good citizens of Ooo. But there is the slight twist in Finn being a child. . . . Finn hasn't fully developed his ability to reason.

Aristotle argues that both children and adults can have good intentions, but the child lacks practical reason. Because of that lack of full reasoning, children are more prone to messing up. Finn, as a child, lacks full understanding of how to do what he intends and the consequences of his actions, due to too little experience. When Finn rids the house people of Donny the obnoxious grass ogre, he's unable to foresee the consequences of his action. When removing Donny he is exposing the house people to the even worse threat of the "Why-wolves." Finn ends up messing up the course of nature itself!

Even so, Finn possesses some virtues (or virtue-like traits) such as tenderness, bravery, and empathy. The only thing that ever really gets in the way of his heroism is his childishness and lack of foresight. Remember how Finn foolishly gets lured in to stealing a chest of gold for Penny in the City of Thieves? Had he used his practical reason and listened to the advice of the old lady he would have suspected that Penny was lying and that the whole setup was a trick. But, as Jake says, "*sucking at something is the first step to being sorta good at something.*" So even though he's not quite there yet, Finn is on the right path! Keeping up the good work will get him where he wants to be— the quest of becoming a good character is a bumpy ride, one must practice and fail to become virtuous and great.

Seeking the Good Life

You mess up-ed, Billy!

—Finn

Finn ages in real time, and we can follow his journey from a boy to teenager, and watch him gain experience and wisdom all the while improving his character and becoming more knowledgeable and virtuous. But what are Finn and Jake really fighting for, and why are they so willing to risk their lives for the cause?

A virtue ethicist would answer: "They seek the good life." Which doesn't mean being rich and comfortable. It means living a life of true virtue and fulfillment. But can it possibly be that simple? There is of course a higher purpose that we learn about in "Memories of Boom Boom Mountain." Here for the first time we meet a baby Finn, who helplessly gets stuck to a huge leaf lying in his own "boom boom." For a while nobody helps Finn, and because of that he remembers his experience as awful. Finn vows to help everyone in need no matter how small their problem is: "At least I have to try!"

The character traits of an epic hero are usually traits of morality, wisdom, strength, courage, and dedication to a cause. Epic heroes have a sense of purpose or duty. They typically fight for things that are good, worthwhile, or noble. They may seek knowledge, truth, enlightenment, or even immortality. Often they battle for honor and justice because of an experience that teaches them the importance of both. Like Finn and his memory of being left helpless, stuck in his own boom boom, virtuous heroes are driven by the lessons they have learned to change the world. That drive is what sends them on their quests.

The Quest to Be a Hero

Why'd you leave me out in the woods when I was a little baby?

—Finn

Finn sure seems driven to help others ever since his trauma as a child, but is Finn a true hero? Well no, *not yet*. He is still too immature, but with some time and work, he could be. I believe that Finn is on a quest to become a genuine hero; his intentions are great, and he should continue to work on his character to become more mature in order to be the hero he wishes to be. He already has the moral foundation; it's only a matter of time and experience. While some heroes quest for justice, others quest for gold, and still others quest for eternal youth, Finn is on a truly admirable quest, the quest to *be* a *real* hero!

Adventure Time is teaching us something about morals. Maybe we can, just by watching, reflect our own virtues—learning to act right, through Finn's achievements and failures. Nussbaum has written about the effects popular culture can have on our moral education. She describes the way it can, through it's often very theatrical story lines and situations, help us understand how to act right in a similar (though less extreme) situations in real life. We can make out small nuances of right and wrong when watching or reading about an exaggerated situation like the ones we see in *Adventure Time*.

We may never fight zombified candy people, but we run into a lot of ethical questions every day, from what kind of animal to kill and eat, to which dictator to help overthrow, to what sweatshop we want to purchase our sneakers from. Who to vote for, what to buy, and how to treat our families are all important ethical questions we deal with regularly. And it is our decision if we are going to be heroes, like Finn, or the villains of our own adventure.

Heroic Motivation

You have more fluff than sense!

—FINN

So, is there something special to being a hero? Something more than profit and gain? Psychologists who have studied that kind of stuff claim there might be signs indicating that heroes are different from the rest of us. They think that heroes have a higher level of empathy and compassion as well as other key characteristics that contribute to heroic behavior. People who rush in to help others in the face of danger and adversity do so because they genuinely care about the safety and well-being of other people.

A study on the social psychology of heroic actions performed by psychologists Franco and Zimbardo found that people who have heroic tendencies also possess a much higher degree of empathy than regular non-heroic people. They suggest that heroes aren't just compassionate and caring; but also able to see things from the perspective of others, and can "walk a mile in another man's shoes."

Jake, who's an older hero than Finn, is aware of the power of empathy (well, sometimes). He's the one who teaches the "Empathy Song" to Donny the grass ogre to make him think about the feelings of others. But empathy isn't just knee-jerk feeling what other's feel, which Finn already seems to have. It's also the ability to step back, reflect, and purposefully imagine yourself in the shoes of someone else. That reflection, that practical reason, seems to require both the natural skill and the desire to understand others!

Heroism also takes self-confidence and courage to rush in where others fear to tread. To do this it seems that people who perform heroic acts tend to feel confident in themselves and their abilities. When faced with a crisis, they have a true belief in that they are capable of handling the challenge and achieving success no matter what the odds. Part of this confidence comes from above-average coping skills and abilities to manage stress. Finn and Jake have a lot of self-confidence and when the situation demands it they stand together cheering each other on, which make them a solid team. "Aw Yeah!"

Zimbardo and Franco also argue that heroes have two important qualities which set them apart from non-heroes: they live by their values and they're willing to endure personal risk to protect those values. In many cases, heroic individuals also tend to have a higher tolerance for risk. Plenty of caring and kind people might shrink back in the face of danger but those who do leap into action are typically more likely to take greater risks in multiple aspects of their lives. Persistence is another quality commonly shared by heroes. People identified as heroes are often more likely to put a positive spin on negative events. When faced with a potentially life-threatening illness, people with heroic tendencies might focus on the good that might come from the situation like renewed appreciation for life or an increased closeness with loved ones.

Finn is excellent at seeing the positive in every situation like for example in "Slumber Party Panic" after surviving a harrowing ordeal including something resembling a zombie apocalypse and ending up accidentally breaking a royal promise he made to Princess Bubblegum with dire consequences, he's still able to see the fun in it all. Finn's take on the whole situation is an appreciation of the fun he had while solving the problem: *"So what is the lesson of breaking a royal promise? It's simple; you get to fight zombies, throw slumber parties, awaken the Gumball Guardians and reverse death itself."* Which reveals yet another aspect of heroism—the awesomeness the hero himself or herself is allowed to feel after a job well done, and heroism therefore comes with a built-in motivation.

How Nobly You Live

Stop talking like a nerd and give it to us straight!

—Finn

So should we all try to be heroes or just leave it to those who're born to be heroes? Is it as simple, and perhaps as sad, as real-izing that true heroes are pretty much destined to be that way? Heroes give us something substantial both inside and outside of Ooo. Rather than spending their time seeking fame and for-tune, they're actually living out values whether we're watching or not. A true hero isn't directing attention to himself, but to something greater, the common good for the citizens of the world. But fret not! Remember *Aristotle.* The virtues of heroism are *habits.* And we can learn habits! The first step to being a hero, then, is realizing we suck cabbage at being heroes. Then, like any good hero, we take the risk of making a change!

Why do we need moral heroes? Because our world is in need of people who will stand in the gap, stand up for each other, set-ting a great example and making the world a better place while doing it. And, what should we learn from Finn? He would tell us to "keep trying!" It's all a matter of trial and error. Do your best, learn from your mistakes, and with time your best will be great, and remember the words of the Stoic writer Seneca: *"What matters most is, not how long you live, but how nobly you live."* But we need more than just Finn and Jake to guide us, we need all of the heroes of Ooo, in their many shapes and sizes, and we need you!

We need to seek out and remember heroes because in order to become moral heroes ourselves, we need to see those values lived out by people who are just as human as ourselves (although perhaps a bit more heroic). My obvious answer is,

"YES!" we should definitely all try to be heroes, because it is that effort at the heart of heroism.

If a thirteen-year-old boy living in an apocalyptic wasteland can make it his goal to help others, can't we do the same? Really, when you think about it, the difference between most of us and Finn isn't courage, strength, loyalty, or wisdom so much as it is the *desire* to be a hero. And, if you listen closely, watch carefully, and pay attention, you can hear faint cries for help off in the distance. . . . It's your call, what are you going to do, hero?

26
Our Heroes!

TRIP MCCROSSIN

"*T*his party is so crazy!"

The Candy Kingdom is jumpin'! The music is pumpin', the dancers are groovin', and Cinnamon Bun is feelin' the awesome party vibes.

"Okay. I'm gonna do it. Okay-okay-okay. Everyone watch! I'm gonna do a flip!"

The partygoers' faces contort from buzzin' amusement to horror as Cinnamon Bun hits his half-baked head against the tower wall. It cracks. And, then, it keeps cracking. Princess Bubblegum is happily unaware, showing off her smooth moves as calamity streaks toward her. As the balcony collapses, she falls. There is nothing between PB and a very messy death. Unless . . .

Finn dives toward the ground and catches the screaming Princess just before she becomes a bubble gum smear on the ground reminiscent of the underside of a jogger's old tennis shoes.

"You truly are my hero this day," Princess Bubblegum says to Finn, who has saved her for the first of what will be many times. And then she ponders, "Hero . . . Hmmm . . . Heeeeerroooo . . .," and realizes it. Who better than Finn to go in search of the "hero's handbook," the Enchiridion?

. . . And so it begins, Finn and Jake's struggle with what it means to be a REAL hero.

Finn's struggle unfolds in three stages. First, Finn overcomes the various trials of Mount Cragdor, secures the book, and is confirmed a hero. Then, Finn's status as a hero is tested by the many challenges that he and Jake face in their adventures.

Finally, Finn's status is doubly confirmed when his own hero, Billy, recognizes him as a hero. And, when this happens, Billy's status as a hero is reconfirmed too! Their meeting changes both heroes, leaving both far better heroes. By the first season's finale, Finn's status as a hero is secure, and it remains so as his adventures continue. (The first stage is reflected in "The Enchiridion!," the second stage in "Business Time," "City of Thieves," "Ocean of Fear," "Freak City," and "Henchman," the third stage in "His Hero.")

Finn's journey give us a hero's handbook of *our own*, to help us to think through what it means to be a hero—a very old question still very much alive today.

To the *Enchiridion*

"Many noble challengers have entered the temple to pass the grueling trials that lie behind these walls," we learn, but "only the truest, most worthy hero can receive the hero's *Enchiridion*."

Finn and Jake face three trials in particular—the old-woman-zapping gnomes, the Jake-devouring ogre, and the Dark Magician's nasty "brain-world." Let's look at these each in turn for what lessons they may hold for Finn, and for us.

Finn and Jake come upon three gnomes, seemingly harmless, trapped in a lava pit. Out of compassion, as good Samaritans, they free them. But once freed, the gnomes start to zap old women to death. They start to torment Finn by killing old women whenever Finn says "What," "Yes," or "No," or "looks sad," or "is a big wuss." Because he helped to free the gnomes, Finn feels responsible for this injustice, is overwhelmed, and runs away, leaving to Jake the business of herding the gnomes back into the lava pit.

The old women are "destroyed because of me," he complains, "I'm not righteous, I'm wrongteous, stupidteous." Finn aspires to heroism, but in failing to save others, not to mention fleeing from the attempt, he doubts himself. This *isn't* Jake's angle though: "Don't let those gnomes and their *illusions* get you down." What in the world, Jake goes on, would sweet old women be doing wandering around Mount Cragdor in the first place? "This place is designed to mess you up," he concludes, it's "all just trials to test your heroic attributes"—which Finn would have realized if he'd *thought things through*. Finn learns that, while partly about mustering courage, *heroism is just as importantly about mustering reason*. Heroes don't lose their courage, but they also *don't lose their heads*.

Next they encounter the giant ogre, which swallows Jake whole. Finn's immediate impulse is to try, courageously given the ogre's size, to physically force Jake's release. When this fails, though, Finn applies the earlier lesson and resorts to reason, figuring that if he steals the ogre's "big money," then he can barter for Jake's release. But when the ogre tells him Jake is dead, Finn loses it and punches the Ogre in the gut (with his whole body!). Without intending it, Finn makes the ogre vomit Jake to safety. What additional lessons do we have here?

Well let's see, firstly. Finn is pretty lucky when he saves Jake, so we can say that, yes, courage is part of heroism, and so is reason, but also basic luck can be crucial to saving the day! So then Finn accidently saves Jake and then they fly straight to the top of the mountain, skipping over whatever tests awaited them between the ogre and the Dark Magician. So we can say, secondly, the effects of luck may be pleasantly and unevenly expected. Okay, and even though he was a pretty mean and whiny baby, Finn gives him his money back, so we see that, finally, retribution can and should be temporary. Finn doesn't hesitate to return the stolen money. "That was righteous," Jake tells Finn.

Finally, Finn faces the Dark Magician. For his "last trial," he must decide first whether or not to slay the Heart Beast, at the magician's urging, which he assures Finn is "completely evil." Finn kills that sucker without hesitation. "I'll slay anything that's evil," he insists, "that's my deal." Suddenly, though, there's a "last, last trial," where he has to "slay" a little ant, not evil, the magician admits, though "not good either," he adds. Finn refuses, absolutely, and, released from the magician's brain-world, Finn slays the Dark Magician instead without hesitation. What are Finn's lessons here? Well, . . . there's always another struggle. And, when considering "the call" (the mission we're given) heroes too have to consider the source.

Having survived the three trials, Finn is lauded as "goodest of heart" and "most righteous hero," and receives the *Enchiridion*. When he consults it, though, it includes not the weightiest of matters—how to kiss a princess, for example, embarrassing Finn. In Season Four's "In Your Footsteps," we find again this sort of ambiguity. "Everything you need to know about being a hero is in this book," he tells the bear, but tells Jake in more or less the same breath that they "never use it, except for, like, sitting on it when the grass is wet and stuff." Here we have two more lessons for Finn. In striving to act heroically, the struggle is at least as important as the end result. And, seriously, heroism isn't easy to define! A "hero's handbook" can never be like a cookbook. It can't just be a set of recipes for being a hero.

Finn is repeatedly challenged, as prospective hero, to relieve the distress of others. He's also challenged by not one but two moral motivations. He may be moved by *justice*, obligated to act to protect their lives and rights. Or he may be moved by *compassion*, and as a good Samaritan, without obligation. Better yet, he may be moved by both. What final lessons are there in this? Well, it's hard to figure out whether we're moved by justice or by compassion. And either's better than neither. But it's best to be both just and compassionate—all the more *heroic!*

The Hero's Greatest Enemy

Let's look now at what troubles and doubts come up for heroes like Finn, and us. . . .

In "Business Time," Finn and Jake use flame-throwers to release items trapped in icebergs after the Great Mushroom War useful for completing their "gauntlet dock." They're torn between happily anticipating the fruits of their labor and how much "hard work sucks." This is complicated by coming upon an iceberg containing a group of businessmen who, once defrosted, are aimless and confused, and offer to complete the dock. "But this dock is our fun pie," Finn insists, and "we should be the ones to bake it." Compassion, though, becomes an important motivator for the boys: "These poor souls are lost without jobs," Jake counters, "We can't ignore their plight." And so the boys give in, out of compassion, and are soon happy they did, given the spectacular dock that the businessmen make! And soon enough, while admitting it "feels weird doing nothing," they do exactly that, growing fat and lazy, eating ice cream and playing with Beemo.

Falling to the evil of laziness, they even let the businessmen perform heroic deeds for them, like saving Lumpy Space

Princess from the Swamp Giant. As a result, the businessmen come to think of *themselves* as heroes, on behalf of the Fuzzy Friends. But clearly they get it wrong. "We're being heroes," they insist, "protecting them, collecting them in our care-sack so they cannot be hurt." "But you're making them unhappy," Finn objects. To the businessmen, though, "their happiness is not a priority." Finn's first impulse is to resist physically, as it was in response to the ogre. But that doesn't work, again, and he's sucked up himself. Trapped and a bit panicked, Finn's still able to think through a strategy that Jake's magical powers, frees himself and the Fuzzy Friends, and, then, banishes the businessmen. Again, his heroism depends not only on his courage, but on his *reason*.

In "City of Thieves," justice is Finn's initial reason to act, as he struggles to rescue Penny's basket of flowers, which she claims has been stolen and taken into the City of Thieves. They're warned that if they enter the city, they will be corrupted and become thieves. Finn doesn't worry about the warning. He's confident that, because as heroes they would never steal, they can enter and rescue Penny's basket while remaining "as pure as the driven snow." Jake's goal is even loftier. "We're gonna purify that city!" None of it goes as planned. Penny convinces Finn that her basket is in the King of Thieves' tower . . . in the king's treasure chest. But Finn doesn't remember one of the important lessons he learned from fighting the Dark Magician: consider the source! Penny turns out to be a thief herself, who can't breach the tower's magical thief-shunning barrier. It turns out she's just tricking him into stealing the chest for her.

Realizing the deception, but blocked from returning the chest because he is now a thief (having stolen from the king's treasure chest), Finn believes he's "ruined," "impure," and "unfit to be a hero." He resolves to "embrace the darkness of this wicked city and use the methods of the criminal to seek vengeance on Penny." He says to her, "You may have soiled my purity, but I think you can still come out clean," and uses a stolen bar of soap to give her a right and proper scrubbing! As a result, she looks clean of her evils and tells the boys that she feels "purified."

They happily rejoice: "The filth of the city and wrongdoings are gone!" Finn and Jake have been purified too! "This good deed we did," Finn exclaims, "has purified us once again." But things aren't what they seem. . . . As the episode closes Penny steals Finn's clothing. Finn cries out in anger, but the moral is a good one: we learn that we should be *really* wary of our sources. Not only that, but retribution can be heroic if guided by good intentions. They boys didn't just want to punish Penny for what she did to Finn, they wanted to clean her up, both for their sakes, and for hers!

In "Ocean of Fear," justice motivates Finn, in response to the boot-stealing fire newt escaping into the ocean. Jake can pursue the newt, but Finn can't, because of his paralyzing fear of the Ocean. His fear takes on the form of the Fear Feaster living inside his belly button. Jake devises a multi-level plan to help Finn overcome his fear, but in the transition from the fourth to the fifth underwater phases, Finn panics, knocks Jake unconscious and swims to the surface, leaving Jake to drown! "You can't even overcome your fear now that your friend is about to die," the Fear Feaster taunts Finn. "Your unheroic body will never let you save Jake." Finn knows it's true, he knows his fear won't let him save Jake. But Finn doesn't give up! He knocks himself unconscious so that he falls into the Ocean. Unconscious he can sink to the bottom without his fear getting in the way. Even if his body is unheroic, *Finn* isn't, and this time, Finn reasons his way out of the problem!

As luck would have it, Finn comes to rest right next to Jake. Roused to consciousness, he wakes Jake up, who saves them both. Back on the surface, the Fear Feaster taunts Finn again. "You just *sank* to the bottom," he insists, "You will *never* be a great hero." Finn regretfully agrees, but from inside of him, from the same place as came the Fear Feaster, come three limo-driving wise men, who *dis*agree. "The mark of a great hero," they insist, "*is* his flaw"—but I think it is not just *having* the flaw that makes Finn a hero, but *overcoming* it; and not just having the courage to overcome it, but being able to use his *reason* in the process.

Stuck between a Steak and the Sunlight

Remember, though, that it isn't just reason that makes a hero, it's justice and compassion too. One of the best examples of Finn's ability to show qualities is when he tries to make

Marceline, the Vampire Queen, stop abusing her henchman. "How're ya gonna pull *that* off," she quips, "*hero?*" Finn bravely tells her, "I'll do what I have to do. I'll even take his place!" There's much that justice requires of us, but taking another's place in servitude may not be one of those things. Still, like the negotiator who takes the hostage's place, Finn's selflessness seems clearly a mark of heroism.

Finn swears to be her new henchman, freeing the poor old man. Here we see true compassion. But we also see Finn worry about justice. "I'm bound by my code of honor to do what she says," he insists, but what if this means helping Marceline bring misery to the innocent? Fortunately, nothing bad ever really happens. Marceline is just messing with Finn who finds himself continually failing to go through with the evil acts she demands. Her demands, though, are just ways to mess with Finn's head.

This is why Finn comes to believe that Marceline is "not how she seems," but, instead, "a radical dame who likes to play games!" In the end, Finn saves everyone, including Marceline. Heroes can go past their abilities out of compassion, though. Sometimes compassion can conflict with justice. Jake believes that Marceline has to be killed, because she's evil, but Finn's compassion makes him want to save her. It seems like Finn can't have both justice and compassion. That's why reason is so important; it's what helps us find the best balance between the two!

When Should Heroes Retire?

When Finn meets his own hero, Billy, he wants to learn the ins and outs of fighting evil. Billy's not interested, though, insisting that however heroically we strive to "kick evil's butt," inevitably "new evil keeps popping up." And those whom we rescue from it inevitably are put at risk again sooner or later. Billy's new and improved way of being a hero is "nonviolently." He tells Finn that the best thing to do is to "help people by being active in your community." We have to notice, though, that locked away in his cave, active in no community, Billy's helping no one.

Still, Finn's determined to meet Billy's challenge, to suppress his "every warrior instinct," and respond to those in need "the Billy way." He's able to do so for a little while, setting violence aside even for the sake of protecting those whose lives are threatened. But, in the long run, the boys do more harm than good. Finn is sincere in his Billy-inspired compassionate impulse to charity, but in the process he's acting outside the typical norms of justice. To help save villagers he spikes his gruel with a "stone skin potion. Finn's intention here is sincere enough. "I thought people would like that," he pleads, in order to "defend against evil monsters!" But the villagers disagree, needless to say. Finn has manipulated their bodies and behavior, without permission—and that's an injustice! We can't turn evil into good, no matter how much compassion we infuse it with.

Finn learns his lesson. "I think us being nonviolent," Finn admits, "is hurting people," though more precisely it's *the way* in which he and Jake are being nonviolent that's doing so. But now he has to choose between Billy and heroism. "The greatest hero in the world told me to help people without being violent," Finn agonizes, "and I promised I would do that and not let him down." In the end, Finn simply can't help himself and saves an old lady using violence. She praises him, "Like a true hero, you were born to punch evil creatures," she insists, "just like I was born to be an old lady." We also take comfort, though, that he did *try* to find a way to save her non-violently, but "couldn't think of anything." Again, *reason* is an essential part of the process by in balancing non-violence with the importance of acting violently when necessary.

Reason and instinct struggle when Finn tries to do what Billy wants and be a hero. Just like in times when our inclination is to react violently, but reason tells us it won't work. Justice and compassion come into conflict too, when justice demands punishment, but compassion calls us to be merciful. In the end, Finn emerges his old butt-kicking hero self again. Billy does too, But Finn hasn't totally *abandoned* "the Billy way," really, he's just changed it to include the righteous choice of violent heroism when nonviolent heroism is not an option.

And so, we see that, really being a hero is a constant balancing act. Heroes have to find the wisest path, sometimes between two things that are good! To strive to be a hero is to struggle willingly in at least these three ways—to reconcile *reason* and *instinct*, *justice* and *compassion*, and *violence* and *non-violence*. This struggle never ends, which is why Finn will always be a hero, even when he messes up, as long as he's always actively and consistently *trying to be one.*

References

Abadeer, Hunson. 2013. *The Adventure Time Encyclopaedia: Inhabitants, Lore, Spells, and Ancient Crypt Warnings of the Land of Ooo Circa 19.56 B.G.E.–501 A.G.E.* Abrams.

Aquinas, St. Thomas. 1981. *The Summa Theologica of St. Thomas Aquinas*. Five volumes. Christian Classics.

Artemidorus. 2012. *Artemidorus' Oneirocritica: Text, Translation, and Commentary*. Oxford University Press.

Augustine, St. 2013. *The Confessions of Saint Augustine*. CreateSpace.

Bergson, Henri. 1910. *Time and Free Will: An Essay on the Immediate Data of Consciousness*. Allen and Unwin.

Berkeley, George. 1979. *Three Dialogues between Hylas and Philonous*. Hackett.

Butler, Judith. 1990. *Gender Trouble*. Routledge.

Callender, Craig, ed. 2011. *The Oxford Handbook of Time*. Oxford University Press.

Cupitt, Don. 2012. *The Time Being*. SCM.

Descartes, René. 1998. *Discourse on Method: Discourse on the Method for Conducting One's Reason Well and for Seeking the Truth in the Sciences*. Hackett.

DeWitt, Bryce, and R, Neill Graham, eds. 1973. *The Many-Worlds Interpretation of Quantum Mechanics*. Princeton University Press.

Dick, Philip K. 1996. *Do Androids Dream of Electric Sheep?* Del Rey.

Doggzone, Jay T. 2010. *Mind Games*. Ooo Press.

Dostoevsky, Fyodor. 2002. *The Brothers Karamazov*. Farrar, Straus, and Giroux.

Epictetus. 2004. *Enchiridion*. Dover.

Erasmus, Desiderius. 1994. *Praise of Folly*. Penguin.

———. 2011. *The Manual of a Christian Knight*. Theophania.

Everett, Hugh. 1973. The Theory of the Universal Wavefunction. In DeWitt and Graham 1973.

Foucault, Michel. 1986. *The Care of the Self.* Vintage.

Freud, Sigmund. 2008. *The Interpretation of Dreams.* Oxford University Press.

———. 2010. *Beyond the Pleasure Principle.* Pacific.

Gadamer, Hans-Georg. 2004. *Truth and Method.* Continuum.

Glob, I.M. 1997. *Holy Bible: New Revised Standard Version.* American Bible Society.

Gran, Meredith. 2014. *Adventure Time: Marceline and the Scream Queens Mathematical Edition.* KaBOOM!

Hobbes, Thomas. 1982. *Leviathan.* Penguin.

Hobson, J.A. 2011. *Dreaming: A Very Short Introduction.* Oxford University Press.

Hume, David. 1978. *A Treatise of Human Nature.* Oxford University Press.

———. 1992. *Writings on Religion.* Open Court.

Kant, Immanuel. 1993. *Grounding for the Metaphysics of Morals.* Hackett.

———. 2005. *Fundamental Principles of the Metaphysics of Morals.* Dover.

Lewis, David. 1973. *Counterfactuals.* Blackwell.

Locke, John. 1980. *Second Treatise of Government.* Hackett.

Matheson, Mark, ed. 2012. *The Tanner Lectures on Human Values.* University of Utah Press.

McTaggart, John. 1908. *The Relation of Time and Eternity.* University of California Press.

Neiman, Susan. 2012. Victims and Heroes. In Matheson 2012.

Nietzsche, Friedrich. 1961. *Thus Spoke Zarathustra: A Book for Everyone and No One.* Penguin.

Nussbaum, Martha C. 1992. *Love's Knowledge: Essays on Philosophy and Literature.* Oxford University Press.

Pepperell, Robert. 2003. *The Posthuman Condition: Consciousness Beyond the Brain.* Intellect.

Pizan, Christine de. 1999. *The Book of Deeds of Arms and of Chivalry.* Penn State University Press.

Plato. 1992. *Republic.* Hackett.

Prior, A.N. 1967. *Past, Present, and Future.* Oxford University Press.

Reeser, Todd W. 2010. *Masculinities in Theory: An Introduction.* Wiley.

Rousseau, Jean-Jacques. 1968. *The Social Contract.* Penguin.

Searle, John R. 1992. *The Rediscovery of the Mind.* MIT Press.

Sorli, Amrit. Dusan Klinar, and David Fiscaletti. 2011. New Insights into the Special Theory of Relativity. *Physics Essays* 24:2.

Stickgold, R., J.A. Hobson, R. Fosse, and M. Fosse. 2001. Sleep, Learning, and Dreams: Off-line Memory Reprocessing. *Science* 294:5544.

Tooley, Michael. 1997. *Time, Tense, and Causation*. Oxford University Press.

Turing, A.M. 1950. Computing Machinery and Intelligence. *Mind* 59:236.

Zimmerman, Dean. 2011. Presentism and the Space-Time Manifold. In Callender 2011.

Our Adventurous Authors

SCOTT F. AIKIN is Assistant Professor of Philosophy at Vanderbilt University. He works in theory of knowledge and ancient philosophy. His recent books are *Epistemology and the Regress Problem* and *Evidentialism and the Will to Believe*. He and his daughters, Madeleine and Iris, regularly have intense debates about popular culture.

ROBERT ARP, PHD has interests in many philosophical areas and works as a researcher for the US Army. He agrees with Jake that you should go sit in the corner and think about your life!

ADAM BARKMAN, PHD is associate professor of philosophy at Redeemer University College, but spends most of his time teaching his three kids at home all the lessons of Ooo—the fun of adventure, the need for candy, and the necessity of virtue.

M. BLANKIER is a PhD candidate in the School of English at Trinity College Dublin and is possessed by the spirit of inquiry and bloodlust. Her arms weren't meant to carry so many rocks, you guys.

DAVID CABALLEROS is but a lowly undergrad student of philosophy at the University of St Andrews in Scotland. When he isn't busy trying to learn the ancient esoteric knowledge of magic (Dustmancy has proven more difficult than at first thought), training to master sword fighting, searching for the Loch Ness monster, questing for treasure and power in underground dungeons, or partying with the Party god, he is attempting to recreate the recipes for Royal tarts and Tree Trunks's apple pies.

DAVID DEGGINGER is in his third year of the English BA program at the University of British Columbia. On weekends he enjoys hiking, sleeping, and looting the occasional dungeon.

BEN GALE is an independent scholar, who, when not thinking about political theory, enjoys eating cheese and listening to music in excess.

Hey Mordecai, if Benson finds out we were writing fan fiction about that weird show that comes before ours, he'll totally fire us! We gotta come up with fake names and stuff. I'll be **MARY GREEN** from Eugene, Oregon and I'll say that I'm studying film to be a screenwriter. What's yours, dude?

You mean once again your "ham-boning" isn't gonna save us, Rigby? All right, Dude, I'll be **RONALD S. GREEN, PHD**, from . . . let's see, Coastal Carolina University. Yeah! I'll be a professor in Philosophy and Religious Studies. OHHHH!!

MARTYN JONES completed his BA at Wheaton College and his MA at the Katholieke Universiteit Leuven, and was an uncredited extra in the *Adventure Time* episode "Reign of Gunters." During filming he waddled away in his Gunter suit, and it hangs in his closet to this day.

Imagine asking *Adventure Time*'s characters if there is one word that best describes the lens through which they view the world. Princess Bubblegum would unquestionably roar "Science!" Finn the Human would enthusiastically yell "Magic!" For **JOHN V. KARAVITIS, CPA, MBA**, it's obviously . . . well . . . you already know the answer, right?

CHRISTOPHER KETCHAM, PHD is a reformed academic living on the set of the dystopian world of an abandoned garnet mine in Pennsylvania. I am down there in the caverns that now grow mushrooms where tiny little characters that look like candies frolic among the fungi and there goes a flaming sprite chased by an icicle thingy. The workers in white hoodies are dancing to a tune that comes from a beembox. But it is all a dream, isn't it?

ABRACADANIEL LEONARD has approximate knowledge of many things, which he gained at Wheaton College in Illinois and Katholieke Universiteit Leuven in Belgium. He authored several pop-psych books under the pen name Jay T. Doggzone during his one million years' dungeon.

GREG LITTMANN is a house-sized monster with six heads, invisible legs, and a scorpion-tail that sprays poison. It is Associate Professor of Philosophy at SIUE, because it is too big and dangerous for anyone to stop it. It has published in meta-philosophy, metaphysics, and the philosophy of logic, and has written more than twenty-five chapters for books relating philosophy to popular culture, including volumes on *Boardwalk Empire, Breaking Bad, Doctor Who, Game of Thrones, Sons of Anarchy,* and *The Walking Dead.* It's said that anyone who slays Greg Littmann and bathes in his blood will become chancellor of the university.

TRIP MCCROSSIN teaches in the Philosophy Department at Rutgers University, where he works on, among other things, the nature, history, and legacy of the Enlightenment. The present essays are part of a broader effort to view literary and other forms of popular culture through the lens of Susan Neiman's understanding of the same. He sometimes dreams of the student who, in receiving this or that assignment, would say, as Finn does to Princess Bubblegum, "Do you think I have the goods . . . 'cause I am *into this stuff!*"

NICOLAS MICHAUD is the editor of numerous popular culture and philosophy texts. He wishes that he could say that he is the adventurous hero of this story, but more likely he is the villain. We all have to make a living somehow. . . .

LIAM MILLER is a lowly PhD student, who toils day and night in the underground caverns beneath his house. Mining the letters he uses to write his thesis, he hopes to find enough vowels to complete his introduction before he dies and his first born takes his place. When he is above ground, he can be found at the University of Queensland in Australia, hammering out all his W's to make E's.

MATTHEW MONTOYA is an MA student in Humanities and Philosophy at Old Dominion University. When not absorbing knowledge through sleepy time osmosis, he traverses dungeons in the hopes of slaying the blood demon who ate his taquito. On his latest adventure, he learned that it is not really Gunter who is the most evil being in the universe, but in actuality that title belongs to the teddy bear living in your closet. The teddy bear is waiting for the eventual stuffed animal revolution . . . waiting for you to fall asleep. Be warned.

MICHAEL J. MUNIZ is locked up in his ivory tower waiting for that special someone. Yes, that special postman to deliver his signed copy of The Enchiridion. Alas, until then, he unlocks the door and goes to beach to write. His hometown of Hialeah, Florida, has sadly been mistaken for the Land of Ooo, way too many times. Though, when he is not waiting around for anything at all, he enjoys fabricating identities of fellow philosophers who write articles about righteous TV shows.

Poom Namvol used to be an MA student in Comparative Literature at Chulalongkorn University, Thailand. But after his dissertation got vaporized by the bomb of the Great Mushroom War, he became a freelance researcher in the fields of magic and legendary scripts. He often travels around Ooo and beyond, digging up junk and ruins of long past civilizations in hope of finding ancient books and scrolls that he could translate and sell for googolplex copies. His dreams are to compose a magnificent book that is comparable to the *Enchiridion* and to marry a bride of a royal bloodline. He often wonders which one of them will come true first.

Rakel Blöndal Sveinsdóttir Toubro has an MA in philosophy of education from Aarhus University. She is an Icelandic-born Valkyrie, interested in ethics, shapeshifting (the secret weapon is hair dye— shhh), tacit knowing, and the philosophy of everything. Currently a lecturer at UCSJ, residing in the Danish countryside where she spends a lot of her spare time defending the family fortress alongside her husband and their flock of kids. The rest of the time she enjoys such clichés as the great outdoors and adventure. She believes the world would be a greater place if we all had more time to contemplate.

You know when your parents ask you, "What will you do with your life if you just play videogames all day?" Daniel Vella might be the answer to that rhetorical question. He is currently a PhD candidate at the IT University of Copenhagen, where he tells us he researches "constructions of subjectivity in digital games." When he's not busy with that, he can be found baking sweet treats that put Tree Trunks's apple pies to shame. Or at least, that's what he says—we await further evidence on this claim. He hails from Malta and lives in a fortress constructed out of perilously teetering piles of books.

Index

DOCTOR WHO

AND PHILOSOPHY
BIGGER ON THE INSIDE

EDITED BY COURTLAND LEWIS AND PAULA SMITHKA